P9-DHI-905

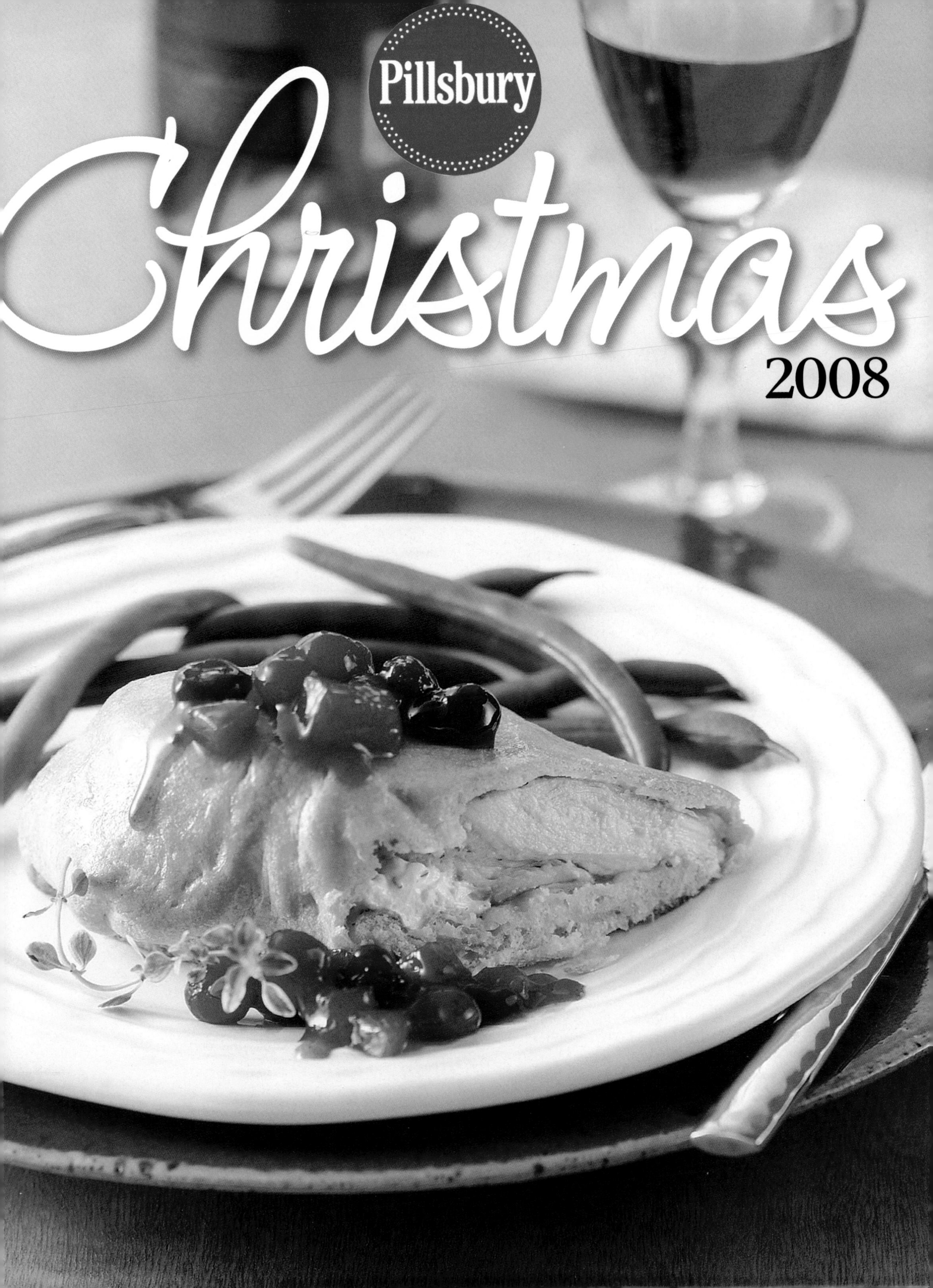
Pillsbury
Christmas
2008

Pillsbury Christmas 2008

published by

Taste of Home Books
Reiman Media Group, Inc.
5400 S. 60th St., Greendale WI 53129
www.tasteofhome.com

This edition published by arrangement with Wiley Publishing, Inc.

All recipes were previously published in a slightly different form.

Cover Photography:
Reiman Publications Photo Studio;
Jim Wieland (Photographer);
Sarah Thompson (Food Stylist);
Jenny Bradley Vent (Set Stylist).

Front Cover Photograph:
Three-Berry Cheesecake, p. 280.

Title Page Photograph:
Chicken Breast Bundles with Cranberry Chutney, p. 100.

credits

GENERAL MILLS, INC.
EDITORIAL DIRECTOR: Jeff Nowak
MANAGER, COOKBOOKS: Lois Tlusty
RECIPE DEVELOPMENT AND TESTING: Pillsbury Test Kitchens
PHOTOGRAPHY: General Mills Photo Studios

REIMAN MEDIA GROUP, INC.
VICE PRESIDENT, EXECUTIVE EDITOR/BOOKS: Heidi Reuter Lloyd
SENIOR EDITOR/BOOKS: Mark Hagen
ART DIRECTOR: Gretchen Trautman
EDITOR: Michelle Bretl
CONTENT PRODUCTION SUPERVISOR: Julie Wagner
LAYOUT DESIGNERS: Kathy Crawford, Nancy Novak
PROOFREADERS: Amy Glander, Linne Bruskewitz
INDEXER: Jean Duerst
GRAPHIC DESIGN INTERN: Heather Miller

CREATIVE DIRECTOR: Ardyth Cope
CREATIVE DIRECTOR/CREATIVE MARKETING: James Palmen
VICE PRESIDENT/BOOK MARKETING: Dan Fink
CHIEF MARKETING OFFICER: Lisa Karpinski
EDITOR IN CHIEF: Catherine Cassidy
PRESIDENT, FOOD & ENTERTAINING: Suzanne M. Grimes
PRESIDENT AND CHIEF EXECUTIVE OFFICER: Mary G. Berner

International Standard Book Number (10): 0-89821-634-6
International Standard Book Number (13): 978-0-89821-634-9
Library of Congress Number: 2008933635
Printed in U.S.A.
Second Printing, December 2008

For additional holiday recipes and other delicious dishes, visit
Pillsbury.com

Back Cover Photographs:
Crafty Crescent Lasagna, p. 134; Chicken Bruschetta, p. 104; Minestrone Salad, p. 74; Cream Cheese French Toast, p. 169; Tropical Fruit Muffins, p. 188.

contents

Comfort and Joy!

Deck the halls and celebrate with hundreds of sensational holiday recipes that are sure to keep all of your special gatherings merry and bright.

p. 45

p. 96

p. 134

p. 157

p. 303

Happy Holidays! It is that magical time of year to celebrate with family, friends and loved ones as you ring in Christmas and anticipate the excitement of a New Year.

Whether you like to host formal dinners filled with impressive specialties, plan cozy get-togethers featuring comforting favorites or host appetizer-buffets filled with fun and laughter, Pillsbury Christmas 2008 *promises to be your most-used recipe source.*

The second volume in this popular line of cookbooks, this edition offers all of the savory sensations and luscious delights guests expect to sample during this merry time of year. Mouthwatering entrees, fantastic side dishes, crowd-pleasing hors d'oeuvres and, of course, those dazzling Christmas desserts that are sure to steal the show.

In fact, this new cookbook offers more than 300 recipes that will make this your most delicious holiday to date. Best of all, each dish has been tested in the Pillsbury Kitchen, so you can rest assured that it meets Pillsbury's standards of simple preparation, reliability and great taste.

With chapters dedicated to holiday entrees (p. 84), side dishes and salads (p. 60) and decadent after-dinner delights (p. 270), creating a memorable holiday meal has never been easier! You'll be amazed at how quickly you can whip up the savory snacks found in the chapter "Festive Bites & Beverages" (p. 6), and if you're looking for something to satisfy the sweet tooth, see page 48 for "Glorious Baked Goods." There you'll find classic coffee cakes, scones and other holiday mainstays.

Christmas is a wonderful time to host change-of-pace gatherings, so why not throw a caroling party, an ice skating get-together or a sledding event? Top off the day with a buffet of good cheer as suggested on page 110. The no-fuss, heartwarming specialties in that chapter are just perfect after a day of fun winter activities.

Because nothing ushers in the holidays like laughter from a tiny tot, we've also included a chapter full of easy edibles that are sure to bring a smile to the little ones on your Christmas list. Turn to "Merry Kitchen Creations" (p. 244) for adorable ideas such as cute Santa Claus Cake (p. 247) and colorful Elf Hat Cookies (p. 256).

And speaking of cookies, you won't want to miss the irresistible sensations in the chapter "Holiday Cookie Exchange" (p. 190). There you'll discover more than 50 treasures...all ideal for cookie platters, hostess gifts, Christmas potlucks and more. Turn here for everything from the traditional cookies folks anticipate all year to special brownies and bars that everyone will be asking about.

In addition, you'll find cook's notes with many of the recipes. These suggestions help shorten prep time, substitute ingredients and more. Hints labeled special touches describe ways to dress up your table and make menus unforgettable. On the other hand, kitchen tips offer advice on everything from streamlining trips to the grocery store to making the most out of your time in the kitchen. We've also included many of our Bake-Off® Contest winners...so you know you're preparing the best of the very best!

With Pillsbury Christmas 2008 *on hand, it's simply a joy to prepare the Yuletide dinners and sweet sensations your loved ones have dreamt about all year. Filled with the many flavors of the season, it's one collection you'll turn to time and again. We hope you cherish* Pillsbury Christmas 2008 *as much as we've enjoyed bringing it to you. Merry Christmas!*

p. 104
p. 287

Festive Bites & Beverages

Memorable hors d'oeuvres and savory snacks make any appetizer buffet merry and bright! From sophisticated to simple, these party starters ring in the holidays with flair.

p. 12

p. 9

p. 29

p. 34

p. 14

cilantro-lime shrimp with chile aïoli p. 10

easy vegetable pizza

easy vegetable pizza

PREP TIME: 20 Minutes ✱ READY IN: 1 Hour 10 Minutes ✱ SERVINGS: 32

- 2 cans (8 oz. each) Pillsbury® Refrigerated Crescent Dinner Rolls
- 1 package (8 oz.) cream cheese, softened
- 1/2 cup sour cream
- 1 teaspoon dried dill weed
- 1/8 teaspoon garlic powder
- 1/2 cup small fresh broccoli florets
- 1/3 cup quartered cucumber slices
- 1 Italian plum tomato, seeded, chopped
- 1/4 cup shredded carrot

1 Heat oven to 375°F. Unroll both cans of dough into 4 long rectangles. Place in ungreased 15x10x1-inch baking pan; press over bottom and up sides to form crust.

2 Bake for 13 to 17 minutes or until golden brown. Cool crust for 30 minutes or until it is completely cooled.

3 In small bowl, combine cream cheese, sour cream, dill and garlic powder; blend until smooth. Spread over cooled crust. Top with vegetables. Serve immediately, or cover and refrigerate 1 to 2 hours. Cut into squares.

NUTRITION INFORMATION PER SERVING: Calories 90 • Total Fat 6g • Saturated Fat 3g • Cholesterol 10mg • Sodium 135mg • Total Carbohydrate 6g • Dietary Fiber 0g • Sugars 1g • Protein 2g. DIETARY EXCHANGES: 1/2 Starch • 1 Fat OR 1/2 Carbohydrate • 1 Fat • 1/2 Carb Choice.

cook's notes

Pressed for time on the party day? Bake the pizza crust and chop the vegetables several hours ahead. Wait until just before serving, however, to spread the cheese onto the crust so it doesn't get soggy.

caramelized onion tartlets

PREP TIME: 30 Minutes ✱ READY IN: 45 Minutes ✱ SERVINGS: 24 Appetizers

- 1 package (15 oz.) Pillsbury® Refrigerated Pie Crusts, softened as directed on package
- 2 tablespoons butter or margarine
- 3/4 cup coarsely chopped red onion
- 2 eggs
- 1/2 cup sour cream
- 1/4 teaspoon salt
- 1/8 teaspoon hot pepper sauce
- 3/4 cup finely shredded Cheddar cheese (3 oz.)
- Additional chopped red onion, if desired

1 Heat oven to 400°F. Remove pie crusts from pouches. Unfold crusts; press out fold lines. With 3-inch round cutter or glass, cut 24 rounds from crusts, rerolling scraps as necessary. Press each round into miniature muffin cup.

2 Melt butter in large skillet over medium-high heat. Add 3/4 cup onion; cook 5 minutes, stirring occasionally. Reduce heat to medium; cook an additional 13 to 15 minutes or until onion is softened and golden brown, stirring occasionally. Remove from heat.

3 Beat eggs in large bowl. Stir in sour cream, salt and hot pepper sauce. Stir in cooked onion and 1/4 cup of the cheese. Spoon onion mixture into crust lined cups. Sprinkle with remaining 1/2 cup cheese.

4 Bake for 10 to 15 minutes or until golden brown and set in center. Serve warm or at room temperature. Garnish with additional onion.

NUTRITION INFORMATION PER SERVING: Calories 115 • Total Fat 8g • Saturated Fat 4g • Cholesterol 30mg • Sodium 140mg • Total Carbohydrate 9g • Dietary Fiber 0g • Sugars 1g • Protein 2g. DIETARY EXCHANGES: 1/2 Starch • 1-1/2 Fat OR 1/2 Carbohydrate • 1-1/2 Fat • 1/2 Carb Choice.

cook's notes

To make this recipe for a sit-down, eat-with-a-fork occasion, double the filling ingredients, except use 3 eggs. Prepare one pie crust in an 11x1-inch tart pan or a 9-inch pie plate. Add the filling and bake about 30 minutes or until set. Let the tart stand for 20 minutes before cutting it into wedges.

cook's notes

This delicious dish can be made up to four hours ahead of time. Prepare the shrimp, lime juice mixture and chile aïoli ahead. Cover and refrigerate. Just before serving, brush the lime juice mixture on the shrimp, then broil. Serve the shrimp with the chile aïoli as directed.

cilantro-lime shrimp with chile aïoli

READY IN: 30 Minutes ✱ SERVINGS: 24 Appetizers

SHRIMP

- 24 fresh uncooked large shrimp (about 1 lb.), shelled with tails left on
- 1 tablespoon chopped fresh cilantro
- 2 tablespoons lime juice
- 1 tablespoon olive oil
- 1 garlic clove, minced

CHILE AÏOLI

- 1 cup mayonnaise
- 3 tablespoons milk
- 2 canned chipotle chiles in adobo sauce, chopped (about 4 teaspoons)
- 2 garlic cloves, chopped
- 2 teaspoons chopped fresh cilantro

1 Heat oven to 350°F. Cut shrimp along outside curve almost to other side; spread open. Remove any visible vein. Place cut side down on ungreased cookie sheet so that tails curve up.

2 In small bowl, combine all remaining shrimp ingredients; mix well. Brush mixture over shrimp. Bake for 5 to 7 minutes or until shrimp turn pink.

3 Meanwhile, in blender container, combine all chile aïoli ingredients except the cilantro; blend until smooth.

4 To serve, drizzle small amount of aïoli onto serving platter. Sprinkle with 2 teaspoons chopped cilantro. Place cooked shrimp over aïoli. Serve with remaining aïoli.

NUTRITION INFORMATION PER SERVING: Calories 80 • Total Fat 8g • Saturated Fat 1g • Cholesterol 15mg • Sodium 70mg • Total Carbohydrate 1g • Dietary Fiber 0g • Sugars 0g • Protein 1g. DIETARY EXCHANGES: 1-1/2 Fat • 0 Carb Choice.

special touch

To dress up a platter of these snacks for a party, surround the edge of the plate with sprigs of curly leaf parsley or sweet basil that have been washed and dried.

crescent wellington spirals

PREP TIME: 20 Minutes ✱ READY IN: 40 Minutes ✱ SERVINGS:16 Appetizers

- 1 can (8 oz.) Pillsbury® Refrigerated Crescent Dinner Rolls
- 1-1/4 cups shredded mozzarella cheese (5 oz.)
- 36 thin slices pepperoni (2-1/2 oz.)
- 1 package (9 oz.) frozen spinach in a pouch, thawed, drained
- 4 tablespoons sliced mushrooms (from 4.5-oz. jar)
- 1/2 teaspoon garlic salt

1 Heat oven to 375°F. Spray large cookie sheet with nonstick cooking spray. Separate dough into 4 rectangles. Firmly press perforations to seal. Press each to form 6x4-inch rectangle.

2 Sprinkle each rectangle with heaping 1/4 cup cheese to within 1 inch of one short side. Top cheese on each rectangle with 9 pepperoni slices, 1/4 of the spinach, 1 tablespoon mushrooms and 1/8 teaspoon garlic salt.

3 Roll up each, starting at short side and rolling to untopped side. Cut each roll into 4 slices. Place slices cut side up on sprayed cookie sheet.

4 Bake for 13 to 18 minutes or until golden brown. Immediately remove from cookie sheet. Cool 2 minutes. Serve warm.

NUTRITION INFORMATION PER SERVING: Calories 100 • Total Fat 6g • Saturated Fat 2g • Cholesterol 10mg • Sodium 350mg • Total Carbohydrate 7g • Dietary Fiber 0g. DIETARY EXCHANGES: 1/2 Starch • 1/2 Medium-Fat Meat • 1/2 Fat OR 1/2 Carbohydrate • 1/2 Medium-Fat Meat • 1/2 Fat • 1/2 Carb Choice.

cilantro-lime shrimp with chile aïoli

creole shrimp and cheese tart

PREP TIME: 15 Minutes ✱ READY IN: 1 Hour 5 Minutes ✱ SERVINGS: 16

STEVE GRIEGER
El Cajon, California
Bake-Off® Contest 41, 2004

- 1/2 lb. cooked deveined shelled shrimp or crawfish, tail shells removed, shrimp coarsely chopped
- 1 to 2 teaspoons dried Creole seasoning
- 1 cup shredded hot pepper-Monterey Jack cheese (4 oz.)
- 1/4 cup finely chopped green onions (4 medium)
- 2 eggs, slightly beaten
- 1 tablespoon butter or margarine, melted
- 1 Pillsbury® Refrigerated Pie Crust (from 15-oz. box), softened as directed on box
- Red pepper sauce, if desired

1 Heat oven to 375°F. In medium bowl, toss shrimp and Creole seasoning to coat. Stir in all remaining ingredients except pie crust and pepper sauce.

2 Remove pie crust from pouch; place crust flat on ungreased cookie sheet. If necessary, press out folds or creases. Spread filling over crust to within 1 inch of edge. Carefully fold 1-inch edge of crust up over filling, pleating crust as necessary.

3 Bake for 32 to 37 minutes or until set in center and crust is golden brown. Cool 10 minutes. Cut into wedges. Serve warm with pepper sauce.

HIGH ALTITUDE (3500-6500 FT): Bake at 375°F for 35 to 40 minutes.

NUTRITION INFORMATION PER SERVING: Calories 110 • Total Fat 7g • Saturated Fat 3g • Cholesterol 65mg • Sodium 150mg • Total Carbohydrate 7g • Dietary Fiber 0g • Sugars 1g • Protein 6g.

goat cheese and sun-dried tomato bread bites

PREP TIME: 30 Minutes ✱ READY IN: 50 Minutes ✱ SERVINGS: 24 Appetizers

- 1 can (11 oz.) Pillsbury® Refrigerated Breadsticks
- 1 cup crumbled chèvre (goat) cheese with basil and garlic or plain chèvre (goat) cheese (4 oz.)
- 1/2 cup oil-packed sun-dried tomatoes, drained, coarsely chopped
- 1 egg
- 1 tablespoon water
- Kosher or coarse salt, if desired

1 Heat oven to 375°F. Spray cookie sheet with nonstick cooking spray. Separate dough into 12 breadsticks; cut each in half crosswise to make 24 small breadsticks. Press each breadstick until 1-1/2 inches wide.

2 With thumb, make indentation in center of each breadstick. Place 1 rounded teaspoon cheese in each indentation; top each with 1 teaspoon tomatoes. Roll up each jelly-roll fashion; place seam side down on sprayed cookie sheet.

3 In small bowl, combine egg and water; beat well. Lightly brush over tops of filled breadsticks. Sprinkle each with salt. Bake for 12 to 17 minutes or until tops are light golden brown. Serve appetizer warm.

NUTRITION INFORMATION PER SERVING: Calories 60 • Total Fat 2g • Saturated Fat 1g • Cholesterol 10mg • Sodium 250mg • Total Carbohydrate 7g • Dietary Fiber 0g • Sugars 1g • Protein 2g. DIETARY EXCHANGES: 1/2 Starch • 1/2 Fat OR 1/2 Carbohydrate • 1/2 Fat • 1/2 Carb Choice.

cook's notes

For a peppered-herb flavor, sprinkle the breadsticks before baking with coarse ground black pepper and dried basil leaves along with the salt.

strawberry sangria

READY IN: 10 Minutes ✱ SERVINGS: 12

- 2 boxes (10 oz. each) frozen sliced strawberries in syrup, thawed
- 1 can (12 oz.) frozen orange, strawberry and banana fruit juice concentrate, thawed
- 2 bottles (750 ml. each) blush white Zinfandel wine, chilled
- 4 cans (12 oz. each) lemon-lime carbonated beverage, chilled
- 6 fresh whole strawberries, halved

1 To make strawberry puree, place strainer over medium bowl; pour strawberries and syrup into strainer. Press mixture with back of spoon through strainer to remove seeds; discard seeds.

2 In 3-quart non-metal bowl or pitcher, mix strawberry puree, fruit juice concentrate and wine. Just before serving, stir in carbonated beverage. Serve in wine glasses over ice. Garnish each serving with strawberry half.

NUTRITION INFORMATION PER SERVING: Calories 230 • Total Fat 0g • Saturated Fat 0g • Trans Fat 0g • Cholesterol 0mg • Sodium 25mg • Total Carbohydrate 38g • Dietary Fiber 1g • Sugars 37g • Protein 0g. • DIETARY EXCHANGES: 2-1/2 Other Carbohydrate • 2 Fat • 2-1/2 Carb Choices.

special touch

Personalize beverages with ribbons, stickers or charms for easy identification during a get-together.

Kitchen tip

Chive and Onion Potato Topper is basically flavored sour cream that is often served as a dip or sandwich spread as well as an enhancement for spuds. If you find the topper in a squeeze bottle, you can even skip the recipe step of spooning the topper into a resealable bag.

holiday herb crescent trees

READY IN: 1 Hour ✱ SERVINGS: 32 Servings (2 Trees)

- 2 cans (8 oz. each) Pillsbury® Refrigerated Crescent Dinner Rolls
- 1/4 cup grated Parmesan cheese
- 1 teaspoon dried Italian seasoning
- 1/2 cup purchased chive and onion potato topper (from 12-oz. container)
- 30 slices cherry tomatoes (about 8 to 10 tomatoes)
- 1/2 yellow bell pepper
- 2 tablespoons chopped fresh parsley
- Green onion curls

1 Heat oven to 375°F. Unroll both cans of dough into 4 long rectangles. Firmly press perforations to seal. Sprinkle each rectangle with 1 tablespoon cheese and 1/4 teaspoon Italian seasoning.

2 Starting at short sides, roll up dough to form 4 rolls. Cut each roll into 8 slices. Place slices cut side down on ungreased cookie sheets to form 2 trees. To form each tree, start by placing 1 slice for top; arrange 2 slices just below, with sides touching. Continue arranging rows of 3 slices, 4 slices and 5 slices. Use remaining slice for tree trunk. Refrigerate 1 tree.

3 Bake first tree for 11 to 13 minutes or until golden brown. Cool 1 minute; carefully loosen with spatula and slide onto wire rack to cool. Bake and cool second tree.

4 Place each tree on serving platter. Spoon potato topper into resealable food storage plastic bag; seal bag. Cut 1/4-inch hole in bottom corner of bag. Pipe potato topper over trees. Place tomato slice on each pinwheel except top ones. From yellow bell pepper, cut 2 small stars using 1-1/4- to 1-1/2-inch cutter; place 1 on top slice of each tree. Chop remaining bell pepper; sprinkle over trees. Sprinkle with parsley. Top with onion curls. Refrigerate until serving time. To serve, pull apart pinwheels of tree.

NUTRITION INFORMATION PER SERVING: Calories 60 • Total Fat 4g • Saturated Fat 1g • Cholesterol 0mg • Sodium 135mg • Total Carbohydrate 6g • Dietary Fiber 0g • Sugars 1g • Protein 1g. DIETARY EXCHANGES: 1/2 Starch • 1/2 Fat OR 1/2 Carbohydrate • 1/2 Fat • 1/2 Carb Choice.

Make it a Mexican fiesta and arrange the warm appetizers on a pretty, colorful plate. Set out bowls of refried beans, tomato salsa and guacamole to serve with the finished foldovers.

green chile and cheese foldovers

PREP TIME: 20 Minutes ✱ READY IN: 45 Minutes ✱ SERVINGS: 16 Appetizers

- 1 cup finely shredded Muenster or Monterey Jack cheese (4 oz.)
- 2 tablespoons finely chopped green onion tops
- 2 tablespoons finely chopped fresh cilantro or parsley
- Dash salt
- 1 can (4.5 oz.) chopped green chiles, drained
- 1 can (16.3 oz.) Pillsbury® Grands!® Refrigerated Buttermilk Biscuits

1 Heat oven to 375°F. Spray large cookie sheet with nonstick cooking spray. In small bowl, combine cheese, onions, cilantro, salt and green chiles; mix well.

2 Separate dough into 8 biscuits. With serrated knife, cut each biscuit in half horizontally to make 16 rounds. Press or roll each to form 3-1/2-inch round. Place 1 tablespoon cheese mixture in center of each round. Fold dough over filling; press edges with fork to seal. Form each filled biscuit into crescent shape. Place on sprayed cookie sheet. Bake for 11 to 16 minutes or until golden brown. Cool 5 minutes. Serve warm.

NUTRITION INFORMATION PER SERVING: Calories 125 • Total Fat 6g • Saturated Fat 2g • Cholesterol 5mg • Sodium 430mg • Total Carbohydrate 14g • Dietary Fiber 0g • Sugars 4g • Protein 4g. DIETARY EXCHANGES: 1 Starch • 1 Fat OR 1 Carbohydrate • 1 Fat • 1 Carb Choice.

holiday herb crescent trees

cherry-cheese spread

cherry-cheese spread

PREP TIME: 15 Minutes ✷ READY IN: 25 Hours 15 Minutes ✷ SERVINGS: 2-1/4 Cups

- 1 package (8 oz.) cream cheese, cubed
- 4 oz. Havarti cheese, cubed
- 1 cup smoky Swiss cheese, shredded (4 oz.)
- 1/4 cup crumbled blue cheese (1 oz.)
- 1/4 cup slivered almonds
- 3 tablespoons cherry-flavored liqueur or 1/4 teaspoon almond extract
- 1 teaspoon chopped shallot
- 1/4 cup dried cherries, chopped

1 Let all cheeses stand at room temperature for at least 30 minutes to soften. If using a mold for the cheese spread, line mold with cheesecloth.

2 Meanwhile, heat oven to 350°F. Spread almonds on ungreased cookie sheet. Bake for 5 to 7 minutes or until golden brown, stirring occasionally. Cool.

3 In food processor bowl with metal blade, combine all cheeses, liqueur and shallot; process until smooth. Add cherries and almonds; process with on/off pulses until almonds are chopped. Spoon cheese spread into mold lined with cheesecloth, crock or small bowl; cover. Refrigerate at least 24 hours to blend flavors.

4 About 30 minutes before serving, unmold cheese spread onto plate; remove cheesecloth. Let spread stand at room temperature for 30 minutes to soften. Serve with thin slices of baguette-style French bread, assorted crackers, celery sticks or fresh pea pods.

NUTRITION INFORMATION PER SERVING: Calories 120 • Total Fat 10g • Saturated Fat 6g • Cholesterol 30mg • Sodium 120mg • Total Carbohydrate 3g • Dietary Fiber 0g • Sugars 2g • Protein 5g. DIETARY EXCHANGES: 1/2 High-Fat Meat • 1-1/2 Fat • 0 Carb Choice.

cook's notes

Crazy for cranberries? Go ahead and use them instead of the dried cherries. Or try substituting golden raisins for the cherries.

italian ham appetizer squares

READY IN: 30 Minutes ✷ SERVINGS: 18 Appetizers

- 1 package (10.6 oz.) Pillsbury® Refrigerated Garlic Breadsticks
- 6 thin slices cooked ham (about 3 oz.)
- 6 thin slices provolone cheese (about 4 oz.)
- 1 medium tomato, chopped
- 6 to 7 large ripe olives, sliced
- 1/2 cup chopped fresh basil
- 2 tablespoons purchased Italian vinaigrette salad dressing

1 Heat oven to 375°F. Unroll dough; separate into 2 equal sections along center perforation. Place 1 inch apart in ungreased 15x10x1-inch baking pan or 13x9-inch (3-quart) glass baking dish. Press perforations to seal. Spread garlic spread from container evenly over each dough section.

2 Bake for 9 to 11 minutes or until light golden brown. Remove partially baked crusts from oven. Top each crust with ham, cheese, tomato and olives. Return to oven; bake an additional 5 minutes or until cheese is melted and edges are golden brown.

3 To serve, cut each topped crust into 9 squares. Sprinkle with basil. Drizzle with salad dressing. Serve warm.

NUTRITION INFORMATION PER SERVING: Calories 90 • Total Fat 5g • Saturated Fat 2g • Cholesterol 5mg • Sodium 300mg • Total Carbohydrate 8g • Dietary Fiber 0g • Sugars 1g • Protein 4g. DIETARY EXCHANGES: 1/2 Starch • 1/2 Lean Meat • 1/2 Fat OR 1/2 Carbohydrate • 1/2 Lean Meat • 1/2 Fat • 1/2 Carb Choice.

kitchen tip

Fresh basil, a key ingredient in these squares, has incomparable flavor and fragrance, but it can wilt quickly in the refrigerator. Trim the stems, as you would with fresh flowers, and set the basil "bouquet" into a glass holding an inch or two of water. Cover the leaves with a plastic bag and store the basil in the refrigerator.

cook's notes

Kiwi fruit slices, mandarin orange wedges and diced fresh mango also make great topping options for these tarts.

mini tart buffet with créme anglaise

PREP TIME: 20 Minutes ✵ READY IN: 1 Hour 20 Minutes ✵ SERVINGS: 6

Créme Anglaise

- 1 cup whipping cream
- 1/2 vanilla bean, split lengthwise, or 1 teaspoon vanilla
- 2 egg yolks
- 1/4 cup sugar

Tarts

- 1 Pillsbury® Refrigerated Pie Crust (from 15-oz. box), softened as directed on box
- 3/4 teaspoon sugar

Toppings

- 2-1/2 cups sliced fresh strawberries
- 1 cup fresh blackberries or raspberries
- 1 cup roasted whole cashews
- 1 jar gourmet chocolate topping, heated
- 1 jar lemon or lime curd

1. In 2-quart saucepan, heat cream and vanilla bean (if using vanilla, add at the end) just to boiling over low heat. In small bowl, beat egg yolks and sugar with wire whisk. Beat small amount of hot cream into yolks. Blend yolk mixture into cream in saucepan; cook over low heat about 10 minutes, stirring constantly, until custard coats a spoon. Do not boil. Remove from heat. Remove vanilla bean and scrape seeds into sauce. Stir until seeds separate. Cool to room temperature, about 30 minutes. Refrigerate until serving time.

2. Heat oven to 450°F. Spray back of 12-cup regular-size muffin pan with nonstick cooking spray. Remove pie crust from pouch; unroll on work surface. Sprinkle crust with sugar; press in lightly. Cut 6 rounds from crust with 4-inch round cookie cutter, or trace 6 rounds with top of large drinking glass and cut out with sharp knife.

3. Fit rounds, sugared side up, alternately over backs of muffin cups. Pinch 5 equally spaced pleats around side of each cup. Prick each generously with fork.

4. Bake 5 to 7 minutes or until lightly browned. Cool 5 minutes. Carefully remove tart shells from muffin cups. Cool completely, about 30 minutes.

5. Just before serving, arrange tart shells on tray with toppings and Créme Anglaise in separate serving containers. Cover and refrigerate any remaining Créme Anglaise.

High Altitude (3500-6500 ft): Bake 5 to 6 minutes.

NUTRITION INFORMATION PER SERVING: 1 Tart Shell (without toppings): Calories 830 • Total Fat 40g • Saturated Fat 16g • Trans Fat 0g • Cholesterol 155mg • Sodium 440mg • Dietary Fiber 5g. DIETARY EXCHANGES: 1/2 Starch • 1/2 Fruit • 6 Other Carbohydrate • 1 High-Fat Meat • 6-1/2 Fat • 7 Carb Choices.

cook's notes

The fruit pieces need to be dry when dipping them into the fondue. If they're slightly wet, the chocolate might not stick as well.

dark chocolate fondue

READY IN: 30 Minutes ✵ SERVINGS: 18

Fondue

- 1/2 cup sugar
- 3/4 cup whipping cream
- 8 oz. mildly sweet dark chocolate, chopped

Dipper Ideas

- Apple wedges
- Orange sections
- Maraschino cherries with stems
- Pineapple chunks
- Strawberries
- Large marshmallows
- Pound cake cubes

1. In 2-quart saucepan, heat all fondue ingredients over medium heat, stirring constantly, just until chocolate is melted. Pour mixture into fondue pot; keep warm over low heat. Spear desired dippers with fondue forks; dip into fondue.

NUTRITION INFORMATION PER SERVING: Calories 120 • Total Fat 7g • Saturated Fat 4g • Trans Fat 0g • Cholesterol 10mg • Sodium 0mg • Total Carbohydrate 14g • Dietary Fiber 0g • Sugars 13g • Protein 0g. DIETARY EXCHANGES: 1 Other Carbohydrate • 1-1/2 Fat • 1 Carb Choice.

cherry fruit punch

READY IN: 15 Minutes ✱ SERVINGS: 31 Cups

- 1 box (4-serving size) cherry-flavored gelatin
- 1 cup boiling water
- 1 can (46 oz.) pineapple juice, chilled
- 1 quart (4 cups) apple cider, chilled
- 1/4 cup lemon juice
- 1 bottle (33.8 oz.) ginger ale, chilled

1 In 3-quart pitcher or bowl, stir gelatin and boiling water until gelatin is dissolved. Stir in pineapple juice, apple cider and lemon juice.

2 If desired, refrigerate until serving time. Just before serving, pour mixture into punch bowl. Gently stir in ginger ale.

NUTRITION INFORMATION PER SERVING: Calories 70 • Total Fat 0g • Saturated Fat 0g • Cholesterol 0mg • Sodium 20mg • Total Carbohydrate 16g • Dietary Fiber 0g. DIETARY EXCHANGE: 1 Other Carbohydrate.

cook's notes

Decorative cocktail picks may be used with cut-up apples or pineapple wedges.

crab puffs

crab puffs

PREP TIME: 25 Minutes ✱ READY IN: 45 Minutes ✱ SERVINGS: 24 Appetizers

- 1 tablespoon butter or margarine, melted
- 1/2 teaspoon garlic powder
- 1 can (8 oz.) Pillsbury® Refrigerated Crescent Dinner Rolls
- 1 egg
- 1/2 cup mayonnaise
- 1 can (6 oz.) crabmeat, drained, flaked
- 3/4 cup shredded sharp Cheddar cheese
- 1/3 cup finely chopped plum (Roma) tomato (1 medium)
- 3 tablespoons finely chopped green onions (3 medium)
- 1 teaspoon hot pepper sauce

1 Heat oven to 375°F. In small bowl, mix butter and garlic powder; set aside. On lightly floured surface, unroll dough; firmly press perforations to seal. Press into 12x8-inch rectangle. Cut into 2-inch squares; place on ungreased cookie sheet. Brush with butter mixture. Bake 4 to 6 minutes or until puffed.

2 Meanwhile, in medium bowl, mix egg and mayonnaise until well blended. Stir in crabmeat, cheese, tomato, onions and hot pepper sauce.

3 Remove baked squares from oven. Spoon generous tablespoon crab mixture on each square. Return to oven; bake 10 to 12 minutes longer or until golden brown and tops are set. Serve warm.

High Altitude (3500-6500 ft): Heat oven to 350°F. Decrease mayonnaise to 1/3 cup. Bake 11 to 13 minutes.

NUTRITION INFORMATION PER SERVING: Calories 100 • Total Fat 8g • Saturated Fat 2.5g • Trans Fat 0.5g • Cholesterol 20mg • Sodium 150mg • Total Carbohydrate 4g • Dietary Fiber 0g • Sugars 0g • Protein 3g. DIETARY EXCHANGES: 1/2 High-Fat Meat • 1 Fat • 0 Carb Choice.

cook's notes

To make ahead, cut the dough squares and place on the cookie sheet; brush with butter mixture. Cover loosely with plastic wrap and refrigerate for up to 2 hours. Make the crabmeat mixture; cover and refrigerate separately.

garlic herb and salmon empanadas

PREP TIME: 30 Minutes ✱ READY IN: 50 Minutes ✱ SERVINGS: 16 Appetizers

- 1 package (15 oz.) Pillsbury® Refrigerated Pie Crusts, softened as directed on package
- 6 oz. smoked salmon, flaked
- 1 package (5.2 oz.) Boursin cheese with garlic and herbs

1 Heat oven to 425°F. Line large cookie sheet with parchment paper or spray with nonstick cooking spray. Remove pie crusts from pouches. Unfold crusts; cut each into 4 wedges.

2 In small bowl, combine salmon and cheese; mix well. Spread about 2 tablespoons mixture evenly over half of each crust wedge to within 1/4 inch of edges. Brush edges of crust with water. Fold untopped dough over filling, forming triangle; press edges to seal. Place on paper-lined cookie sheet.

3 Bake for 12 to 17 minutes or until golden brown. Remove from cookie sheet; place on wire rack. Cool 10 minutes. To serve, cut each warm empanada in half, forming 2 triangles.

NUTRITION INFORMATION PER SERVING: Calories 160 • Total Fat 10g • Saturated Fat 5g • Cholesterol 10mg • Sodium 240mg • Total Carbohydrate 13g • Dietary Fiber 0g • Sugars 1g • Protein 4g. DIETARY EXCHANGES: 1 Starch • 2 Fat OR 1 Carbohydrate • 2 Fat • 1 Carb Choice.

special touch

Try serving these rich, smoky empanadas with a side of sour cream topped with chopped fresh chives or green onions.

cook's notes

Get a head start by making this snack a day early. Prepare the ravioli and the sauce and cool separately. Cover and refrigerate both for one day. To serve, arrange the ravioli in a single layer on a cookie sheet and reheat in a 350°F oven for 10 minutes or until the ravioli are hot. Reheat the sauce on the stovetop.

fried ravioli with tomato sauce

READY IN: 45 Minutes ✷ SERVINGS: 40 Appetizers

- 1 can (15 oz.) tomato sauce
- 1 cup finely chopped fresh tomato (about 1 large)
- 1/2 cup finely chopped sun-dried tomatoes packed in olive oil and herbs
- 1 teaspoon dried Italian seasoning
- 1 quart (4 cups) vegetable oil for deep-frying
- 1 package (25 oz.) frozen small square cheese-filled ravioli, thawed, or 1 package (20 oz.) refrigerated 4-cheese ravioli, thawed
- 2 tablespoons chopped green onion tops

1 In medium saucepan, combine tomato sauce, fresh tomato, sun-dried tomatoes and Italian seasoning; mix well. Bring to a boil. Reduce heat to medium-low; simmer 15 to 20 minutes or until thickened, stirring occasionally.

2 Meanwhile, heat oil in large heavy saucepan over medium-high heat to 375°F. Pat ravioli dry with paper towels. Fry ravioli, about 6 at a time, for 1 to 3 minutes or until golden and crisp, turning ravioli once.

3 Drain ravioli on paper towels. Pour sauce into serving bowl; sprinkle with onions. Serve warm ravioli with warm dipping sauce.

NUTRITION INFORMATION PER SERVING: Calories 50 • Total Fat 3g • Saturated Fat 1g • Cholesterol 20mg • Sodium 210mg • Total Carbohydrate 4g • Dietary Fiber 0g • Sugars 1g • Protein 2g. DIETARY EXCHANGES: 1/2 Medium-Fat Meat • 1/2 Fat • 0 Carb Choice.

asiago, bacon and olive roll-ups

PREP TIME: 20 Minutes ✷ READY IN: 40 Minutes ✷ SERVINGS:16 Appetizers

Roll-Ups

- 5 slices bacon, cut into small pieces
- 1/2 cup Asiago cheese, finely shredded (2 oz.)
- 8 pitted medium-sized ripe olives, chopped
- 1 can (8 oz.) Pillsbury® Refrigerated Crescent Dinner Rolls
- 1 to 2 teaspoons purchased sun-dried tomato paste or Italian tomato paste

Dipping Sauce

- 1/4 cup sour cream
- 1/4 cup purchased ranch salad dressing
- 1/4 teaspoon salt

1 Heat oven to 350°F. Cook bacon until crisp. Drain on paper towel. In small bowl, combine bacon, cheese and olives; toss to mix.

2 Separate dough into 8 triangles; press out slightly. Cut each triangle in half lengthwise to make 16 triangles.

3 Spread thin layer of tomato paste on each triangle. Spoon 1-1/2 teaspoons olive mixture on shortest side of each triangle; spread slightly. Roll up each, starting at shortest side of triangle and rolling to opposite point. Place point side down on ungreased cookie sheet. Bake for 13 to 18 minutes or until golden brown.

4 Meanwhile, in small bowl, combine all dipping sauce ingredients; mix well. Place bowl of sour cream mixture in center of serving plate. Arrange warm roll-ups around bowl.

NUTRITION INFORMATION PER SERVING: Calories 110 • Total Fat 8g • Saturated Fat 2g • Cholesterol 5mg • Sodium 280mg • Total Carbohydrate 6g • Dietary Fiber 0g • Sugars 1g • Protein 3g. DIETARY EXCHANGES: 1/2 Starch • 1-1/2 Fat OR 1/2 Carbohydrate • 1-1/2 Fat • 1/2 Carb Choice.

cook's notes

You'll be one step ahead if you make the sour cream dipping sauce a day in advance. Cover and refrigerate the dip until you're ready to serve these tasty snacks.

fried ravioli with tomato sauce

Kitchen tip

Unlike whiskey, gin isn't aged, so it was an easy, popular choice for bootleggers during Prohibition. The homemade spirit was called bathtub gin.

bathtub gin fizz

READY IN: 5 Minutes ✷ SERVINGS: 8

- 1 bottle (2 liters) lemon-lime flavored carbonated beverage
- 1 can (12 oz.) frozen lemonade concentrate, thawed
- 1/2 cup lime juice
- 1/4 cup powdered sugar
- 2-1/4 cups gin
- Ice

1 In large punch bowl, combine carbonated beverage, lemonade concentrate, lime juice and powdered sugar; stir to blend.

2 Gently stir in the gin. Serve over ice in tall glasses. If desired, garnish individual glasses with lime slices.

NUTRITION INFORMATION PER SERVING: Calories 390 • Total Fat 0g • Saturated Fat 0g • Cholesterol 0mg • Sodium 35mg • Total Carbohydrate 57g • Dietary Fiber 0g • Sugars 52g • Protein 0g. DIETARY EXCHANGES: 4 Fruit • 4 Other Carbohydrate • 3-1/2 Fat.

poinsettia brie with breadstick bites

READY IN: 45 Minutes ✱ SERVINGS: 8

- 1 round (8 oz.) Brie cheese
- 1 can (11 oz.) Pillsbury® Refrigerated Breadsticks
- 2 tablespoons butter or margarine, melted
- 1 teaspoon sesame seed
- 1/2 teaspoon herbes de Provence
- 1/4 teaspoon garlic powder
- 5 pieces (1 inch each) roasted red bell peppers (from a jar)
- 1 teaspoon chopped yellow bell pepper
- 3 basil leaves

1 Heat oven to 375°F. Cut 15-inch piece of foil. Fold in half lengthwise; cut on fold to make 2 strips. Overlap 2 ends; fold together to make 29-inch strip. Fold lengthwise twice to make long strip 1-1/2 inches wide. Overlap and fold remaining ends to form 8-inch diameter circle for collar. Spray inside of collar with nonstick cooking spray. Place on ungreased cookie sheet. Place cheese in center of collar.

2 Separate dough into 12 breadsticks. Cut each into 4 pieces; place in medium bowl. Drizzle dough with melted butter. Sprinkle with sesame seed, herbes de Provence and garlic powder; toss to coat. Spoon breadstick pieces to fill space between cheese and foil collar on cookie sheet.

3 Bake for 15 minutes. Remove foil collar; bake an additional 5 to 10 minutes or until breadstick pieces are golden brown and cheese is soft.

4 Cut roasted pepper pieces into shapes to resemble poinsettia petals. Place in center of cheese. Sprinkle yellow bell pepper pieces in center of poinsettia. Place basil leaves around roasted pepper pieces to resemble leaves. Slide onto serving plate. Serve melted cheese with warm breadstick pieces.

NUTRITION INFORMATION PER SERVING: Calories 230 • Total Fat 13g • Saturated Fat 6g • Cholesterol 30mg • Sodium 500mg • Total Carbohydrate 19g • Dietary Fiber 1g • Sugars 3g • Protein 9g. DIETARY EXCHANGES: 1 Starch • 1 High-Fat Meat • 1 Fat OR 1 Carbohydrate • 1 High-Fat Meat • 1 Fat • 1 Carb Choice.

Kitchen tip

Herbes de Provence is an herb blend that's popular in southern France. To substitute for the dried blend, you can improvise by mixing 1/8 teaspoon each of dried marjoram, thyme, summer savory, crushed rosemary and ground sage. If you prefer, just pick your favorite from the listed herbs and sprinkle it onto the breadsticks.

crescent-crab purses

PREP TIME: 20 Minutes ✱ READY IN: 40 Minutes ✱ SERVINGS: 12 Appetizers

- 1 can (6 oz.) crabmeat, well drained
- 2 tablespoons grated Parmesan cheese
- 2 tablespoons sharp process cheese spread (from 5-oz. jar)
- 1 tablespoon chopped fresh parsley, if desired
- 1/8 teaspoon ground red pepper (cayenne)
- 1 clove garlic, finely chopped
- 1 can (8 oz.) refrigerated crescent dinner rolls

1 Heat oven to 375°F. In small bowl, mix all ingredients except dough. Unroll dough into 1 large rectangle; press into 12x9-inch rectangle, firmly pressing perforations to seal. Cut rectangle into twelve 3-inch squares.

2 Place about 1 tablespoon crab mixture on each dough square. Bring all sides together in center; press to seal. With fingers, pinch dough firmly about 1/4 inch below edges, making a pouch with points extending over top. Place on ungreased cookie sheet.

3 Bake 12 to 17 minutes or until deep golden brown. Immediately remove from the cookie sheet. Serve warm.

NUTRITION INFORMATION PER SERVING: Calories 90 • Total Fat 5g • Saturated Fat 2g • Trans Fat 1g • Cholesterol 15mg • Sodium 240mg • Total Carbohydrate 8g • Dietary Fiber 0g • Sugars 2g • Protein 5g. DIETARY EXCHANGES: 1/2 Starch • 1/2 Lean Meat • 1/2 Fat • 1/2 Carb Choice.

Kitchen tip

"Purses" are a take on steamed Chinese appetizer buns and resemble drawstring pouches. Pinch the dough together firmly over the filling so each "pouch" stays sealed.

cook's notes

This appetizer cheesecake is so impressive and utterly delicious. If you have trouble finding the Creole seasoning, go ahead and use Cajun seasoning instead.

savory crab cheesecake

PREP TIME: 20 Minutes ✷ READY IN: 4 Hours 30 Minutes ✷ SERVINGS: 20

Crust

- 1/2 cup Italian-style dry bread crumbs
- 1/4 cup shredded Parmesan cheese (1 oz.)
- 2 tablespoons butter or margarine, melted

Filling

- 20 oz. cream cheese, softened
- 2 tablespoons finely chopped green onions (2 medium)
- 1-1/2 teaspoons dried Creole seasoning
- 1 teaspoon sugar
- 1/2 teaspoon ground mustard
- Dash ground red pepper (cayenne)
- 1/2 cup whipping cream
- 1 tablespoon cocktail sauce
- 1 teaspoon Worcestershire sauce
- 1/2 teaspoon red pepper sauce
- 4 eggs
- 1 can (6 oz.) lump crabmeat, drained
- Fresh parsley sprigs or leaf lettuce
- 1/2 to 3/4 cup cocktail sauce
- Assorted crackers

1 Heat oven to 350°F. In small bowl, mix all crust ingredients. Press mixture in bottom of ungreased 8- or 9-inch springform pan. Bake 5 to 9 minutes or until light golden brown.

2 Meanwhile, in large bowl, beat all filling ingredients except eggs and crabmeat with electric mixer on medium speed until well blended. Beat in 1 egg at a time until well blended. Stir in crabmeat. Pour filling over partially baked crust.

3 Bake 60 to 70 minutes longer for 8-inch pan; 40 to 50 minutes for 9-inch pan or until filling is set. Cool 30 minutes.

4 With small metal spatula or knife, loosen edge of cheesecake. Cool 30 minutes longer. Refrigerate before serving, at least 2 hours.

5 To serve, remove side of pan; place cheesecake on serving platter. Arrange parsley around outer edge. Serve with cocktail sauce and crackers.

High Altitude (3500-6500 ft): Use 9-inch springform pan. Before baking cheesecake, place baking pan filled with about 2 inches water on oven rack below middle rack. Place cheesecake on middle oven rack over pan.

NUTRITION INFORMATION PER SERVING: Calories 250 • Total Fat 19g • Saturated Fat 10g • Trans Fat 1.5g • Cholesterol 90mg • Sodium 460mg • Total Carbohydrate 14g • Dietary Fiber 0g • Sugars 4g • Protein 7g. DIETARY EXCHANGES: 1 Starch • 1/2 High-Fat Meat • 3 Fat • 1 Carb Choice.

special touch

For a finishing touch, garnish each pinwheel with a small fresh basil leaf. If you grow your own basil, pinch off flowers as they form so the plant will continue to produce leaves.

roasted red pepper and pesto pinwheels

PREP TIME: 15 Minutes ✷ READY IN: 35 Minutes ✷ SERVINGS: 16 Appetizers

- 1 can (8 oz.) Pillsbury® Refrigerated Crescent Dinner Rolls
- 1/3 cup purchased pesto
- 1/4 cup chopped purchased roasted red bell peppers (from a jar)

1 Heat oven to 350°F. Unroll dough into 2 long rectangles. Firmly press perforations to seal. Spread rectangles with pesto to within 1/4 inch of edges. Sprinkle with bell peppers.

2 Starting at short side, roll up each rectangle; pinch edges to seal. Cut each roll into 8 slices. Place cut side down on ungreased cookie sheet.

3 Bake for 13 to 17 minutes or until golden brown. Immediately remove from cookie sheet. Serve pinwheels warm.

NUTRITION INFORMATION PER SERVING: Calories 60 • Total Fat 4g • Saturated Fat 1g • Cholesterol 0mg • Sodium 125mg • Total Carbohydrate 6g • Dietary Fiber 0g • Sugars 1g • Protein 1g. DIETARY EXCHANGES: 1/2 Starch • 1/2 Fat OR 1/2 Carbohydrate • 1/2 Fat • 1/2 Carb Choice.

savory crab cheesecake

mini swiss quiches

mini swiss quiches

PREP TIME: 25 Minutes ✱ READY IN: 1 Hour 10 Minutes ✱ SERVINGS: 24 Appetizers

- 1 box (15 oz.) Pillsbury® Refrigerated Pie Crusts, softened as directed on box
- 1-1/2 cups shredded Swiss cheese (6 oz.)
- 2 tablespoons sliced green onions (2 medium)
- 1 tablespoon chopped pimientos
- 2 eggs
- 1/2 cup milk
- 1/4 teaspoon salt
- Dash ground nutmeg

1 Heat oven to 375°F. Spray 24 miniature muffin cups with nonstick cooking spray. Remove 1 crust from pouch; place on cutting board. With 2-1/2-inch round cookie cutter, cut 12 rounds from crust. Repeat with remaining crust. Press 1 round of dough into the bottom and up the sides of each muffin cup.

2 Place 1 tablespoon cheese in each cup. Top each with onion and pimientos. In small bowl, beat eggs, milk, salt and nutmeg with a fork until blended. Pour into the crusts, filling to within 1/4 inch of the top.

3 Bake 25 to 30 minutes or until golden brown. Cool slightly. Carefully lift quiches from muffin cups with tip of knife. Serve warm.

NUTRITION INFORMATION PER SERVING: Calories 80 • Total Fat 5g • Saturated Fat 2.5g • Cholesterol 25mg • Sodium 90mg • Total Carbohydrate 6g • Dietary Fiber 0g. DIETARY EXCHANGES: 1/2 Starch • 1 Fat.

Kitchen tip

If you don't have a 2-1/2-inch round cookie cutter, measure some of the small cans and jars in your recycling bin. A large clean juice concentrate can or a soup can is just about the right size.

tomato-basil appetizer wedges

PREP TIME: 20 Minutes ✱ READY IN: 1 Hour 10 Minutes ✱ SERVINGS:12

- 1 Pillsbury® Refrigerated Pie Crust (from 15-oz. package), softened as directed on package
- 1/2 cup Italian-style dry bread crumbs
- 1/3 cup chopped fresh basil
- 1/4 cup grated Romano cheese
- 1/4 teaspoon salt
- 1/4 teaspoon freshly ground black pepper
- 1 cup ricotta cheese
- 3 tablespoons extra-virgin or regular olive oil
- 3 Italian plum tomatoes, seeded, diced

1 Heat oven to 400°F. Remove crust from pouch; unfold crust. Place on ungreased cookie sheet; press out fold lines. With rolling pin, roll to form 12-inch round.

2 In medium bowl, combine bread crumbs, basil, Romano cheese, salt, pepper, ricotta cheese and oil; mix well. Stir in tomatoes. Spoon and spread over crust to within 3 inches of edge. Fold edge of crust 3 inches over filling; crimp crust slightly.

3 Bake for 25 to 35 minutes or until golden brown. Cool 15 minutes. Cut into 12 wedges. Serve wedges warm or cool.

NUTRITION INFORMATION PER SERVING: Calories 175 • Total Fat 11g • Saturated Fat 4g • Cholesterol 11mg • Sodium 230mg • Total Carbohydrate 14g • Dietary Fiber 0g • Sugars 2g • Protein 5g. DIETARY EXCHANGES: 1 Starch • 2 Fat OR 1 Carbohydrate • 2 Fat • 1 Carb Choice.

special touch

Add a fresh finish to these appetizers by garnishing each serving with a thin slice of fresh plum tomato and shredded fresh basil.

Kitchen tip

Crescents and other refrigerated dough products should be stored on a shelf in the main part of the refrigerator. Temperatures in the refrigerator's door shelves or crisper may be too warm or too cold. Be sure to keep dough refrigerated until just before baking.

seafood appetizers

PREP TIME: 15 Minutes ✷ READY IN: 35 Minutes ✷ SERVINGS: 24 Appetizers

- 2 cups frozen cooked cocktail or salad shrimp
- 1 can (8 oz.) Pillsbury® Refrigerated Crescent Dinner Rolls
- 1 cup flaked imitation crabmeat (surimi), cut into small pieces
- 1 teaspoon seafood seasoning blend
- 1 teaspoon garlic powder
- 1-1/2 cups shredded Mexican cheese blend (6 oz.)
- 1 teaspoon dried parsley flakes

1 Heat oven to 375°F. Thaw shrimp as directed on package. Drain well; press between paper towels to remove excess liquid. Cut shrimp into small pieces.

2 Unroll dough onto ungreased cookie sheet. Press to form 12x8-inch rectangle. Firmly press perforations to seal. Top dough with shrimp and all remaining ingredients.

3 Bake for 15 to 20 minutes or until the crust is golden brown. Cut dough into 24 squares. Serve squares warm.

NUTRITION INFORMATION PER SERVING: Calories 80 • Total Fat 4g • Saturated Fat 2g • Cholesterol 30mg • Sodium 210mg • Total Carbohydrate 5g • Dietary Fiber 0g • Sugars 1g • Protein 5g. DIETARY EXCHANGES: 1/2 Starch • 1/2 Very Lean Meat • 1/2 Fat OR 1/2 Carbohydrate • 1/2 Very Lean Meat • 1/2 Fat • 0 Carb Choice.

peachy keen slush

PREP TIME: 15 Minutes ✷ READY IN: 8 Hours 15 Minutes ✷ SERVINGS: 22

- 1/4 cup sugar
- 5 cups water
- 1 can (12 oz.) frozen orange juice concentrate, thawed
- 1 can (12 oz.) frozen lemonade concentrate, thawed
- 2-1/2 cups peach-flavored schnapps
- 1/3 cup lemon juice
- 1 bottle (2 liters) ginger ale, chilled

1 In medium saucepan, mix sugar and 2 cups of the water. Heat to boiling. Boil 3 minutes. Set aside to cool slightly.

2 In large non-metal freezer container, blend juice concentrates, remaining 3 cups water, the schnapps and lemon juice. Stir in sugar mixture. Cover; freeze at least 8 hours or overnight, stirring 2 or 3 times after 2 hours, until frozen.

3 To serve, spoon 1/2 cup slush mixture into each glass. Add about 1/3 cup ginger ale to each; stir gently.

NUTRITION INFORMATION PER SERVING: Calories 170 • Total Fat 0g • Saturated Fat 0g • Trans Fat 0g • Cholesterol 0mg • Sodium 15mg • Total Carbohydrate 30g • Dietary Fiber 0g • Sugars 28g • Protein 0g. DIETARY EXCHANGES: 2 Other Carbohydrate • 1 Fat • 2 Carb Choices.

goat cheese, marinara and pine nut braid

PREP TIME: 20 Minutes ✱ READY IN: 55 Minutes ✱ SERVINGS: 10

- 1 package (10.6 oz.) Pillsbury® Refrigerated Garlic Breadsticks
- 1/2 cup purchased marinara sauce
- 1/4 cup crumbled chèvre (goat) cheese (1 oz.)
- 1/4 cup grated Parmesan cheese or shredded fresh Parmesan cheese
- 1/4 to 1/2 teaspoon dried rosemary leaves, crushed
- 1/4 cup pine nuts, toasted
- 2 tablespoons chopped fresh basil

1 Heat oven to 375°F. Spray cookie sheet with nonstick cooking spray. Unroll dough; separate into 2 equal sections along center perforation. Place dough sections next to each other on sprayed cookie sheet forming 10 parallel strips. Press to form 12x7-inch rectangle.

2 Spread marinara sauce lengthwise in 3-inch-wide strip down center of dough to within 1/2 inch of edges. Sprinkle chèvre cheese, 2 tablespoons of the Parmesan cheese, rosemary and pine nuts over sauce.

3 Cut dough on perforation lines up to filling. Fold strips of dough over filling, stretching slightly; press edges of dough together. Carefully spread garlic spread from container over dough. Sprinkle with remaining 2 tablespoons Parmesan cheese.

4 Bake for 17 to 22 minutes or until golden brown. Sprinkle with basil. Cool 10 minutes. Cut into crosswise slices. Serve warm.

NUTRITION INFORMATION PER SERVING: Calories 140 • Total Fat 7g • Saturated Fat 2g • Cholesterol 5mg • Sodium 390mg • Total Carbohydrate 14g • Dietary Fiber 1g • Sugars 2g • Protein 5g. DIETARY EXCHANGES: 1 Starch • 1-1/2 Fat OR 1 Carbohydrate • 1-1/2 Fat • 1 Carb Choice.

Kitchen tip

Be sure to store chèvre or goat cheese in the refrigerator, tightly wrapped in plastic and away from eggs, butter and other foods that might easily pick up other flavors.

garlic and herb crescent ornament

garlic and herb crescent ornament

PREP TIME: 30 Minutes ✱ READY IN: 1 Hour ✱ SERVINGS: 20

ORNAMENT

2 cans (8 oz. each) Pillsbury® Refrigerated Crescent Dinner Rolls

TOPPING

4 oz. cream cheese, softened

1/3 cup whipping cream

1/2 cup garlic and herb spreadable cheese

GARNISH

2 gold or silver baking cups

Sprigs fresh rosemary

Choice of red, yellow or green bell peppers, carrots, zucchini, cherry tomatoes and fresh chopped thyme

1 Heat oven to 375°F. Spray 12-inch pizza pan with nonstick cooking spray. Remove dough from 1 can, keeping dough in one piece; do not unroll. With palms of hands, gently roll dough in one direction into 12-inch log. With serrated knife, cut log into 20 slices. Repeat with the second can of dough.

2 At center of spray-coated pizza pan, arrange 2 slices side by side, pressing together to flatten inside edges and to form a circle. Place 7 slices in ring around center slices; press together lightly. Arrange 12 slices in the next ring; press together lightly. Arrange 19 slices in the last ring, overlapping edges slightly in ring. (See photo.) Press together gently.

3 Bake for 13 to 18 minutes or until edges are golden brown. Gently loosen ornament from pan; cool 5 minutes. Gently remove ornament from pan; slide onto wire rack. Cool 15 minutes or until completely cooled.

4 Meanwhile, in medium bowl, beat cream cheese at medium speed until soft and fluffy. Slowly beat in whipping cream, continue beating until fluffy. Beat in spreadable cheese until well blended. Cover; refrigerate until serving time.

5 Place cooled ornament on large round serving tray, rearranging as necessary if crescent slices have separated. Spread entire ornament with cream cheese mixture. Shape one foil baking cup to resemble metal ornament top, folding in half at base of cup. Cut small slit in top. Fold second baking cup inward from outside edges to make metal strip. Twist together at base to make loop for ornament top. Insert base into slit. Slide springs of rosemary through loop to resemble branch of pine tree. Garnish as desired with vegetables and thyme.

NUTRITION INFORMATION PER SERVING: Calories 140 • Total Fat 10g • Saturated Fat 4g • Cholesterol 15mg • Sodium 230mg • Total Carbohydrate 10g • Dietary Fiber 0g • Sugars 2g • Protein 2g. DIETARY EXCHANGES: 1/2 Starch • 1/2 Other Carbohydrate • 2 Fat.

kitchen tip

Be sure to keep cans of dough refrigerated until you're ready to use them. In this recipe, keep one can refrigerated while you begin assembling the recipe with the first can.

chile cheese puffs

PREP TIME: 20 Minutes ✱ READY IN: 45 Minutes ✱ SERVINGS: 32 Appetizers

1 can (11 oz.) Pillsbury® Refrigerated Breadsticks

2 eggs

2 cups shredded Cheddar cheese (8 oz.)

1/4 cup finely chopped onion

1/2 cup mayonnaise

1/4 teaspoon salt

1/4 teaspoon pepper

1/4 teaspoon ground red pepper (cayenne)

1 can (4.5 oz.) chopped green chiles, drained

1 Heat oven to 375°F. Lightly grease 13x9-inch pan. Unroll dough into 1 long rectangle in greased pan. Starting at center, press out dough to edges of pan; press perforations to seal.

2 Beat eggs in medium bowl. Add all remaining ingredients; mix well. Spoon and spread mixture evenly over dough.

3 Bake for 17 to 22 minutes or until filling is set and edges are light golden brown. Cool 5 minutes. Cut into small squares. Serve warm.

NUTRITION INFORMATION PER SERVING: Calories 90 • Total Fat 6g • Saturated Fat 2g • Cholesterol 25mg • Sodium 170mg • Total Carbohydrate 5g • Dietary Fiber 0g • Sugars 1g • Protein 3g. DIETARY EXCHANGES: 1/2 Starch • 1 Fat OR 1/2 Carbohydrate • 1 Fat • 0 Carb Choice.

special touch

Stir up a quick homemade salsa to serve with these cheese puff squares. To improvise, mix chopped fresh tomatoes, green chiles and finely chopped onion with some lime juice and a dash of ground cumin.

For a burst of flavor, add basil or rosemary sprigs to each cup.

spicy shrimp cups

PREP TIME: 20 Minutes ✱ READY IN: 1 Hour 30 Minutes ✱ SERVINGS: 24 Appetizers

- 1 box (15 oz.) Pillsbury® Refrigerated Pie Crusts, softened as directed on box
- 12 oz. cream cheese, softened
- 1 tablespoon chopped fresh parsley
- 4 teaspoons honey
- 3 teaspoons hot pepper sauce
- 24 cooked deveined peeled medium shrimp
- Fresh parsley sprigs
- Grated lime peel, if desired

1 Heat oven to 425°F. Remove pie crusts from pouches; unroll on work surface. Cut each crust into 12 (2-1/2-inch) squares. Discard scraps.

2 Turn mini muffin pans upside down (you will need 24 cups). Press square of dough over top of each ungreased inverted mini muffin cup. Prick top and sides of each with fork; fold and pinch corners to shape cups.

3 Bake 8 to 10 minutes or until golden brown. Cool 5 minutes. Remove from muffin cups to cooling racks. Cool completely, about 30 minutes.

4 In medium bowl, mix cream cheese, chopped parsley, honey and pepper sauce until smooth. Spoon about 1 tablespoon mixture into each pastry cup. Top each with 1 shrimp. Refrigerate 30 minutes or until cold. Garnish each cup with parsley sprig and lime peel.

High Altitude (3500-6500 ft): Bake 10 to 12 minutes.

NUTRITION INFORMATION PER SERVING: Calories 120 • Total Fat 8g • Saturated Fat 4.5g • Cholesterol 30mg • Sodium 115mg • Total Carbohydrate 8g • Dietary Fiber 0g. DIETARY EXCHANGES: 1/2 Starch • 1-1/2 Fat.

Love the taste of garlic? Chop a clove of garlic and heat with the olive oil in the microwave for about 20 seconds before brushing it onto the bread.

beef crostini with caper mayonnaise

READY IN: 30 Minutes ✱ SERVINGS: 24 Appetizers

- 24 slices (1/4- to 1/2-inch-thick) baguette or small French bread
- 2 tablespoons olive oil
- 1/2 cup mayonnaise
- 1/4 cup grated Parmesan cheese
- 2 tablespoons chopped fresh chives
- 2 to 4 tablespoons drained capers
- 1/4 teaspoon garlic powder
- 1/2 lb. thinly sliced cooked roast beef (from deli), cut into 24 pieces
- 2 Italian plum tomatoes, cut into 24 thin slices
- Chopped fresh chives, if desired

1 Heat oven to 350°F. Place bread slices on ungreased cookie sheet; brush lightly with oil. Bake for 8 to 10 minutes or until crisp. Cool 5 minutes or until completely cooled.

2 Meanwhile, in small bowl, combine mayonnaise, cheese, 2 tablespoons chives, the capers and garlic powder; mix well.

3 Spread about 1/2 tablespoon mayonnaise mixture on each toasted bread slice. Top each with 1 piece of roast beef and 1 slice of tomato. Garnish with chives.

NUTRITION INFORMATION PER SERVING: Calories 80 • Total Fat 6g • Saturated Fat 1g • Cholesterol 10mg • Sodium 190mg • Total Carbohydrate 3g • Dietary Fiber 0g • Sugars 0g • Protein 3g. DIETARY EXCHANGES: 1/2 Medium-Fat Meat • 1 Fat • 0 Carb Choice.

spicy shrimp cups

taco crescent wreath

taco crescent wreath

PREP TIME: 40 Minutes ✱ READY IN: 1 Hour ✱ SERVINGS: 20

- 2 cans (8 oz. each) Pillsbury® Refrigerated Crescent Dinner Rolls
- 2 dried chipotle chiles, if desired
- 1/3 cup sour cream
- 1/4 cup chopped fresh cilantro
- 1/4 cup mayonnaise
- 1 teaspoon sugar
- 1/4 teaspoon salt
- 1/4 teaspoon ground cumin
- Assorted toppings (chopped avocado, tomato and yellow bell pepper; sliced ripe olives; finely shredded Cheddar cheese)

1 Heat oven to 375°F. Invert 10-ounce custard cup on center of ungreased large cookie sheet. Remove dough from 1 can, keeping dough in 1 piece; do not unroll. (Keep remaining can of dough in refrigerator.) With palms of hands, roll dough in one direction to form 12-inch log. Cut log into 20 slices. Arrange 16 slices, slightly overlapping and in clockwise direction, around custard cup on cookie sheet.

2 Repeat with second can of dough, cutting log into 20 slices. Arrange slices from second can and remaining 4 slices from first can (total of 24 slices), slightly overlapping each other and in counterclockwise direction, close to but not overlapping first ring. Remove custard cup from center of wreath shape.

3 Bake 15 to 18 minutes or until light golden brown. Gently loosen wreath from cookie sheet; carefully slide onto cooling rack. Cool completely, about 30 minutes.

4 Meanwhile, cover chipotle chiles with water; let stand 10 to 15 minutes. Drain; finely chop. In medium bowl, mix chiles, sour cream, cilantro, mayonnaise, sugar, salt and cumin.

5 Place cooled wreath on serving tray or platter. Spread sour cream mixture over wreath. Decorate with assorted toppings. Store in refrigerator.

High Altitude (3500-6500 ft): In Step 3, bake 17 to 19 minutes.

NUTRITION INFORMATION PER SERVING: Calories 150 • Total Fat 10g • Saturated Fat 3g • Cholesterol 5mg • Sodium 270mg • Total Carbohydrate 11g • Dietary Fiber 1g. DIETARY EXCHANGES: 1/2 Starch • 1/2 Other Carbohydrate • 2 Fat.

cook's notes

Assemble and bake the crescent wreath up to 8 hours ahead. Just before serving, top it with the sour cream mixture and garnish.

goat cheese and olive phyllo purses

READY IN: 45 Minutes ✱ SERVINGS: 12

- 6 (17x12-inch) sheets frozen phyllo (filo) pastry, thawed
- 1/4 cup butter, melted
- 2 logs (3.5 to 4 oz.) chèvre (goat cheese), cut into 12 pieces
- 12 pitted kalamata olives, drained, patted dry and each cut in half

1 Heat oven to 400°F. Place 1 sheet of phyllo pastry on cutting board. (Cover remaining sheets with slightly damp towel.) Brush sheet with melted butter. Cut sheet in half lengthwise; cut each half into 4 equal pieces. Stack 4 pieces on top of one another, offsetting corners each time to fan. Repeat with other 4 pieces.

2 Place 1 piece of chèvre in center of each stack. Top each with 2 olive halves. Gather and pleat pastry around cheese to form "purse"; place on ungreased cookie sheet. Repeat with remaining sheets of phyllo pastry, cheese and olives.

3 Bake for 12 to 14 minutes or until deep golden brown and crisp. Immediately remove from cookie sheet; place on wire rack. Cool 5 minutes before serving.

NUTRITION INFORMATION PER SERVING: Calories 135 • Total Fat 9g • Saturated Fat 6g • Cholesterol 25mg • Sodium 190mg • Total Carbohydrate 8g • Dietary Fiber 0g • Sugars 1g • Protein 5g. DIETARY EXCHANGES: 1/2 Starch • 1/2 High-Fat Meat • 1 Fat • 1/2 Carbohydrate Choice.

special touch

To make these "purses" look more like holiday presents, tie the green portion of a green onion around the skinny part of the appetizer.

ham-filled biscuit wreath with honey-mustard dipping sauce

READY IN: 35 Minutes ✱ SERVINGS: 20 Appetizers

Biscuits
- 1 can (12 oz.) Pillsbury® Golden Homestyle® Refrigerated Buttermilk Biscuits
- 1 tablespoon stone-ground mustard

Filling
- 2 tablespoons chopped green onions
- 1/4 cup butter, softened
- 5 slices (6x4-inch) cooked ham

Dipping Sauce
- 3 tablespoons stone-ground mustard
- 2 tablespoons mayonnaise
- 2 tablespoons honey

1 Heat oven to 400°F. Remove biscuits from can. Cut each biscuit in half crosswise; place on ungreased cookie sheet. With back of teaspoon, spread 1 tablespoon mustard evenly over tops.

2 Bake biscuits for 10 to 14 minutes or until golden brown. Remove from cookie sheet; place on wire rack. Cool 10 minutes.

3 Meanwhile, in small bowl, combine onions and butter; mix well. Split each cooled biscuit; spread both halves of each with about 1/2 teaspoon butter mixture.

4 Cut each ham slice into 4 pieces. Place ham slices on bottom biscuit halves; cover the ham with top halves.

5 In small serving bowl, combine all dipping sauce ingredients; blend well. Place in center of serving platter. Arrange ham-filled biscuits in wreath shape around dip.

NUTRITION INFORMATION PER SERVING: Calories 100 • Total Fat 6g • Saturated Fat 3g • Cholesterol 10mg • Sodium 360mg • Total Carbohydrate 9g • Dietary Fiber 0g • Sugars 3g • Protein 3g. DIETARY EXCHANGES: 1/2 Starch • 1/2 Other Carbohydrate • 1 Fat.

cook's notes

To make Mustard Biscuits to serve with soup or salads, do not divide the unbaked biscuits. Spread the mustard evenly over the tops and bake as directed. Omit the filling and dipping sauce.

pastrami and pepper roll-ups

PREP TIME: 25 Minutes ✱ READY IN: 2 Hours 25 Minutes ✱ SERVINGS: 40 Appetizers

- 1/2 lb. thinly sliced pastrami (from deli)
- 1/3 cup chive and onion cream cheese spread (from 8-oz. container)
- 1/2 cup roasted red bell peppers (from a jar), drained, cut into 3/4-inch-wide strips
- Fresh rosemary sprigs, if desired

1 Spread each pastrami slice with cream cheese spread. Top each with roasted pepper piece at one edge. Starting at roasted pepper edge, roll up each tightly. Cover; refrigerate at least 2 hours or until firm.

2 To serve, cut each roll into 1-inch-thick pieces. Secure each with fresh rosemary sprig or cocktail toothpick.

NUTRITION INFORMATION PER SERVING: Calories 15 • Total Fat 1g • Saturated Fat 1g • Cholesterol 5mg • Sodium 80mg • Total Carbohydrate 0g • Dietary Fiber 0g • Sugars 0g • Protein 1g. DIETARY EXCHANGES: Free • 0 Carb Choice.

cook's notes

Involve the whole family when making this appetizer. One person can spread the cream cheese, another can top with the roasted peppers and a third can be in charge of rolling up the appetizers.

ham-filled biscuit wreath
with honey-mustard dipping sauce

LARRY ELDER
Charlotte, North Carolina
Bake-Off® Contest 33, 1988

italian spinach torta

PREP TIME: 15 Minutes ✳ READY IN: 1 Hour 15 Minutes ✳ SERVINGS: 12

CRUST

1 box (15 oz.) Pillsbury® Refrigerated Pie Crusts, softened as directed on box

FILLING

1 box (9 oz.) Green Giant® frozen spinach, thawed, squeezed to drain
1 cup ricotta cheese
1/2 cup grated Parmesan cheese
1/4 to 1/2 teaspoon garlic salt
1/4 teaspoon pepper
1 egg, separated
1 teaspoon water

1 Make pie crusts as directed on box for two-crust pie using 10-inch tart pan with removable bottom or 9-inch glass pie pan. Place 1 pie crust in pan; press in bottom and up sides of pan. Trim edges if necessary.

2 Place oven rack in lowest rack position; heat oven to 400°F. In medium bowl, mix spinach, ricotta cheese, Parmesan cheese, garlic salt, pepper and egg yolk until well blended; spread evenly in crust-lined pan.

3 To make lattice top, cut remaining pie crust into 3/4-inch-wide strips; arrange in lattice design over spinach mixture. Trim and seal edges. In small bowl with fork, beat egg white and water; gently brush over lattice.

4 Bake on lowest oven rack 45 to 50 minutes or until dark golden brown. If necessary, cover torta with foil during last 5 to 10 minutes of baking to prevent excessive browning. Cool 10 minutes; remove sides of pan.

NUTRITION INFORMATION PER SERVING: Calories 200 • Total Fat 11g • Saturated Fat 4.5g • Cholesterol 30mg • Sodium 290mg • Total Carbohydrate 20g • Dietary Fiber 0g • Sugars 3g • Protein 6g.

mexican chili dip

READY IN: 15 Minutes ✱ SERVINGS: 24

- 1/4 cup chopped onion (1/2 medium)
- 1 garlic clove, minced
- 2 tablespoons water
- 1 can (14.5 oz.) stewed tomatoes, undrained
- 1 can (4.5 oz.) Old El Paso® chopped green chiles, drained
- 1/2 teaspoon salt
- 1/2 teaspoon chili powder
- Dash ground red pepper (cayenne) or red pepper sauce
- 1/2 cup shredded Monterey Jack cheese (2 oz.)
- 1 package (8 oz.) 1/3-less-fat cream cheese (Neufchâtel), cut into small cubes
- Chili powder, if desired
- Assorted cut-up fresh vegetables or tortilla chips

1 In 2-quart saucepan, cook onion, garlic and water over medium heat 2 to 4 minutes, stirring occasionally, until onion is tender and water has evaporated.

2 Stir in tomatoes, chiles, salt, chili powder and ground red pepper. Cook about 2 minutes until hot, stirring occasionally.

3 Reduce heat to medium-low. Add cheeses; cook, stirring constantly, just until melted. Sprinkle with chili powder. Serve with cut-up fresh vegetables.

NOTE: To make dip in microwave, in 1-1/2-quart microwavable bowl, microwave onion, garlic and water on High 2 to 3 minutes or until onion is tender and water has evaporated. Stir in cheeses; microwave on High 1-1/2 to 2 minutes or until cheeses are melted. Stir in tomatoes, chiles, salt, chili powder and ground red pepper. Microwave on High 2 minutes or until mixture is hot.

NUTRITION INFORMATION PER SERVING: Calories 45 • Total Fat 3g • Saturated Fat 2g • Cholesterol 10mg • Sodium 190mg • Total Carbohydrate 3g • Dietary Fiber 0g • Sugars 2g • Protein 2g.

smoked salmon on endive

READY IN: 25 Minutes ✱ SERVINGS: 24 Appetizers

- 1 container (8 oz.) chive and onion cream cheese spread
- 1 package (4.5 oz.) smoked salmon, skin removed, finely chopped
- 2 tablespoons mayonnaise
- 1/8 teaspoon hot pepper sauce
- 24 leaves Belgian endive (2 to 3 heads)
- Chopped fresh chives, if desired

1 In medium bowl, combine all ingredients except endive and chives; mix well. Spoon or pipe scant tablespoon mixture into each endive leaf.

2 Serve immediately, or cover and refrigerate until serving time. Just before serving, sprinkle appetizers with chives.

NUTRITION INFORMATION PER SERVING: Calories 50 • Total Fat 4g • Saturated Fat 2g • Cholesterol 10mg • Sodium 80mg • Total Carbohydrate 1g • Dietary Fiber 0g • Sugars 0g • Protein 2g. DIETARY EXCHANGES: 1/2 Lean Meat • 1/2 Fat • 0 Carb Choice.

special touch

A large open star tip works well if piping the cheese mixture onto the Belgian endive leaves. The star tip adds an artistic touch and works better than a small tip, which will become clogged with the bits of salmon in the cheese.

cook's notes

To efficiently use cooler space, freeze the slush in a 2-gallon resealable plastic bag placed flat on a cookie sheet. Frozen flat, the slush will be easy to break up.

frozen white wine mar-grías

PREP TIME: 5 Minutes ✱ READY IN: 24 Hours 5 Minutes ✱ SERVINGS: 24

- 1 container (64 oz.) refrigerated pineapple-orange juice (8 cups)
- 1 bottle (750 ml.) regular or nonalcoholic dry white wine
- 1 can (10 oz.) frozen margarita mix concentrate, thawed
- 1-1/2 cups brandy
- 4 cans (12 oz. each) sour citrus soda

1 In 4-quart resealable plastic container, mix all ingredients except soda until blended. Seal container; freeze 24 hours or until mixture is firm, stirring twice.

2 To serve, spoon about 3/4 cup slush mixture into each large margarita glass. Pour about 1/4 cup soda over each. If desired, garnish each with lime wedge.

NUTRITION INFORMATION PER SERVING: Calories 135 • Total Fat 5g • Saturated Fat 0g • Cholesterol 0mg • Sodium 10mg • Total Carbohydrate 23g • Dietary Fiber 0g • Sugars 22g • Protein 0g. DIETARY EXCHANGES: 1-1/2 Fruit • 1-1/2 Other Carbohydrate • 1 Fat.

beef tenderloin and caramelized onion sandwiches

PREP TIME: 45 Minutes ✱ READY IN: 1 Hour 30 Minutes ✱ SERVINGS: 36 Appetizers

- 1 teaspoon salt
- 1/4 teaspoon garlic powder
- 1/4 teaspoon paprika
- 1/4 teaspoon coarse ground black pepper
- 1 beef tenderloin (1 lb.), trimmed
- 3 tablespoons butter
- 1 tablespoon vegetable oil
- 2 tablespoons brown sugar
- 3 medium onions, cut into 1/4-inch-thick slices
- 2 tablespoons dry red wine or water
- 1/2 cup sour cream
- 1 tablespoon purchased horseradish sauce
- 1 round (10-inch) loaf focaccia (Italian flat bread)
- 1-1/2 cups firmly packed baby spinach leaves
- Cocktail toothpicks

1 Heat oven to 450°F. In small bowl, combine 1/2 teaspoon of the salt, the garlic powder, paprika and pepper; mix well. Rub mixture on all surfaces of beef tenderloin. Place beef in small shallow roasting pan; tuck thin end under.

2 Bake for 20 to 25 minutes or until meat thermometer inserted in center registers 140°F for rare. Cool 30 minutes or until completely cooled; slice very thin.

3 Meanwhile, in large skillet, heat butter and oil over medium heat until butter melts. Add brown sugar and onions; stir to coat. Cook over medium heat for 10 minutes or until onions begin to soften, stirring occasionally. Add wine. Reduce heat to medium-low; cover and cook 10 to 15 minutes or until onions are very tender.

4 Combine sour cream, horseradish sauce and remaining 1/2 teaspoon salt; mix well. Heat focaccia as directed on package; cut in half horizontally. Spread both cut sides with sour cream mixture. Arrange spinach leaves on bottom half of focaccia; top with beef slices. Top with onions and top half of focaccia; press down.

5 Insert toothpicks through all layers at 1-1/4- to 1-1/2-inch intervals. Cut between toothpicks to form tiny sandwich squares.

NUTRITION INFORMATION PER SERVING: Calories 80 • Total Fat 4g • Saturated Fat 2g • Cholesterol 10mg • Sodium 170mg • Total Carbohydrate 7g • Dietary Fiber 0g • Sugars 1g • Protein 4g. DIETARY EXCHANGES: 1/2 Starch • 1/2 Lean Meat • 1/2 Fat • 1/2 Carb Choice.

cook's notes

You can bake the beef tenderloin and cook the onions as directed, but wrap the tenderloin and place the onions in a covered container, and refrigerate up to 24 hours. Just before serving, prepare the sauce and assemble sandwiches as directed.

frozen white wine mar-grías

orange-ginger shrimp snacks
cracker bread rolls

orange-ginger shrimp snacks

PREP TIME: 15 Minutes ✷ READY IN: 35 Minutes ✷ SERVINGS: 15 Appetizers

- 1/2 cup vegetable oil
- 1/4 cup vinegar
- 1/4 cup frozen orange juice concentrate, thawed
- 1 tablespoon chopped red onion
- 2 teaspoons grated gingerroot
- 3/4 teaspoon crushed red pepper flakes
- 1 lb. uncooked deveined peeled medium shrimp
- 5 bamboo skewers (12 inch)

1 In a blender, place all of the ingredients except the shrimp and the skewers; process until the ingredients are well blended.

2 In large resealable food-storage plastic bag, place shrimp. Pour oil mixture over shrimp; let stand at room temperature 15 minutes to marinate. Soak bamboo skewers in water while shrimp are marinating.

3 Drain shrimp, discarding marinade. Thread shrimp onto bamboo skewers; place on ungreased cookie sheet.

4 Broil 6 inches from heat 3 to 5 minutes, turning once, until shrimp turn pink. With kitchen scissors, cut each skewer into 3 pieces.

NUTRITION INFORMATION PER SERVING: Calories 40 • Total Fat 2g • Saturated Fat 0g • Cholesterol 45mg • Sodium 50mg • Total Carbohydrate 1g • Dietary Fiber 0g • Sugars 0g • Protein 5g. DIETARY EXCHANGE: 1 Lean Meat.

kitchen tip

Gingerroot is found in the supermarket produce department. Use a microplane grater to grate unpeeled gingerroot. Tightly wrap any leftover fresh gingerroot and freeze for up to 6 months.

cracker bread rolls

PREP TIME: 15 Minutes ✷ READY IN: 35 Minutes ✷ SERVINGS: 28 Appetizers

- 1 soft cracker bread (16 inch), room temperature
- 4 oz. (half 8-oz. package) 1/3-less-fat cream cheese (Neufchâtel), softened
- 1 tablespoon chopped fresh or 1 teaspoon dried basil leaves
- 1 tablespoon chopped fresh or 1 teaspoon dried oregano leaves
- 4 oz. thinly sliced cooked ham
- 12 large spinach leaves, stems removed
- 1/2 medium red bell pepper, cut into thin bite-size strips

1 Cut cracker bread in half crosswise. In small bowl, mix cream cheese, basil and oregano. Spread half of cream cheese mixture on 1 cracker bread half to within 1/4 inch of edges.

2 Arrange half of ham slices over cream cheese to within 1 inch of rounded edge. Top with 6 spinach leaves. Starting about 1 inch from straight edge, arrange half of bell pepper strips in rows parallel to straight edge.

3 Starting with straight edge, roll up tightly. Wrap roll tightly in plastic wrap. Repeat with remaining ingredients to make second roll. Refrigerate rolls until firm enough to slice, at least 20 minutes. Cut rolls into 1-inch-thick slices.

NUTRITION INFORMATION PER SERVING: Calories 35 • Total Fat 1g • Saturated Fat 1g • Cholesterol 5mg • Sodium 110mg • Total Carbohydrate 4g • Dietary Fiber 0g • Sugars 1g • Protein 2g. DIETARY EXCHANGE: 1/2 Starch.

kitchen tip

Look for cracker bread in the deli department of your supermarket.

cook's notes

Spanish smoked chorizo is another linked sausage that's right on the money when it comes to making these tasty coins. Use it in place of the Polish sausage or the kielbasa links.

saucy sausage medallions

READY IN: 30 Minutes ✱ SERVINGS: 20 Appetizers

- 1 tablespoon olive oil
- 1/4 cup finely chopped onion
- 3 garlic cloves, minced
- 1 lb. cooked Polish sausage or kielbasa links, cut into 1/2-inch-thick slices
- 1 teaspoon paprika
- 1/2 teaspoon coriander
- Dash ground red pepper (cayenne)
- 1 can (8 oz.) tomato sauce
- 1/4 cup dry red wine or water

1 Heat oil in large skillet over medium heat until hot. Add onion; cook 4 to 5 minutes or until softened, stirring occasionally.

2 Add garlic; cook and stir 30 to 60 seconds or until fragrant. Add sausage slices; cook 2 to 4 minutes or until lightly browned, turning once.

3 Stir in paprika, coriander and ground red pepper. Add tomato sauce and wine; mix well. Cook about 5 minutes to reduce liquid slightly, stirring occasionally. Serve with cocktail toothpicks.

NUTRITION INFORMATION PER SERVING: Calories 85 • Total Fat 7g • Saturated Fat 2g • Cholesterol 15mg • Sodium 300mg • Total Carbohydrate 2g • Dietary Fiber 0g • Sugars 1g • Protein 3g. DIETARY EXCHANGES: 1/2 High-Fat Meat • 1/2 Fat • 0 Carb Choice.

mini reuben turnovers

PREP TIME: 30 Minutes ✱ READY IN: 45 Minutes ✱ SERVINGS: 24 Appetizers

- 2 oz. corned beef (from deli), cut into pieces
- 1/4 cup shredded Swiss cheese (1 oz.)
- 2 tablespoons well-drained sauerkraut, squeezed dry with paper towel
- 2 tablespoons stone-ground mustard
- 1 can (8 oz.) refrigerated crescent dinner rolls
- 1 egg, beaten, if desired
- Thousand Island dressing, if desired

1 Heat oven to 375°F. In food processor bowl with metal blade, place corned beef, cheese, sauerkraut and mustard. Cover; process with on-and-off pulses until finely chopped.

2 Remove half of dough in rolled section from can; refrigerate remaining half of dough in can. Unroll half of dough and separate into 2 rectangles; press each into 7-1/2x5-inch rectangle, firmly pressing perforations to seal. Cut each rectangle into six 2-1/2-inch squares.

3 Place 1 teaspoon corned beef mixture on each square. Fold 1 corner to opposite corner, forming triangle and pressing edges to seal; place on ungreased cookie sheet. With fork, prick top of each to allow steam to escape. Brush tops with egg. Repeat with remaining half of dough and corned beef mixture.

4 Bake 9 to 14 minutes or until golden brown. Immediately remove from cookie sheet. Serve warm with dressing.

NUTRITION INFORMATION PER SERVING: Calories 45 • Total Fat 3g • Saturated Fat 1g • Trans Fat 0.5g • Cholesterol 0mg • Sodium 140mg • Total Carbohydrate 4g • Dietary Fiber 0g • Sugars 0g • Protein 1g. DIETARY EXCHANGES: 1/2 Starch • 1/2 Fat • 0 Carb Choice.

cook's notes

If corned beef isn't your favorite, try Mini Rachel Turnovers by substituting cooked turkey for the corned beef.

tomato-topped onion bread wedges

PREP TIME: 30 minutes ✱ READY IN: 50 Minutes ✱ SERVINGS: 6

SALAD

- 1 tablespoon olive or vegetable oil
- 2 large tomatoes, chopped (about 2 cups)
- 1 medium red bell pepper, chopped (1 cup)
- 1 tablespoon chopped fresh parsley
- 1 tablespoon tarragon vinegar
- 1/2 teaspoon dried basil leaves
- 1/2 teaspoon dried oregano leaves
- 1/8 teaspoon pepper

BREAD

- 1/3 cup olive or vegetable oil
- 1/3 cup chopped onion
- 1 clove garlic, minced
- 1 can (13.8 oz.) Pillsbury® Refrigerated Pizza Crust
- 1/4 cup grated Parmesan cheese

1 In 10-inch skillet, heat 1 tablespoon oil over medium heat. Add tomatoes and bell pepper; cook 10 to 15 minutes, stirring occasionally, until most of liquid has evaporated. Remove from heat. Stir in remaining salad ingredients; place in medium bowl and set aside to cool. Wipe skillet clean with paper towel.

2 Heat oven to 400°F. In same skillet, heat 1/3 cup oil over medium heat. Add onion and garlic; cook and stir 2 to 3 minutes or until onion is tender. Set onion mixture aside. With 1 tablespoon of the oil from onion mixture, grease 9-inch round pan.

3 Unroll dough; fold in half. Place dough in pan; gently press evenly in pan. With fork, poke holes in dough every 2 inches. Spread onion mixture evenly over dough. Sprinkle Parmesan cheese over top.

4 Bake 18 to 20 minutes or until golden brown and slightly puffed. Cool slightly, about 10 minutes. Remove from pan; place on serving plate. Top warm bread with salad.

HIGH ALTITUDE (3500-6500 FT): Bake at 400°F 20 to 22 minutes.

NUTRITION INFORMATION PER SERVING: Calories 330 • Total Fat 18g • Saturated Fat 3.5g • Cholesterol 0mg • Sodium 550mg • Total Carbohydrate 36g • Dietary Fiber 2g • Sugars 7g • Protein 8g.

SANDRA J. BANGHAM
Rockville, Maryland
Bake-Off® Contest 36, 1994

cook's note

For color variation in the salad, substitute 1 medium green bell pepper for the red bell pepper.

Glorious Baked Goods

Golden breads, aromatic biscuits and classic coffee cakes…this holiday, let these comforting mainstays warm up frosty mornings as well as winter's chilliest nights.

p. 53

p. 51

p. 55

p. 52

p. 56

cranberry upside-down muffins p. 59

caraway breadstick twists

caraway breadstick twists

READY IN: 30 Minutes ✷ SERVINGS 10

- 1 package (10.6 oz.) Pillsbury® Refrigerated Garlic Breadsticks
- 1 teaspoon deli-style brown mustard
- 1/2 cup finely shredded Swiss cheese (2 oz.)
- 3 tablespoons finely chopped onion
- 2 teaspoons finely chopped fresh parsley
- 1 to 2 teaspoons caraway seed

1 Heat oven to 375°F. Spray cookie sheet with nonstick cooking spray. Unroll dough; separate into 2 equal sections along center perforation. Spread half of the garlic spread from container evenly over 1 dough section. Spread with mustard. Top with cheese, onion, parsley and caraway seed; press in firmly.

2 Place remaining dough section over topped dough; press edges to seal. Spread remaining garlic spread over top of dough.

3 With sharp knife, cut filled dough in half lengthwise; cut into pieces along perforations. Twist each dough strip 2 times, stretching slightly. Place 1 inch apart on sprayed cookie sheet. Firmly press down ends. Bake for 10 to 15 minutes or until golden brown. Serve warm.

NUTRITION INFORMATION PER SERVING: Calories 110 • Total Fat 5g • Saturated Fat 2g • Cholesterol 5mg • Sodium 310mg • Total Carbohydrate 13g • Dietary Fiber 1g • Sugars 2g • Protein 4g. DIETARY EXCHANGES: 1 Starch • 1 Fat OR 1 Carbohydrate • 1 Fat.

special touch

Serve these savory twists warm from the oven with spicy mustard for dipping.

poppy seed swirl loaf

PREP TIME: 15 Minutes ✷ READY IN: 1 Hour 25 Minutes ✷ SERVINGS: 12

BREAD

- 1/2 cup poppy seed filling (from 12-1/2-oz. can)
- 2 teaspoons grated lemon peel
- 1 can (11 oz.) Pillsbury® Refrigerated Crusty French Loaf
- 1/3 cup golden raisins

FROSTING

- 1/3 cup powdered sugar
- 1 to 2 teaspoons water

1 Heat oven to 350°F. Grease cookie sheet. In small bowl, combine poppy seed filling and lemon peel; mix well.

2 Unroll dough onto floured surface, forming 13x12-inch rectangle. Drop poppy seed mixture by small teaspoonfuls over dough to within 1/2 inch of edges; gently spread being careful not to stretch dough. Sprinkle with raisins. Starting with one long side, loosely roll up dough; pinch edges to seal. Place seam side down on greased cookie sheet.

3 Bake for 28 to 35 minutes or until bread is deep golden brown and sounds hollow when tapped with finger. Cool 30 minutes.

4 In small bowl, blend frosting ingredients until smooth, adding enough water for desired spreading consistency. Spread frosting over top of cooled bread. Let stand 5 minutes or until set. Cut into crosswise slices. Serve warm.

NUTRITION INFORMATION PER SERVING: Calories 130 • Total Fat 2g • Saturated Fat 0g • Cholesterol 0mg • Sodium 160mg • Total Carbohydrate 24g • Dietary Fiber 2g • Sugars 12g • Protein 3g. DIETARY EXCHANGES: 1 Starch • 1/2 Fruit • 1/2 Fat OR 1-1/2 Carbohydrate • 1/2 Fat.

special touch

If you like lemon, you'll love this swirled loaf. For extra lemon flavor, use lemon juice instead of water for the frosting and stir in a little extra grated lemon peel. To serve, slice the bread, then arrange the slices on a pretty platter garnished with long, twisted curls of lemon peel.

Pillsbury Bake-Off®

Lois Ann Groves
San Antonio, Texas
Bake-Off® Contest 27, 1976
Grand Prize Winner

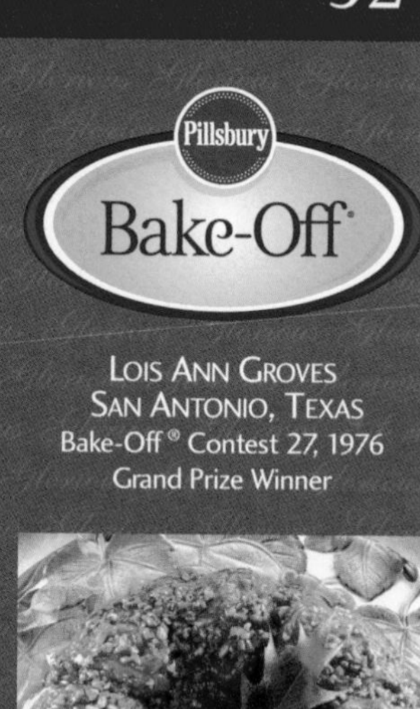

crescent caramel swirl

SERVINGS: 12

- 1/2 cup butter (do not use margarine)
- 1/2 cup chopped nuts
- 3/4 cup firmly packed brown sugar
- 1 tablespoon water
- 2 cans (8 oz. each) Pillsbury® Refrigerated Crescent Dinner Rolls

1 Heat oven to 350°F. Melt butter in small saucepan. Coat bottom and sides of 12-cup fluted tu pan with 2 tablespoons of the melted butter; sprinkle pan with 3 tablespoons of the nuts. Ad remaining nuts, brown sugar and water to remaining 6 tablespoons melted butter. Bring to a boil stirring occasionally. Boil 1 minute, stirring constantly.

2 Remove dough from cans; do not unroll. Cut each roll into 4 slices (for total of 16 slices). Arrange 8 slices, cut side down, in nut-lined pan; separate layers of each pinwheel slightly. Spoon half of brown sugar mixture over dough. Place remaining dough slices alternately over bot layer. Spoon remaining brown sugar mixture over slices.

3 Bake for 23 to 33 minutes or until deep golden brown. Cool 3 minutes. Invert onto serving platter or waxed paper.

NUTRITION INFORMATION PER SERVING: Calories 280 • Total Fat 18g • Sodium 400mg • Total Carbohydrate 29g • Protein 3g.

cook's notes

If you want to get a head start on making this recipe, chop the apples ahead of time, then cover them with cold water mixed with a teaspoon or two of lemon juice. This will help prevent the apples from turning brown. Drain the apples and pat dry just before using them in the recipe.

upside-down apple-walnut coffee cake

PREP TIME: 20 Minutes ✷ READY IN: 1 Hour ✷ SERVINGS: 8

- 1-1/2 cups chopped peeled apples
- 1 can (12.4 oz.) Pillsbury® Refrigerated Cinnamon Rolls with Icing
- 1/2 cup chopped walnuts
- 1/3 cup firmly packed brown sugar
- 2 tablespoons butter or margarine, melted
- 2 tablespoons corn syrup

1 Heat oven to 350°F. Spray 9-inch glass pie pan with nonstick cooking spray. Spread 1 cup of apples in sprayed pan.

2 Separate dough into 8 rolls; cut each into quarters. Place dough pieces in large bowl. Add remaining 1/2 cup apples and walnuts.

3 In small bowl, combine brown sugar, butter and corn syrup; mix well. Add brown sugar mixtur to dough mixture; toss gently to combine. Spoon mixture over apples in pan.

4 Bake for 28 to 38 minutes or until deep golden brown. Cool 5 minutes. Invert onto serving platter.

5 Remove lid from icing. Microwave icing on High for 10 to 15 seconds or until of drizzling consistency. Drizzle over warm coffee cake. Serve warm.

NUTRITION INFORMATION PER SERVING: Calories 290 • Total Fat 13g • Saturated Fat 2g • Cholesterol 10mg • Sodium 400mg • Total Carbohydrate 39g • Dietary Fiber 2g • Sugars 20g • Protein 4g. DIETARY EXCHANGES: 1-1/2 Starch • 1 Fruit • 2-1/2 Fat OR 2-1/2 Carbohydrate • 2-1/2 Fat.

white chocolate-iced blueberry loaf

PREP TIME: 10 Minutes ✻ READY IN: 3 Hours 10 Minutes ✻ SERVINGS: 12

LOAF

- 2-1/2 cups all-purpose flour
- 1 cup granulated sugar
- 3 teaspoons baking powder
- 1/2 teaspoon salt
- 1/4 teaspoon ground allspice, if desired
- 1 cup buttermilk
- 1/4 cup butter or margarine, melted
- 2 eggs
- 1-1/2 cups fresh or frozen (do not thaw) blueberries
- 1/2 cup chopped pecans

ICING

- 1/4 cup white vanilla baking chips
- 3 tablespoons powdered sugar
- 1 to 2 tablespoons milk

1 Heat oven to 350°F. Grease bottom only of 9x5-inch loaf pan. In large bowl, mix flour, sugar, baking powder, salt and allspice with spoon. Beat in buttermilk, butter and eggs until blended. Stir in blueberries and pecans. Spread batter in pan.

2 Bake 1 hour 15 minutes to 1 hour 20 minutes or until toothpick inserted in center comes out clean. Cool in pan on wire rack 10 minutes.

3 Run knife around edges of pan to loosen loaf. Remove loaf from pan; place on wire rack. Cool completely, about 1 hour 30 minutes.

4 In small microwavable bowl, microwave vanilla baking chips on High 30 seconds. Stir until melted; if necessary, microwave in additional 10-second increments until melted. Beat in powdered sugar and enough milk until smooth and desired drizzling consistency. Drizzle icing over loaf. Let stand until icing is set before storing.

HIGH ALTITUDE (3500-6500 FT): Decrease baking powder to 1-1/2 teaspoons.

NUTRITION INFORMATION PER SERVING: Calories 290 • Total Fat 9g • Saturated Fat 3g • Cholesterol 45mg • Sodium 280mg • Total Carbohydrate 45g • Dietary Fiber 2g • Sugars 23g • Protein 5g.

special touch

This delicious loaf makes a great gift. Place toothpicks into the top surface of the loaf to protect the icing from sticking. Then wrap the loaf in colored cellophane and tie with a pretty bow.

sweet potato streusel muffins

breadstick focaccia

cranberry upside-down muffins

cranberry upside-down muffins

PREP TIME: 15 Minutes ✱ READY IN: 35 Minutes ✱ SERVINGS: 12 Muffins

- 3/4 cup whole-berry cranberry sauce
- 1/4 cup firmly packed brown sugar
- 2 cups all-purpose flour
- 2 tablespoons sugar
- 3 teaspoons baking powder
- 1/2 teaspoon salt
- 1 cup skim milk
- 1/4 cup vegetable oil
- 1 teaspoon grated orange peel
- 2 egg whites

1 Heat oven to 400°F. Place wire rack over sheet of waxed paper. Spray 12 medium muffin cups with nonstick cooking spray. Spoon 1 tablespoon cranberry sauce into each muffin cup. Top each with 1 teaspoon brown sugar.

2 In large bowl, combine flour, sugar, baking powder and salt; mix well. In small bowl, combine milk, oil, orange peel and egg whites; blend well. Add to flour mixture all at once; stir just until dry ingredients are moistened. Divide batter evenly over cranberries and brown sugar in muffin cups.

3 Bake for 14 to 18 minutes or until toothpick inserted in center comes out clean. Cool in pan for 1 minute. Run knife around edges of cups to loosen. Invert muffins onto wire rack over waxed paper; remove pan. Cool 5 minutes. Serve warm.

NUTRITION INFORMATION PER SERVING: Calories 180 • Total Fat 5g • Saturated Fat 0g • Cholesterol 0mg • Sodium 250mg • Total Carbohydrate 31g • Dietary Fiber 0g • Sugars 14g • Protein 3g. DIETARY EXCHANGES: 1 Starch • 1 Fat • 1 Other Carbohydrate.

special touch

These citrus muffins look even more appealing when served with orange slices and a sprig of fresh mint.

red and green biscuit pull-apart

PREP TIME: 20 Minutes ✱ READY IN: 35 Minutes ✱ SERVINGS: 10

- 1/4 teaspoon garlic powder
- 1/4 teaspoon salt, if desired
- 1/4 teaspoon dried basil leaves, crushed
- 1/4 teaspoon dried oregano leaves, crushed
- 1 can (12 oz.) Pillsbury® Golden Layers™ Refrigerated Flaky Biscuits
- 4-1/2 teaspoons olive oil
- 1/4 cup chopped green bell pepper
- 1/4 cup chopped red bell pepper
- 1/4 cup shredded mozzarella cheese (1 oz.)
- 2 tablespoons grated Romano or Parmesan cheese

1 Heat oven to 400°F. In small bowl, combine garlic powder, salt, basil and oregano; mix well. Separate dough into 10 biscuits.

2 Place 1 biscuit in center of ungreased cookie sheet. Arrange remaining biscuits in circle, edges slightly overlapping, around center biscuit. Gently press out to form 10-inch round.

3 Brush biscuits with oil. Top with bell peppers and cheeses. Sprinkle garlic powder mixture over top. Bake for 12 to 15 minutes or until golden brown. To serve, pull apart warm biscuits.

NUTRITION INFORMATION PER SERVING: Calories 120 • Total Fat 7g • Saturated Fat 2g • Cholesterol 3mg • Sodium 390mg • Total Carbohydrate 12g • Dietary Fiber 0g • Sugars 2g • Protein 3g. DIETARY EXCHANGES: 1 Starch • 1 Fat OR 1 Carbohydrate • 1 Fat.

kitchen tip

This colorful holiday bread is great for a snack or to serve as a bread for supper or brunch. Double the spice mixture in this recipe and keep it on hand to season soups and stews or to sprinkle on cooked vegetables or buttered rolls and breads.

Seasonal Soups, Sides & Salads

Holiday meals shine bright when simmering soups, savory side dishes and colorful salads complete dinner lineups. See this chapter for chowders, vegetables and more.

p.63

p. 63

p.64

p. 68

p. 82

minestrone salad p. 74

pear-almond tossed salad

pear-almond tossed salad

PREP TIME: 10 Minutes ✱ READY IN: 10 Minutes ✱ SERVINGS: 12

- 4 cups torn romaine lettuce
- 1/4 cup diced dried cherries
- 1/4 cup butter toffee-glazed sliced almonds
- 1 red-skinned pear, unpeeled, cored and cubed
- 4 green onions, sliced (1/4 cup)
- 1/4 cup orange marmalade
- 2 tablespoons olive oil
- 1 tablespoon lemon juice

1 In large bowl, combine the romaine lettuce, dried cherries, toffee-glazed almonds, red-skinned pear and the green onions.

2 In small bowl, mix marmalade, oil and lemon juice until well blended. Drizzle over the salad; toss to mix.

NUTRITION INFORMATION PER SERVING: Calories 80 • Total Fat 3g • Saturated Fat 0g • Cholesterol 0mg • Sodium 5mg • Total Carbohydrate 12g • Protein 0g. DIETARY EXCHANGES: 1 Other Carbohydrate • 1/2 Fat.

Kitchen tip

Look for toffee-glazed sliced almond salad toppers near the greens in the produce aisle. After one bite you'll want to add these tasty nuts to all of your salads.

garlic smashed red potatoes

PREP TIME: 15 Minutes ✱ READY IN: 4 Hours 45 Minutes ✱ SERVINGS: 14

- 3 lbs. small red potatoes (2 to 3 inches)
- 4 cloves garlic, minced
- 1 teaspoon salt
- 1/2 cup water
- 2 tablespoons olive oil
- 1/2 cup chive-and-onion cream cheese spread (from 8-oz. container)
- 1/2 to 3/4 cup milk

1 Cut potatoes into halves or quarters as necessary to make similar-size pieces; place in 4- to 6-quart slow cooker.

2 Stir in garlic, salt, water and oil until potato pieces are coated. Cover; cook on High setting 3-1/2 to 4-1/2 hours or until potatoes are tender.

3 With fork or potato masher, mash potatoes and garlic. Stir in cream cheese spread until well blended. Stir in enough milk for soft serving consistency. Serve immediately, or cover and hold in slow cooker on Low setting up to 2 hours.

NUTRITION INFORMATION PER SERVING: Calories 130 • Total Fat 5g • Saturated Fat 2g • Cholesterol 10mg • Sodium 210mg • Total Carbohydrate 18g • Dietary Fiber 2g • Sugars 2g • Protein 3g.

cook's notes

Keep these green beans in mind when serving turkey or chicken. Their savory flavor makes them perfect alongside poultry.

parmesan-garlic butter green beans

READY IN: 15 Minutes ✱ SERVINGS: 6

- 1 package (14 oz.) frozen whole green beans
- 2 tablespoons butter
- 1 small garlic clove, minced
- 1 tablespoon grated Parmesan cheese

1 Cook green beans as directed on package. Drain. Meanwhile, melt butter in small saucepan over medium-low heat.

2 Add garlic; cook 2 to 3 minutes or until garlic is tender, stirring frequently. Pour garlic butter over cooked green beans; stir to coat. Sprinkle with cheese; toss gently.

NUTRITION INFORMATION PER SERVING: Calories 55 • Total Fat 4g • Saturated Fat 3g • Cholesterol 10mg • Sodium 50mg • Total Carbohydrate 4g • Dietary Fiber 1g • Sugars 2g • Protein 1g. DIETARY EXCHANGES: 1 Vegetable • 1 Fat.

cook's notes

Southern-style hashbrowns are ideal for this side dish, but use the cubed variety if that's what you have on hand.

swiss potato casserole

PREP TIME: 20 Minutes ✱ READY IN: 1 Hour 25 Minutes ✱ SERVINGS: 12

- 1 package (2 lb.) frozen southern-style hash-brown potatoes
- 2 cups shredded Swiss cheese (8 oz.)
- 1/4 cup butter or margarine
- 3 tablespoons all-purpose flour
- 3 cups milk
- 1 teaspoon salt
- 1 teaspoon onion powder
- 1/2 teaspoon white pepper
- 1/2 teaspoon ground nutmeg

1 Heat oven to 350°F. Spray 13x9-inch (3-quart) glass baking dish with nonstick cooking spray. In baking dish, mix potatoes and cheese.

2 In large saucepan, melt butter over medium heat. Stir in flour; cook until bubbly, stirring constantly. Gradually add milk, stirring constantly. Stir in salt, onion powder, pepper and nutmeg. Cook and stir until mixture comes to a boil. Pour over potato mixture. Bake 55 to 65 minutes or until mixture is set and top is lightly browned.

NUTRITION INFORMATION PER SERVING: Calories 210 • Total Fat 11g • Saturated Fat 5g • Cholesterol 20mg • Sodium 320mg • Total Carbohydrate 19g • Dietary Fiber 1g • Protein 9g. DIETARY EXCHANGES: 1-1/2 Starch • 1-1/2 Other Carbohydrate • 1/2 High-Fat Meat • 1 Fat.

kitchen tip

Look for soup base near the instant bouillon in the grocery store. It produces a richer flavor than broth or bouillon.

beef barley soup

PREP TIME: 25 Minutes ✱ READY IN: 1 Hour 45 Minutes ✱ SERVINGS: 6

- 1 tablespoon oil
- 1 lb. lean beef stew meat, cubed
- 2 quarts water (8 cups)
- 2 tablespoons beef soup base
- 1/2 cup uncooked barley
- 1 teaspoon dried basil leaves
- 2 cups thinly sliced carrots
- 1 cup Green Giant® frozen sweet peas
- 1/4 cup chopped onion

1 Heat oil in Dutch oven over high heat until hot. Add beef; cook and stir until browned. Drain. Add water and soup base; bring to a boil. Add barley and basil. Reduce heat to low; cover and simmer 1 hour.

2 Add carrots, peas and onion; cover and simmer an additional 15 to 20 minutes or until vegetables are tender.

NUTRITION INFORMATION PER SERVING: Calories 230 • Total Fat 7g • Saturated Fat 2g • Cholesterol 50mg • Sodium 990mg • Total Carbohydrate 21g • Dietary Fiber 5g • Sugars 5 g • Protein 21g. DIETARY EXCHANGES: 1 Starch • 1 Vegetable • 2-1/2 Lean Fat Meat OR 1 Carbohydrate • 1 Vegetable • 2-1/2 Lean Meat.

parmesan-garlic butter green beans

alfredo beef-topped potatoes

alfredo beef-topped potatoes

READY IN: 25 Minutes ✷ SERVINGS: 4

- 4 medium baking potatoes
- 1 lb. lean (at least 80%) ground beef
- 1/2 teaspoon seasoned salt
- 1/4 teaspoon pepper
- 2 cups Green Giant® frozen broccoli florets
- 1 medium red bell pepper, cut into bite-sized strips
- 1 container (10 oz.) refrigerated Alfredo sauce (1-1/4 cups)
- 2 tablespoons chopped fresh basil, if desired

1 Pierce potatoes with fork several times; place on microwavable plate. Microwave on High 6 to 8 minutes, turning once, until fork-tender.

2 Meanwhile, in 12-inch nonstick skillet, break up ground beef; sprinkle with seasoned salt and pepper. Cook over medium-high heat, stirring frequently, until beef is thoroughly cooked; drain.

3 Stir in broccoli, bell pepper and Alfredo sauce. Reduce heat to low; cook about 6 minutes, stirring occasionally, until broccoli is crisp-tender.

4 Place potatoes on individual serving plates. Cut potatoes in half lengthwise; mash slightly. Top each potato half with beef mixture. Sprinkle with basil.

NUTRITION INFORMATION PER SERVING: Calories 630 • Total Fat 35g • Saturated Fat 19g • Cholesterol 140mg • Sodium 520mg • Total Carbohydrate 47g • Dietary Fiber 6g. DIETARY EXCHANGES: 2-1/2 Starch • 1/2 Other Carbohydrate • 1 Vegetable • 3 Medium-Fat Meat • 3-1/2 Fat.

cook's notes

Roasted bell peppers from a jar or the deli can be substituted for the red bell pepper. Drain them well before adding.

spicy black beans and rice

READY IN: 30 Minutes ✷ SERVINGS: 12

- 2 cups uncooked regular long-grain white rice
- 4 cups water
- 2 tablespoons oil
- 1 tablespoon minced garlic (3 to 4 medium cloves)
- 3 teaspoons dried oregano leaves
- 1 teaspoon crushed red pepper flakes
- 2 cans (15 oz. each) Progresso® black beans, undrained
- 1/4 cup diced red bell pepper

1 Cook rice in water as directed on package. Meanwhile, heat oil in large saucepan over medium heat until hot. Add garlic, oregano and red pepper flakes; cook and stir 1 to 2 minutes.

2 Add beans; bring to a boil. Reduce heat; simmer 10 minutes to blend flavors, stirring occasionally. Serve over rice; sprinkle with bell pepper.

NUTRITION INFORMATION PER SERVING: Calories 130 • Total Fat 2g • Saturated Fat 0g • Cholesterol 0mg • Sodium 170mg • Total Carbohydrate 22g • Dietary Fiber 3g. DIETARY EXCHANGES: 1-1/2 Starch • 1-1/2 Other Carbohydrate • 1/2 Fat.

cook's notes

Wary of spicy food? Start by cooking 1/2 teaspoon of the red pepper flakes with the seasonings. Continue with the recipe as directed. After adding the beans, simmer for 5 minutes and taste. Season to taste with the remaining red pepper flakes.

special touch

For extra flair, garnish the salad with fruit, champagne grapes and figs.

jiggle bell salad

PREP TIME: 10 Minutes ✳ READY IN: 5 Hours 5 Minutes ✳ SERVINGS: 8

- 1-1/2 cups cranberry-apple juice drink
- 2 boxes (4-serving size each) wild strawberry flavored gelatin
- 2 cups sparkling water, chilled
- 1 can (15 oz.) mandarin orange segments, drained
- Lettuce leaves

1. Oil 7-cup mold with vegetable oil. In 2-quart saucepan, heat cranberry-apple juice drink to boiling. Remove from heat. Stir in gelatin until dissolved. Refrigerate 15 minutes.
2. Stir in sparkling water. Refrigerate 40 minutes longer. Fold orange segments into gelatin; spoon into mold. Refrigerate until firm, about 4 hours.
3. To serve, line serving platter with lettuce. Unmold gelatin onto lined platter. Cut gelatin into wedges to serve.

NUTRITION INFORMATION PER SERVING: Calories 130 • Total Fat 0g • Saturated 0g • Cholesterol 0mg • Sodium 100mg • Total Carbohydrate 30g • Dietary Fiber 0g • Sugars 28g • Protein 2g.

ground beef stew over garlic mashed potatoes

READY IN: 20 Minutes ✳ SERVINGS: 4

- 1/2 lb. lean (at least 80%) ground beef
- 1/4 cup chopped onion
- 1 cup Green Giant® frozen mixed vegetables
- 1 can (14.5 oz.) diced tomatoes, drained
- 1 jar (12 oz.) beef gravy
- 1/4 teaspoon dried marjoram leaves
- 1/4 teaspoon pepper
- 1 cup water
- 2 tablespoons margarine or butter
- 1/2 teaspoon garlic salt
- 1/2 cup milk
- 1-1/3 cups plain mashed potato mix (dry)
- 1 tablespoon chopped fresh parsley

1. In 12-inch nonstick skillet, cook ground beef and onion over medium-high heat, stirring frequently, until beef is thoroughly cooked; drain.
2. Stir in mixed vegetables, tomatoes, gravy, marjoram and pepper. Heat to boiling. Reduce heat to low; simmer 8 to 10 minutes, stirring occasionally, until vegetables are tender.
3. In 2-quart saucepan, heat water, margarine and garlic salt to boiling. Remove from heat; add the milk.
4. Stir in potato mix and parsley; let stand about 30 seconds or until liquid is absorbed. Fluff potatoes with fork. Serve beef mixture over potatoes.

NUTRITION INFORMATION PER SERVING: Calories 350 • Total Fat 15g • Saturated Fat 5g • Cholesterol 40mg • Sodium 870mg • Total Carbohydrate 35g • Dietary Fiber 4g. DIETARY EXCHANGES: 1 Starch • 1 Other Carbohydrate • 1 Vegetable • 2 Medium-Fat Meat • 1 Fat.

cook's notes

Oregano can be used in place of the marjoram; both are mint-family herbs from the Mediterranean mountains. In place of the potatoes, try this thick, rich stew over biscuits, rice or pasta.

ground beef stew
over garlic mashed potatoes

melon salad with orange-mint syrup

melon salad with orange-mint syrup

PREP TIME: 40 Minutes ✱ READY IN: 1 Hours 10 Minutes ✱ SERVINGS: 12

- 1/2 cup sugar
- 2 teaspoons grated orange peel
- 1/2 cup fresh orange juice (1 large orange)
- 1 teaspoon cornstarch
- 1 tablespoon thinly sliced mint leaves
- 1 medium honeydew melon, cut in half, seeded
- 1 medium cantaloupe
- Fresh mint sprigs, if desired

1 In 1-quart saucepan, mix sugar, orange peel, orange juice and cornstarch. Heat to boiling over medium heat, stirring occasionally. Reduce heat to low; simmer uncovered about 8 minutes, stirring frequently, until sugar has dissolved and syrup has thickened. Stir in sliced mint. Cover; refrigerate at least 30 minutes, stirring occasionally.

2 Meanwhile, cut honeydew melon in half; remove and discard seeds. With melon baller, scoop out melon into balls; place in medium bowl. Cut cantaloupe in half; remove and discard seeds. Remove rind; cut cantaloupe into 1-inch-thick wedges. Arrange cantaloupe on serving platter.

3 Gently toss melon balls with cooled syrup. To serve, spoon melon balls on top and around cantaloupe; drizzle with remaining syrup. Garnish with mint sprigs.

NUTRITION INFORMATION PER SERVING: Calories 80 • Total Fat 0g • Saturated Fat 0g • Trans Fat 0g • Cholesterol 0mg • Sodium 10mg • Total Carbohydrate 18g • Dietary Fiber 0g • Sugars 17g • Protein 0g. DIETARY EXCHANGES: 1/2 Fruit • 1/2 Other Carbohydrate • Carbohydrate Choices 1.

cook's notes

If you're entertaining a crowd, make the syrup a day ahead of your gathering. The melon pieces left after making the balls can be stored in the refrigerator for snacking.

frosty cranberry salad squares

PREP TIME: 10 Minutes ✱ READY IN: 6 Hours 40 Minutes ✱ SERVINGS: 12

- 1 package (8 oz.) cream cheese, softened
- 1 can (14 oz.) sweetened condensed milk (not evaporated)
- 1/4 cup mayonnaise
- 2 tablespoons lemon juice
- 1 can (16 oz.) jellied cranberry sauce
- 1 bag (16 oz.) frozen dark sweet cherries
- 1 can (20 oz.) crushed pineapple, drained
- 2 tablespoons chopped nuts

1 In large bowl, beat cream cheese, condensed milk, mayonnaise and lemon juice with electric mixer on low speed until smooth and fluffy.

2 Add cranberry sauce; beat on low speed until blended. Fold in cherries and pineapple. Spoon evenly into ungreased 13x9-inch (3-quart) glass baking dish. Sprinkle with nuts.

3 Cover; freeze 6 hours or until firm. To serve, let stand at room temperature 30 minutes or until slightly softened. Cut into squares.

NUTRITION INFORMATION PER SERVING: Calories 330 • Total Fat 14g • Saturated Fat 7g • Cholesterol 35mg • Sodium 135mg • Total Carbohydrate 46g • Dietary Fiber 1g • Protein 5g. DIETARY EXCHANGES: 1 Starch • 2 Fruit • 3 Other Carbohydrate • 3 Fat.

cook's notes

Due to its velvety texture, sweet flavor and crunchy nuts, the squares also make a fine holiday dessert.

potatoes alfredo with garden peas
smoky cheese and potato bake

potatoes alfredo with garden peas

PREP TIME: 10 Minutes ✳ READY IN: 4 Hours 40 Minutes ✳ SERVINGS: 10

- 2 lb. small (2 to 3 inches) red potatoes, cut into 1/4-inch-thick slices (8 cups)
- 1/4 cup sliced green onions
- 2 garlic cloves, minced
- 1 container (10 oz.) refrigerated Alfredo sauce
- 1/2 cup half-and-half or milk
- 1/2 teaspoon salt
- 1/8 teaspoon pepper
- 1-1/2 cups Green Giant® frozen sweet peas

1 Spray 3-1/2- to 4-quart slow cooker with nonstick cooking spray. Layer half each of potatoes, onions and garlic in sprayed slow cooker.

2 In medium bowl, combine Alfredo sauce, half-and-half, salt and pepper; mix well. Spoon half of mixture over top. Layer with remaining potatoes, onions, garlic and sauce mixture. Do not stir. Cover; cook on High setting for 3 to 4 hours.

3 About 30 minutes before serving, sprinkle peas over potato mixture. Cover; cook on High setting an additional 20 to 30 minutes. Stir gently to mix the peas with the potatoes before serving.

NUTRITION INFORMATION PER SERVING: Calories 215 • Total Fat 11g • Saturated Fat 7g • Cholesterol 30mg • Sodium 270mg • Total Carbohydrate 24g • Dietary Fiber 2g • Sugars 3g • Protein 5g. DIETARY EXCHANGES: 1-1/2 Starch • 1-1/2 Other Carbohydrate • 2 Fat.

special touch

For added flavor, toss 1 teaspoon dried dill weed into the slow cooker when you add the peas.

smoky cheese and potato bake

PREP TIME: 10 Minutes ✳ READY IN: 6 Hours 10 Minutes ✳ SERVINGS: 14

- 1 can (10-3/4 oz.) condensed cream of mushroom soup
- 1 container (8 oz.) sour cream (about 1 cup)
- 1 round (7 oz.) hickory-smoked Gouda cheese, cut into 1/2-inch cubes
- 1/3 cup roasted red bell pepper strips (from a jar)
- 1 package (32 oz.) frozen southern-style cubed hash-brown potatoes (8 cups), thawed

1 Spray 3-1/2- to 4-quart slow cooker with nonstick cooking spray. In medium bowl, combine soup, sour cream and cheese; mix well. Gently stir in roasted pepper strips.

2 Arrange half of potatoes in sprayed slow cooker. Top with half of sour cream mixture; spread evenly. Top with remaining potatoes and sour cream mixture, spreading evenly. Do not stir. Cover; cook on Low setting for 5 to 6 hours.

NUTRITION INFORMATION PER SERVING: Calories 180 • Total Fat 8g • Saturated Fat 5g • Cholesterol 25mg • Sodium 320mg • Total Carbohydrate 21g • Dietary Fiber 1g • Sugars 2g • Protein 6g. DIETARY EXCHANGES: 1-1/2 Starch • 1-1/2 Other Carbohydrate • 1/2 High-Fat Meat • 1 Fat.

cook's notes

Remove the red wax coating from the cheese before cutting it into cubes. To thaw the potatoes, microwave them in a covered, 2-quart, microwavable glass dish on High for 5 to 6 minutes or until thawed, stirring twice.

cook's notes

Any medium-sized pasta can be used in place of the bow tie pasta called for in this salad.

minestrone salad

READY IN: 20 Minutes ✱ SERVINGS: 12

- 5 cups uncooked bow tie pasta (farfalle)
- 1 can (15.5 or 15 oz.) Green Giant®, Joan of Arc® or Progresso® red kidney beans, drained, rinsed
- 1 package (3.5 oz.) sliced pepperoni
- 4 Italian plum tomatoes, coarsely chopped
- 1/2 cup chopped green bell pepper
- 1/4 cup chopped fresh parsley
- 1/4 cup shredded fresh Parmesan cheese (1 oz.)
- Freshly ground black pepper, if desired
- 1 bottle (8 oz.) Italian salad dressing (3/4 cup)

1 Cook pasta to desired doneness as directed on package. Drain in a colander; rinse pasta well with cold water to cool.

2 In large bowl, combine cooked pasta and all remaining ingredients; mix well. Serve immediately, or cover and refrigerate until serving time.

NUTRITION INFORMATION PER SERVING: Calories 270 • Total Fat 14g • Saturated 3g • Cholesterol 10mg • Sodium 400mg • Total Carbohydrate 29g • Dietary Fiber 2g • Sugars 4g • Protein 8g.

cook's notes

To gussy up Creamy Chicken-Vegetable Chowder without much work, drain a small jar of diced pimientos and stir it into the heartwarming dish. For even more flair, replace 1 of the cups of cooked chicken with a cup of cooked and cubed ham. Garnish individual servings with additional chopped green onions or a little fresh parsley.

creamy chicken-vegetable chowder

PREP TIME: 25 Minutes ✱ SERVINGS: 6

Chowder

- 1-1/2 cups milk or half-and-half
- 1 cup chicken broth
- 1 can (10-3/4 oz.) condensed cream of potato soup
- 1 can (10-3/4 oz.) condensed cream of chicken soup
- 2 cups cubed cooked chicken or turkey
- 1/3 cup chopped green onions
- 1 can (11 oz.) whole kernel corn with red and green peppers, drained
- 1 jar (11 oz.) sliced mushrooms, drained
- 1 can (4.5 oz.) chopped green chiles
- 6 oz. shredded Cheddar cheese (1-1/2 cups)

Crescent Rolls

- 1 can (8 oz.) refrigerated crescent dinner rolls
- 1/4 cup crushed nacho-flavored tortilla chips

1 In 4-quart saucepan or Dutch oven, combine milk, broth, potato soup and chicken soup; blend well. Add all remaining chowder ingredients except cheese; mix well. Cook over medium heat for 5 to 8 minutes or until onions are tender, stirring occasionally. Remove from heat. Add cheese; stir until melted.

2 While chowder is heating, bake crescent rolls. Heat oven to 375°F. Shape dough as directed on can. Gently press top of each roll in crushed chips. Place on ungreased cookie sheet.

3 Bake at 375°F for 11 to 13 minutes or until golden brown. Serve chowder with crescent rolls.

NUTRITION INFORMATION PER SERVING: Calories 535 • Total Fat 25g • Saturated Fat 11g • Cholesterol 80mg • Sodium 1920mg • Total Carbohydrate 47g • Dietary Fiber 3g • Sugars 12g • Protein 30g. DIETARY EXCHANGES: 3 Starch • 3 Lean Meat • 3 Fat.

minestrone salad

winter fruit salad with lemon poppy seed dressing

winter fruit salad with lemon poppy seed dressing

READY IN: 25 Minutes ✷ SERVINGS: 12

Dressing

- 1/2 cup sugar
- 1/3 cup lemon juice
- 2 teaspoons finely chopped onion
- 1 teaspoon Dijon mustard
- 1/2 teaspoon salt
- 2/3 cup vegetable oil
- 1 tablespoon poppy seed

Salad

- 1 large head romaine lettuce, torn into bite-sized pieces (about 10 cups)
- 1 cup shredded Swiss cheese (4 oz.)
- 1 cup cashews
- 1/4 cup sweetened dried cranberries
- 1 apple, cubed
- 1 pear, cubed

1 In blender container or food processor bowl with metal blade, place sugar, lemon juice, onion, mustard and salt. Cover; blend until smooth. With machine running, add oil in slow, steady stream, blending until thick and smooth. Add poppy seed; blend a few seconds to mix.

2 In large serving bowl, toss all of the salad ingredients together. Pour dressing over the salad; toss salad to coat.

NUTRITION INFORMATION PER SERVING: Calories 280 • Total Fat 20g • Saturated Fat 4g • Cholesterol 10mg • Sodium 200mg • Total Carbohydrate 20g • Dietary Fiber 2g • Protein 5g. DIETARY EXCHANGES: 1 Starch • 1 Other Carbohydrate • 1 Vegetable • 4 Fat.

cook's notes

Add some cooked and cooled chicken or shrimp to this salad for a light entree.

savory crescent palmiers

PREP TIME: 15 Minutes ✷ READY IN: 30 Minutes ✷ SERVINGS: 16 Pastries

- 2 tablespoons grated Parmesan cheese
- 1 can (8 oz.) refrigerated crescent dinner rolls
- 2 tablespoons yellow mustard
- 1/8 teaspoon onion powder

1 Heat oven to 375°F. Lightly grease cookie sheets with shortening. Sprinkle cutting board or waxed paper with cheese. Separate dough into 4 rectangles; firmly press perforations to seal. Lightly press dough into cheese.

2 In small bowl, blend mustard and onion powder. Brush rectangles with mustard mixture. Using 2 rectangles, place 1 rectangle, mustard side up, on top of the other. Starting with shortest sides, roll up both ends jelly-roll fashion to meet in center; cut into 8 slices. Repeat with remaining rectangles. Place, cut side down, 2 inches apart on cookie sheets.

3 Bake 6 to 12 minutes or until deep golden brown. Gently recoil if necessary. Immediately remove from cookie sheets. Serve warm.

NUTRITION INFORMATION PER SERVING: Calories 60 • Total Fat 3.5g • Saturated Fat 1g • Trans Fat 1g • Cholesterol 0mg • Sodium 125mg • Total Carbohydrate 6g • Dietary Fiber 0g • Sugars 1g • Protein 2g. DIETARY EXCHANGES: 1/2 Starch • 1/2 Fat.

cook's notes

Not only are these flaky pastries great with soup, stew, chili or salad, but they are a tasty little appetizer.

kitchen tip

Red pepper flakes are pieces of fried hot chiles. Chili paste, chili sauce and ground red pepper are all made from hot chiles.

antipasto jumble

PREP TIME: 15 Minutes ✻ READY IN: 1 Hour 15 Minutes ✻ SERVINGS: 14

ANTIPASTO

- 1 pint grape tomatoes (2 cups)
- 1 cup fresh baby carrots
- 1 cup pitted kalamata olives
- 6 oz. string cheese, cut into 1/2-inch chunks (about 1 cup)
- 1 jar (7 oz.) stuffed large Queen green olives (about 1 cup), drained
- 1 jar (6 oz.) Green Giant® whole mushrooms, drained

MARINADE

- 1/4 cup refrigerated basil pesto
- 1/4 cup Italian dressing
- 1 teaspoon grated orange peel
- 1/2 teaspoon crushed red pepper flakes

1 In large glass or ceramic serving bowl, mix all antipasto ingredients. In small bowl, mix all of the marinade ingredients until blended.

2 Pour the marinade over the antipasto; toss well. Refrigerate antipasto for at least 1 hour or until serving time.

NUTRITION INFORMATION PER SERVING: Calories 120 • Total Fat 9g • Saturated Fat 2g • Cholesterol 10mg • Sodium 540mg • Total Carbohydrate 5g • Dietary Fiber 1g • Protein 2g. DIETARY EXCHANGES: 1/2 Medium-Fat Meat • 1-1/2 Fat.

cook's notes

Light Creamed Corn is an obvious choice for the hurried holiday season. Prepare the side dish the night before and refrigerate. Simply reheat in the slow cooker before dinner the next day.

light creamed corn

PREP TIME: 10 Minutes ✻ READY IN: 3 Hours 10 Minutes ✻ SERVINGS: 10

- 2 bags (1 lb. each) Green Giant® Niblets® frozen corn
- 2 packages (3 oz. each) reduced-fat cream cheese (Neufchatel), cut into cubes
- 3/4 cup fat-free milk
- 2 tablespoons butter or margarine, melted
- 1 teaspoon sugar
- 1 teaspoon salt
- 1/4 teaspoon pepper
- 2 tablespoons bacon flavor bits

1 In 3- to 4-quart slow cooker, spread corn to cover bottom. Top with cream cheese cubes. In small bowl, mix milk, butter, sugar, salt and pepper; pour over corn and cream cheese. Cover; cook on High setting 3 to 4 hours.

2 Cream cheese may look curdled. Sprinkle bacon bits over top; stir until cream cheese is smooth and creamy. If necessary, add additional milk until desired creamy consistency.

NUTRITION INFORMATION PER SERVING: Calories 160 • Total Fat 7g • Saturated Fat 4g • Cholesterol 20mg • Sodium 350mg • Total Carbohydrate 19g • Dietary Fiber 2g • Sugars 3g • Protein 5g.

antipasto jumble

tarragon green peas
italian mixed green salad

tarragon green peas

READY IN: 15 Minutes ✱ SERVINGS: 6

- 1 package (1 lb.) frozen sweet peas
- 3 tablespoons butter
- 2 green onions, sliced
- 1/8 teaspoon dried tarragon leaves

1 Cook peas as directed on package. Drain. Meanwhile, melt butter in small saucepan over medium heat.

2 Stir in the onions; cook 2 to 3 minutes or until onions are tender, stirring occasionally. Stir in tarragon. Pour onion-butter mixture over cooked peas; stir to coat.

NUTRITION INFORMATION PER SERVING: Calories 110 • Total Fat 6g • Saturated Fat 4g • Cholesterol 15mg • Sodium 95mg • Total Carbohydrate 10g • Dietary Fiber 3g • Sugars 4g • Protein 4g. DIETARY EXCHANGES: 1/2 Starch • 1-1/2 Fat.

cook's notes

Jazz up the green peas with a dash of garlic powder, onion salt or dried basil.

italian mixed green salad

READY IN: 20 Minutes ✱ SERVINGS: 12

- 9 cups torn mixed salad greens (such as romaine, iceberg, leaf or Bibb lettuce, arugula, escarole and/or curly endive)
- 3 medium tomatoes, cut into wedges
- 1/2 large red onion, cut in half, thinly sliced
- 2 green bell peppers, cut into thin bite-sized strips
- 1/2 cup chopped fresh parsley
- 2 tablespoons chopped fresh basil
- 1/2 teaspoon salt
- 1/2 cup olive or vegetable oil
- 1/3 cup red or white wine vinegar

1 In large bowl, combine salad greens, tomatoes, onion and bell peppers. Sprinkle with parsley, basil and salt.

2 Just before serving, drizzle the salad with the olive or vegetable oil and the red or white wine vinegar; toss until well coated.

NUTRITION INFORMATION PER SERVING: Calories 105 • Total Fat 9g • Saturated Fat 1g • Cholesterol 0mg • Sodium 115mg • Total Carbohydrate 5g • Dietary Fiber 1g • Sugars 2g • Protein 1g. DIETARY EXCHANGES: 1 Vegetable • 2 Fat • 1 Carb Choice.

cook's notes

Make the most of your time by replacing the 9 cups of torn mixed salad greens with an equal amount of baby spring greens. Buy them prepackaged or in bulk from your grocer's produce department.

broccoli with walnut-garlic butter

READY IN:10 Minutes ✱ SERVINGS: 6

- 1 package (14 oz.) frozen broccoli florets
- 1 tablespoon butter
- 1 garlic clove, minced
- 1/4 cup walnut pieces

1 Cook broccoli as directed on package. Drain. Meanwhile, melt butter in small saucepan over low heat. Add garlic; cook until butter is lightly browned, stirring constantly. Stir in walnuts. Pour walnut mixture over cooked broccoli; toss gently to coat.

NUTRITION INFORMATION PER SERVING: Calories 75 • Total Fat 5g • Saturated Fat 2g • Cholesterol 5mg • Sodium 25mg • Total Carbohydrate 4g • Dietary Fiber 2g • Sugars 1g • Protein 3g. DIETARY EXCHANGES: 1 Vegetable • 1 Fat.

cook's notes

Doubling this dish for a crowd? Microwave the broccoli in two batches. It won't take up any extra time, and the smaller batches cook more evenly.

special touch

These polenta stars are particularly pretty when they are cut in different sizes. Purchase several sizes or a graduated set of star cookie cutters from a cookware store and get the whole family involved in cutting out shapes.

baked herbed polenta stars

PREP TIME: 15 Minutes ✱ READY IN: 1 Hour ✱ SERVINGS: 10

- 5 cups water
- 1-1/2 teaspoons salt
- 1-1/2 cups yellow cornmeal
- 1/2 cup whipping cream
- 1/4 cup grated Parmesan cheese
- 2 teaspoons dried Italian seasoning
- 1 tablespoon olive oil

1 Grease 15x10x1-inch baking pan. In large saucepan, bring 5 cups water and salt to a boil. While stirring water in a circular motion with wire whisk, add cornmeal in a slow steady stream, keeping water boiling continuously. Reduce heat to low; continue cooking, stirring constantly, until mixture is thick, 5 to 15 minutes depending on type of cornmeal.

2 Add cream, cheese and Italian seasoning; mix well. Pour into greased pan. Cool 15 minutes. At this point, polenta can be covered and refrigerated until serving time.

3 To serve, heat oven to 400°F. With assorted star-shaped cookie cutters, cut polenta into stars. (Polenta scraps can be combined and rerolled to cut additional stars.) Brush both sides of each star with oil; place on ungreased cookie sheets. Bake at 400°F for 10 to 15 minutes or until thoroughly heated.

NUTRITION INFORMATION PER SERVING: Calories 135 • Total Fat 6g • Saturated Fat 3g • Cholesterol 15mg • Sodium 410mg • Total Carbohydrate 17g • Dietary Fiber 1g • Sugars 2g • Protein 3g. DIETARY EXCHANGES: 1 Starch • 1 Fat.

cook's notes

Combine all of the ingredients except the spinach several hours before serving time. Cover and refrigerate the salad. Just before serving, toss in the spinach.

spinach waldorf salad with cinnamon-apple dressing

READY IN: 20 Minutes ✱ SERVINGS: 8

- 1/2 cup mayonnaise
- 2 tablespoons frozen apple juice concentrate, thawed
- 1/4 teaspoon ground cinnamon
- 2 large red eating apples, cubed (about 4 cups)
- 1/2 cup seedless red grapes, halved
- 1/2 cup chopped celery (1 medium stalk)
- 1/2 cup chopped walnuts
- 4 cups torn fresh spinach leaves

1 In large bowl, mix the mayonnaise, juice concentrate and cinnamon until well blended. Stir in the apples, grapes, celery and walnuts to coat.

2 Before serving, place spinach in large salad bowl. Spoon apple mixture over spinach; toss to mix and coat.

NUTRITION INFORMATION PER SERVING: Calories 210 • Total Fat 16g • Saturated Fat 2g • Trans Fat 0g • Cholesterol 10mg • Sodium 100mg • Total Carbohydrate 15g • Dietary Fiber 3g • Sugars 10g • Protein 2g. DIETARY EXCHANGES: 1/2 Fruit • 1/2 Other Carbohydrate • 3 Fat.

spinach waldorf salad with cinnamon-apple dressing

Dazzling Yuletide Dinner

Gather family and friends for Christmas dinner and create memories that last a lifetime. Menu planning is easy when you start with the succulent entrées featured here.

p. 106

p. 104

p. 91

p. 95

p. 100

honey-mustard roasted chicken and squash p. 96

roast salmon provençal

roast salmon provençal

PREP TIME: 20 Minutes ✱ READY IN: 40 Minutes ✱ SERVINGS: 4

- 4 salmon fillets (1/2-inch thick) or steaks (4 to 6 oz. each)
- 3 cups refrigerated unpeeled potato wedges (from 1 lb. 4 oz. package)
- 1-1/2 cups small whole fresh mushrooms
- 1/2 red bell pepper, cut into 1-inch pieces
- 1 medium zucchini, cut into 1/2-inch pieces
- 1/2 cup purchased Italian salad dressing
- 1/2 teaspoon dried basil leaves
- 1/2 cup large pitted kalamata or ripe olives

1 Heat oven to 425°F. Spray 15x10-inch baking pan with sides with nonstick cooking spray. Place salmon, potatoes, mushrooms, red pepper and zucchini in sprayed pan. Brush with half of the salad dressing. Sprinkle with basil. Bake for 20 minutes.

2 Remove pan from oven. Add olives to pan and stir vegetables slightly. Drizzle remaining salad dressing over salmon and vegetables.

3 Return to oven; bake an additional 5 to 10 minutes or until fish flakes easily with fork and potatoes are tender.

NUTRITION INFORMATION PER SERVING: Calories 445 • Total Fat 21g • Saturated Fat 3g • Cholesterol 80mg • Sodium 490mg • Total Carbohydrate 35g • Dietary Fiber 4g • Sugars 6g • Protein 29g. DIETARY EXCHANGES: 2 Starch • 1 Vegetable • 3 Lean Meat • 2 Fat.

cook's notes

A green bell pepper and a medium yellow summer squash can be used instead of the red pepper and zucchini.

crescent chicken newburg

PREP TIME: 25 Minutes ✱ READY IN: 55 Minutes ✱ SERVINGS: 6

- 2 tablespoons butter or margarine
- 6 boneless skinless chicken breast halves, cut into 1/2-inch pieces
- 1/4 cup all-purpose flour
- 1/4 to 1/2 teaspoon salt
- 1/4 teaspoon white pepper
- 1-1/2 cups half-and-half
- 3 tablespoons dry sherry
- 1 package (16 oz.) frozen broccoli, carrots and water chestnuts, cooked, drained
- 3 tablespoons grated Parmesan cheese
- 1 can (8 oz.) refrigerated crescent dinner rolls
- 1 tablespoon butter or margarine, melted
- 1/4 teaspoon paprika

1 Heat oven to 350°F. Melt 2 tablespoons butter in large skillet over medium-high heat. Add chicken; cook and stir until browned and no longer pink in center. Reduce heat to medium; stir in flour, salt, pepper, half-and-half and sherry. Cook until mixture boils and thickens, stirring constantly.

2 Stir in cooked vegetables and 2 tablespoons of the Parmesan cheese. Cook an additional 4 to 6 minutes or until thoroughly heated, stirring frequently. Spoon into ungreased 12x8-inch (2-quart) glass baking dish.

3 Remove dough from can in rolled section; do not unroll. Cut roll into 12 slices; cut each slice in half crosswise. Arrange slice halves, curved side up, around outside of chicken mixture. Brush with 1 tablespoon melted butter. Sprinkle with remaining tablespoon Parmesan cheese. Sprinkle entire casserole with paprika. Bake for 23 to 27 minutes or until rolls are deep golden brown.

NUTRITION INFORMATION PER SERVING: Calories 485 • Total Fat 23g • Saturated Fat 11g • Cholesterol 115mg • Sodium 770mg • Total Carbohydrate 35g • Dietary Fiber 3g • Sugars 10g • Protein 34g. DIETARY EXCHANGES: 2 Starch • 1 Vegetable • 3-1/2 Very Lean Meat • 4 Fat • 2 Carb Choices.

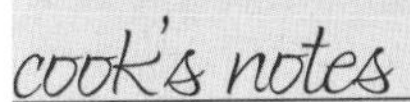

This family-friendly Newburg pairs a typical Newburg sauce, made from butter, cream and sherry, with chicken and uses refrigerated crescent rolls. If you prefer to twist the concept a bit more, you can use a different mix of frozen vegetables than the kind called for in this rich recipe.

Kitchen tip

Salmon is a good source of Omega-3 oils which benefit the heart and brain; these oils are found almost exclusively in seafood.

salmon with vegetable pilaf

READY IN: 20 Minutes ✱ SERVINGS: 2

Salmon

- 1 small carrot, thinly sliced (about 1/3 cup)
- 1-1/2 teaspoons chicken-flavor instant bouillon
- 1 teaspoon dried dill weed
- 1-1/2 cups water
- 1 cup uncooked instant brown rice
- 1 cup frozen French-style green beans
- 1 salmon fillet, 1/2 to 3/4 inch thick (8 oz.)
- 1/4 teaspoon lemon-pepper seasoning

Sauce

- 2 tablespoons light sour cream
- 1 tablespoon mayonnaise or salad dressing
- 1/2 teaspoon Dijon mustard
- 1/4 teaspoon dried dill weed
- Fresh dill, if desired

1 In large nonstick skillet, place carrot, bouillon, 1 teaspoon dill weed and water. Heat to boiling. Reduce heat; cover and simmer 2 minutes.

2 Uncover skillet; stir in rice and green beans. Cut salmon fillet into 2 serving pieces. Place salmon over rice and green beans, skin side down. Sprinkle salmon only with lemon-pepper seasoning. Return to a boil. Reduce heat to medium-low; cover and cook 8 to 10 minutes or until liquid is absorbed and thickest part of fish flakes easily with fork.

3 Meanwhile, in small bowl, mix all sauce ingredients until well blended. To serve, remove salmon from skillet; place on serving platter. Fluff rice mixture with fork before serving. Serve sauce with salmon. Garnish with fresh dill.

NUTRITION INFORMATION PER SERVING: Calories 575 • Total Fat 16g • Saturated Fat 4g • Cholesterol 85mg • Sodium 1180mg • Total Carbohydrate 81g • Dietary Fiber 8g. DIETARY EXCHANGES: 4-1/2 Starch • 1 Vegetable • 2-1/2 Lean Meat • 1-1/2 Fat.

prime rib-eye roast

PREP TIME: 10 Minutes ✱ READY IN: 4 Hours ✱ SERVINGS: 12

- 1/2 cup dry red wine
- 1/4 cup balsamic vinegar
- 2 tablespoons Worcestershire sauce
- 3 medium garlic cloves, minced
- 1-1/2 teaspoons salt
- 1/2 teaspoon coarse ground black pepper
- 2 (5- to 5-1/2 lb.) boneless beef small-end rib-eye roasts

1 In medium bowl, combine all ingredients except beef roasts; mix well. Divide marinade between 2 large resealable plastic food storage bags or two 12x8-inch (2-quart) glass baking dishes.

2 Add 1 beef roast to each bag or baking dish, turning to coat all sides. Seal bags or cover dishes with plastic wrap. Refrigerate 1 to 8 hours to marinate, turning occasionally.

3 To serve, heat oven to 350°F. Place beef roasts, fat side up, on racks in shallow roasting pans; discard marinade.

4 Bake for 1-3/4 to 2 hours for medium-rare or until meat thermometer inserted in center registers 135°F, or 2 to 2-1/2 hours for medium doneness or until meat thermometer registers 150°F. Let roasts stand 15 to 20 minutes. Cut roasts into slices.

NUTRITION INFORMATION PER SERVING: Calories 595 • Total Fat 27g • Saturated Fat 10g • Cholesterol 215mg • Sodium 510mg • Total Carbohydrate 1g • Dietary Fiber 0g • Sugars 1g • Protein 81g. DIETARY EXCHANGES: 1 Lean Meat • 0 Carb Choice.

cook's notes

Don't let the fact that this recipe calls for wine intimidate you. Simply use your favorite drinking wine, or get a recommendation from a specialty shop. Both Merlot and Cabernet Sauvignon are good choices.

salmon with vegetable pilaf

maple roast chicken and squash

maple roast chicken and squash

PREP TIME: 10 Minutes ✱ READY IN: 2 Hours 5 Minutes ✱ SERVINGS: 4

- 1 whole chicken (3 to 5 lb.)
- 1/2 teaspoon seasoned salt
- 1/2 teaspoon dried marjoram leaves
- 1/4 teaspoon pepper
- 1 medium acorn squash, quartered, seeds removed
- 1 can (8 oz.) crushed pineapple in unsweetened juice, undrained
- 1/2 cup real maple syrup
- 2 tablespoons soy sauce
- 2 tablespoons Dijon mustard

1 Heat oven to 375°F. Remove and discard giblets from chicken. Rinse chicken inside and out with cold water; drain. Pat dry with paper towels. Rub chicken with seasoned salt, marjoram and pepper. In shallow roasting pan, place chicken. Insert ovenproof meat thermometer so tip is in thickest part of inside thigh and does not touch bone. Bake 45 minutes. Arrange squash, cut side up, around chicken. Bake 30 minutes longer.

2 In small bowl, mix pineapple with its juice, maple syrup, soy sauce and mustard until well blended. Spoon about 1 cup pineapple mixture over chicken and squash. Bake 15 to 30 minutes longer or until thermometer reads 180°F and legs move easily when lifted or twisted, and squash is tender, basting chicken and squash with pan juices once.

3 Remove chicken and squash from pan; cover to keep warm. Pour drippings from pan into medium saucepan. Add remaining pineapple mixture; mix well. Cook over medium heat 5 to 10 minutes or until mixture is reduced slightly, stirring occasionally. Serve pineapple mixture with chicken and squash.

NUTRITION INFORMATION PER SERVING: Calories 570 • Total Fat 21g • Saturated Fat 6g • Cholesterol 130mg • Sodium 940mg • Total Carbohydrate 53g • Dietary Fiber 2g • Sugars 34g • Protein 42g. DIETARY EXCHANGES: 2 Starch • 1/2 Fruit • 1 Other Carbohydrate • 5 Lean Meat • 1 Fat.

cook's notes

Don't have real maple syrup on hand? Maple-flavored syrup can be used instead.

To make this squash easier to cut, use a knife to pierce 2 to 4 holes in the skin so steam can escape. Microwave the squash on High for 2 to 3 minutes or just until it's soft enough to cut.

southern turkey-stuffing bake

PREP TIME: 15 Minutes ✱ READY IN: 1 Hour 30 Minutes ✱ SERVINGS: 6

- 1 cup chopped onions (2 medium)
- 4 slices bacon, cut into small pieces
- 4 cups seasoned cornbread stuffing mix
- 1-1/2 cups water
- 2 cups Green Giant® frozen cut broccoli
- 1/2 teaspoon dried thyme leaves
- 1/2 teaspoon seasoned salt
- 1/2 teaspoon garlic powder
- 1/8 teaspoon ground red pepper (cayenne)
- 2 turkey breast tenderloins (3/4 lb. each)

1 Heat oven to 350°F. Spray 11x7-inch (2-quart) glass baking dish with nonstick cooking spray. In Dutch oven, cook onions and bacon over medium-high heat for 4 to 5 minutes or until bacon is browned and onions are tender, stirring occasionally. Remove from heat. Add cornbread mix and water; mix well. Stir in broccoli. Spread in sprayed baking dish.

2 In small bowl, combine thyme, seasoned salt, garlic powder and ground red pepper; mix well. Rub on turkey tenderloins. Arrange over stuffing mixture; press into stuffing slightly. Cover with foil.

3 Bake covered for 1 hour. Uncover baking dish; bake an additional 10 to 15 minutes or until turkey is no longer pink in center. To serve, cut turkey into crosswise slices.

HIGH ALTITUDE (3500-6500 FT): Bake covered at 350°F for 1 hour 15 minutes. Uncover baking dish; bake an additional 15 minutes.

NUTRITION INFORMATION PER SERVING: Calories 355 • Total Fat 5g • Saturated Fat 1g • Cholesterol 80mg • Sodium 1000mg • Total Carbohydrate 42g • Dietary Fiber 3g • Sugars 4g • Protein 35g. DIETARY EXCHANGES: 3 Starch • 3-1/2 Very Lean Meat • 1/2 Fat.

cook's notes

Don't feel like chopping onions? Look for bags of chopped onions near the other frozen vegetables in your grocer's freezer.

Kitchen tip

Luxurious shavings of fresh Parmigiano-Reggiano–Italian Parmesan cheese aged at least 2 years–give pasta a restaurant touch. Use the large single opening on your grater to shave the cheese.

parmesan chicken with pasta rags

READY IN: 30 Minutes ✱ SERVINGS: 4

Chicken

- 3 garlic cloves, minced
- 1/2 teaspoon seasoned salt
- 3 tablespoons olive oil
- 1 tablespoon butter
- 1/2 cup Progresso® garlic herb bread crumbs
- 1/2 cup grated fresh Parmesan cheese (2 oz.)
- 1-1/2 lb. boneless skinless chicken breast halves or thighs

Pasta

- 8 oz. uncooked lasagna noodles, broken into random 2-inch pieces
- 1/4 cup olive oil
- 1 garlic clove, minced
- 1 package (9 oz.) Green Giant® frozen spinach, thawed, drained
- 1/2 teaspoon seasoned salt
- 1 cup cherry tomatoes, halved
- 2 tablespoons chopped fresh basil

Garnish, If Desired

- Fresh basil sprigs
- Shaved Parmesan cheese

1 Heat oven to 475°F. In shallow microwave-safe bowl, combine 3 garlic cloves, 1/2 teaspoon seasoned salt, 3 tablespoons oil and the butter. Microwave on High for 1 minute or until butter is melted; stir to mix.

2 In another shallow bowl, combine bread crumbs and grated cheese; mix well. Coat chicken breast halves with garlic mixture; coat with crumb mixture. Place in ungreased 15x10x1-inch baking pan. Bake at 475°F for 20 minutes or until chicken is fork-tender and juices run clear.

3 Meanwhile, cook broken lasagna noodles to desired doneness as directed on package. Drain; cover to keep warm.

4 Heat 1/4 cup oil in large skillet over medium-high heat until hot. Add 1 garlic clove; cook and stir 1 minute or until tender. Add spinach and 1/2 teaspoon seasoned salt; mix well. Cook 2 to 3 minutes or until spinach is cooked, stirring frequently.

5 Add cooked noodles, tomatoes and basil; cook 1 to 2 minutes or until thoroughly heated, stirring occasionally. Serve pasta mixture with chicken. Garnish with basil and cheese.

NUTRITION INFORMATION PER SERVING: Calories 800 • Total Fat 38g • Saturated Fat 10g • Cholesterol 120mg • Sodium 1100mg • Total Carbohydrate 60g • Dietary Fiber 4g • Sugars 4g • Protein 54g. DIETARY EXCHANGES: 3-1/2 Starch • 3-1/2 Other Carbohydrate • 1 Vegetable • 6 Very Lean Meat • 7 Fat.

Kitchen tip

To broil pork chops, place on broiler pan; broil 4 to 6 inches from heat using the recipe times as a guide, turning once.

spice-rubbed pork chops

PREP TIME: 15 Minutes ✱ READY IN: 45 Minutes ✱ SERVINGS: 4

- 1 tablespoon brown sugar
- 1 teaspoons chili powder
- 1/4 teaspoon salt
- 1/4 teaspoon cumin
- 1/4 teaspoon pepper
- 1/8 teaspoon allspice
- 4 pork loin chops (3/4 inch thick)

1 In small bowl, combine all ingredients except pork chops; mix well. Rub pork chops on both sides with spice mixture. Let stand at room temperature for 30 minutes.

2 Meanwhile, heat grill. When ready to grill, place pork chops on gas grill over medium heat or on charcoal grill 4 to 6 inches from medium coals. Cook 8 to 10 minutes or until pork is no longer pink in center, turning once.

NUTRITION INFORMATION PER SERVING: Calories: 180 • Total Fat 8g • Saturated Fat 3g • Cholesterol 65mg • Sodium 190mg • Total Carbohydrate 4g • Dietary Fiber 0g • Sugars 3g • Protein 23g. DIETARY EXCHANGE: 3 Lean Meat.

parmesan chicken with pasta rags

oven-roasted pork chops and vegetables

honey-mustard roasted chicken and squash

cherry-balsamic cornish hen with rice

chicken breast bundles with cranberry chutney

balsamic sirloin and pasta sauté

balsamic sirloin and pasta sauté

READY IN: 20 Minutes ✳ SERVINGS: 3

- 1 teaspoon olive or vegetable oil
- 1 teaspoon butter or margarine
- 1 boneless beef sirloin steak (10 oz.), cut into 2x1/2x1/4-inch strips
- 1/2 teaspoon dried basil leaves
- 3 tablespoons water
- 2 tablespoons balsamic vinegar
- 1 package (1 lb.) Green Giant® Pasta Accents® garlic frozen vegetables with pasta
- 1 cup diced seeded tomatoes
- Fresh cilantro, if desired

1 Heat oil and butter in large nonstick skillet over medium-high heat until hot. Add beef strips and basil; cook and stir 2 to 3 minutes or until beef is browned.

2 Stir in water and vinegar. Add frozen vegetables with pasta; mix well. Bring to a boil. Reduce heat to medium; cover and simmer 4 minutes, stirring once. Add tomatoes; cover and cook 1 minute or until thoroughly heated. To serve, spoon mixture onto serving platter. Garnish with fresh cilantro or basil.

NUTRITION INFORMATION PER SERVING: Calories 360 • Total Fat 14g • Saturated Fat 6g • Cholesterol 65mg • Sodium 580mg • Total Carbohydrate 33g • Dietary Fiber 3g • Sugars 7g • Protein 25g. DIETARY EXCHANGES: 2 Starch • 2 Other Carbohydrate • 1 Vegetable • 2-1/2 Lean Meat • 1 Fat.

cook's notes

Use beef sirloin steak in this sauté; it's more tender than beef sirloin tip steak, and turns out perfectly when briefly cooked.

grilled rosemary chicken

READY IN: 35 Minutes ✳ SERVINGS: 6

- 6 boneless chicken breast halves (with skin)
- 12 sprigs fresh rosemary or 2 tablespoons dried rosemary leaves, crushed
- 12 sprigs fresh oregano or 2 tablespoons dried oregano leaves, crushed
- 6 garlic cloves, halved lengthwise

1 Heat grill. Loosen skin on one edge of each chicken breast half. Under the skin of each, place 2 sprigs rosemary or 1 teaspoon dried rosemary, 2 sprigs oregano or 1 teaspoon dried oregano and 2 garlic clove halves. Smooth skin over seasonings and chicken breast halves.

2 When ready to grill, place chicken on gas grill over medium heat or on charcoal grill 4 to 6 inches from medium coals. Cook 10 to 12 minutes or until chicken is fork-tender and juices run clear, turning once halfway through cooking. Cool slightly.

3 To serve, remove skin and seasonings from chicken. Slice crosswise into strips. Arrange on serving platter. Garnish as desired.

NUTRITION INFORMATION PER SERVING: Calories 90 • Total Fat 8g • Saturated 2g • Cholesterol 80mg • Sodium 70mg • Total Carbohydrate 1g • Dietary Fiber 0g • Sugars 0g • Protein 29g. DIETARY EXCHANGES: 4 Very Lean Meat • 1 Fat.

cook's notes

To broil the seasoned chicken, place it on broiler pan. Broil 4 to 6 inches from heat for 10 to 12 minutes or until chicken is fork-tender and juices run clear, turning once halfway through cooking.

cook's notes

To boost Italian flavor, use fresh garlic on the chicken breasts; mince 1 or 2 cloves and rub into poultry. Another Italian grating cheese can be used in place of the Parmesan; try Asiago or Romano.

chicken bruschetta

READY IN: 20 Minutes ✷ SERVINGS: 4

Chicken

- 4 boneless skinless chicken breast halves
- 1 teaspoon garlic powder
- 1/4 teaspoon salt
- 1/8 teaspoon pepper

Topping

- 2 tablespoons olive oil
- 1 jar (4.5 oz.) Green Giant® sliced mushrooms, drained
- 5 garlic cloves, minced
- 1/4 teaspoon salt
- 1/2 cup chopped red onion
- 1/2 cup loosely packed chopped fresh basil or 1 teaspoon dried basil leaves
- 3 medium Italian plum tomatoes, seeded, chopped
- 4 teaspoons balsamic vinegar
- 1/8 teaspoon freshly ground black pepper
- 1/4 cup shredded fresh Parmesan cheese (1 oz.)
- Fresh basil sprigs, if desired

1 Spray broiler pan with nonstick cooking spray. Sprinkle chicken breast halves with garlic powder, 1/4 teaspoon salt and 1/8 teaspoon pepper; place on sprayed broiler pan. Broil 4 to 6 inches from heat for 12 to 16 minutes or until fork-tender and juices run clear, turning once.

2 Meanwhile, heat oil in large nonstick skillet over medium-high heat until hot. Add mushrooms, garlic and 1/4 teaspoon salt; cook 1 to 2 minutes or until garlic is tender, stirring occasionally. Add onion, chopped basil, tomatoes, vinegar and 1/8 teaspoon pepper; cook and stir 30 to 45 seconds or until thoroughly heated.

3 To serve, arrange chicken on individual plates. Sprinkle with half of the cheese. Top each serving with mushroom mixture; sprinkle with remaining cheese. Garnish with basil sprigs.

High Altitude (3500-6500 ft): Broil chicken 16 to 20 minutes.

NUTRITION INFORMATION PER SERVING: Calories 275 • Total Fat 13g • Saturated Fat 3g • Cholesterol 80mg • Sodium 630mg • Total Carbohydrate 8g • Dietary Fiber 1g. DIETARY EXCHANGES: 1/2 Starch • 1/2 Other Carbohydrate • 4 Very Lean Meat • 2 Fat.

steak neapolitan

READY IN: 20 Minutes ✷ SERVINGS: 4

- 1 teaspoon vegetable oil
- 2 tablespoons lemon juice
- 4 beef tenderloin steaks (4 oz. each and about 1-inch thick)
- 1 cup finely chopped onions (2 medium)
- 1 cup dry Marsala wine
- 2 tablespoons chopped fresh Italian parsley

1 Heat oil in large skillet over medium-high heat until hot. Add lemon juice and steaks; cook 8 to 10 minutes or until of desired doneness, turning once. Remove steaks from skillet; cover to keep warm.

2 Add onions and wine to juice mixture in skillet; cook and stir 4 minutes or until liquid is reduced to about 1/2 cup. To serve, spoon onion mixture over steaks. Sprinkle with fresh parsley.

NUTRITION INFORMATION PER SERVING: Calories 290 • Total Fat 10g • Saturated Fat 3g • Cholesterol 65mg • Sodium 65mg • Total Carbohydrate 11g • Dietary Fiber 1g • Sugars 4g • Protein 25g. DIETARY EXCHANGES: 3 Medium-Fat Meat • 1 Other Carbohydrate.

chicken bruschetta

Kitchen tip

Allow about 1 pound of uncooked whole turkey per serving. This is enough for a feast plus leftovers.

roast turkey with sausage-apple stuffing

PREP TIME: 30 Minutes ✱ READY IN: 5 Hours ✱ SERVINGS: 12

- 1/2 lb. bulk pork sausage
- 1/2 cup chopped onion (1 medium)
- 1/2 cup chopped celery (1 medium stalk)
- 8 cups unseasoned stuffing cubes (about 14 oz.)
- 2 tablespoons finely chopped fresh parsley
- 2 teaspoons poultry seasoning
- 1 teaspoon salt
- 1/4 teaspoon pepper
- 1/4 cup butter or margarine, melted
- 2 cups chopped peeled apples (2 medium)
- 2/3 cup raisins
- 2 cups chicken broth or water
- 1 whole turkey (10 to 12 lb.)

1 Heat oven to 325°F. In 8-inch skillet, cook pork sausage, onion and celery over medium-high heat, stirring frequently, until sausage is no longer pink; do not drain.

2 In large bowl, mix stuffing cubes, parsley, poultry seasoning, salt, pepper and butter. Stir in apples, raisins, broth and sausage mixture with drippings.

3 Remove and discard giblets and neck from turkey. Rinse turkey inside and out with cold water; pat dry with paper towels. Spoon stuffing loosely into neck and body cavities of turkey; do not pack tightly. Cover and refrigerate remaining stuffing. Turn wings back and tuck tips over shoulder joints. Refasten drumsticks with metal piece or tuck under skin at tail. Fasten neck skin to back with skewers.

4 Place stuffed turkey, breast side up, in shallow roasting pan. Insert ovenproof meat thermometer so tip is in thickest part of inside thigh and does not touch bone.

5 Tent sheet of foil loosely over turkey; roast 3 hours 30 minutes to 4 hours 30 minutes, removing foil during last 30 to 60 minutes of roasting to allow browning, until thermometer reads 180°F and legs move easily when lifted or twisted. Spoon or brush drippings over turkey several times during roasting. Remove from oven. Cover turkey with foil and allow to stand 10 to 15 minutes before carving.

6 Meanwhile, mix remaining stuffing with additional chicken broth or water to moisten. Spoon into microwavable casserole. Microwave on High for 5 minutes, turning halfway through cooking until thoroughly heated.

NUTRITION INFORMATION PER SERVING: Calories 560 • Total Fat 27g • Saturated 8g • Cholesterol 140mg • Sodium 1150mg • Total Carbohydrate 36g • Dietary Fiber 2g • Sugars 9g • Protein 44g. DIETARY EXCHANGES: 2 Starch • 1/2 Fruit • 5-1/2 Lean Meat • 1-1/2 Fat.

lemon and herb-roasted turkey breast

PREP TIME: 15 Minutes ✱ READY IN: 3 Hours ✱ SERVINGS: 8

- 1 medium lemon
- 2 cloves garlic, minced
- 2 tablespoons finely chopped fresh parsley
- 1/2 teaspoon salt
- 1/2 teaspoon dried sage leaves
- 1/2 teaspoon dried marjoram leaves
- 1/4 teaspoon pepper
- 1 tablespoon olive oil
- 1 fresh or frozen bone-in whole turkey breast (5 to 5-1/2 lb.), thawed

1 Heat oven to 325°F. Spray 13x9-inch pan and 16x12-inch sheet of foil with nonstick cooking spray. Grate peel from lemon. Cut lemon into quarters; set aside. In small bowl, mix lemon peel, garlic, parsley, salt, sage, marjoram, pepper and oil.

2 Loosen skin covering turkey breast and pull away, leaving attached at neck. If necessary, use sharp knife to loosen. Rub herb mixture evenly over turkey breast meat. Replace skin over breast, tucking under bottom of breast. Rub any remaining mixture over skin.

3 Place lemon quarters in neck opening. Place turkey, skin side up, in pan; cover tightly with foil, sprayed side down.

4 Bake 1 hour. Uncover pan; insert meat thermometer into turkey so bulb reaches center of thickest part of breast meat but does not rest on bone.

5 Bake uncovered 1-1/4 to 1-3/4 hours longer or until turkey is fork-tender, its juices run clear and meat thermometer reads 170°F. Let stand 5 minutes before serving. Remove and discard lemon from neck opening before cutting turkey into slices.

HIGH ALTITUDE (3500-6000 FT): Bake covered at 350°F for 2 hours. Uncover; bake 15 to 45 minutes longer.

NUTRITION INFORMATION PER SERVING: Calories 360 • Total Fat 16g • Saturated 4g • Cholesterol 145mg • Sodium 270mg • Total Carbohydrate 0g • Dietary Fiber 0g • Sugars 0g • Protein 54g. DIETARY EXCHANGES: 7-1/2 Very Lean Meat • 2-1/2 Fat.

Kitchen tip

Coarsley chop leftover parsley, sprinkle with salt and freeze for later use.

italian roasted salmon

READY IN: 30 Minutes ✱ SERVINGS: 4

- 1/4 cup purchased Italian salad dressing
- 2 tablespoons chopped fresh parsley
- 1/2 teaspoon dried basil leaves
- 1 tablespoon lemon juice
- 1 salmon fillet (1 lb.)
- Lemon slices

1 Heat oven to 425°F. Line shallow baking pan with foil. Spray foil with nonstick cooking spray. In shallow dish, combine salad dressing, parsley, basil and lemon juice; mix well.

2 Place salmon, skin side down, in sprayed foil-lined pan. Spoon about half of salad dressing mixture over salmon.

3 Bake for 15 to 20 minutes or until fish flakes easily with fork, spooning remaining salad dressing mixture over fish once or twice during baking. Serve fish with lemon slices.

NUTRITION INFORMATION PER SERVING: Calories 225 • Total Fat 13g • Saturated Fat 2g • Cholesterol 80mg • Sodium 200mg • Total Carbohydrate 2g • Dietary Fiber 0g • Sugars 2g • Protein 25g. DIETARY EXCHANGES: 3-1/2 Lean Meat • 1/2 Fat.

Kitchen tip

Foil is a handy tool for all busy cooks. Using it to line baking pans cuts down on clean-up, shaving time off the clock.

cook's notes

Try using unpeeled small red potatoes, cut into wedges or quarters, in place of the refrigerated potatoes.

skillet chicken and winter vegetables

READY IN: 45 Minutes ✷ SERVINGS: 4

- 3 tablespoons all-purpose flour
- 3/4 teaspoon peppered seasoned salt
- 4 chicken drumsticks, skin removed
- 4 chicken thighs, skin removed
- 2 cups refrigerated red or new potato wedges (from 20-oz. pkg.)
- 1 cup fresh baby carrots
- 1 medium onion, cut into thin wedges
- 1 can (14.5 oz.) Italian-style stewed tomatoes, undrained

1 Spray 12-inch nonstick skillet with nonstick cooking spray. Heat over medium-high heat until hot. In shallow bowl, combine flour and seasoned salt; mix well. Coat chicken pieces with flour mixture; add to skillet. Cook 6 to 10 minutes or until browned on all sides.

2 Add all remaining ingredients; stir gently to mix. Increase heat to high; cook 2 minutes. Reduce heat to medium-low; cover and simmer 20 to 25 minutes or until chicken is fork-tender, its juices run clear and vegetables are tender, stirring occasionally.

NUTRITION INFORMATION PER SERVING: Calories 315 • Total Fat 8g • Saturated Fat 2g • Cholesterol 90mg • Sodium 690mg • Total Carbohydrate 30g • Dietary Fiber 4g • Sugars 6g • Protein 31g. DIETARY EXCHANGES: 1-1/2 Starch • 1 Vegetable • 3-1/2 Lean Meat • 2 Carb Choices.

peppered beef tenderloin with wine sauce

PREP TIME: 20 Minutes ✷ READY IN: 2 Hours 35 Minutes ✷ SERVINGS: 8

Sauce
- 6 shallots (about 6 oz.)
- 1 small carrot, cut into 1/4-inch pieces
- 1 teaspoon olive oil
- 1 can (14 oz.) beef broth
- 2 cups dry red wine
- 1 tablespoon tomato paste
- 1 teaspoon dried thyme leaves
- 1 bay leaf

Tenderloin
- 1 beef tenderloin (3-1/2 lb.)
- 1 tablespoon olive oil
- 1 tablespoon cracked black pepper

1 Heat oven to 400°F. Peel shallots; cut lengthwise into 1/4-inch-wide slices. Place shallots and carrot in ungreased 13x9-inch pan. Add 1 teaspoon oil; toss to coat. Bake for 20 to 25 minutes or until vegetables are tender.

2 Use small amount of broth to loosen any browned bits from bottom of pan; pour into large saucepan. Add roasted vegetables, remaining broth, the wine, tomato paste, thyme and bay leaf; blend well. Bring to a boil over medium-high heat. Cook 30 minutes or until reduced to about 2 cups (about half of total). Cool 30 minutes.

3 Remove bay leaf. In blender container, blend vegetables with liquid until pureed. Return to saucepan. Cover; refrigerate.

4 Increase oven temperature to 450°F. Place beef tenderloin in shallow metal roasting pan. Rub tenderloin with 1 tablespoon oil. Sprinkle top and sides with pepper. Place pan over medium-high heat; cook until tenderloin is browned on all sides. Place pan in 450°F oven. Immediately reduce oven temperature to 375°F; bake 40 to 50 minutes or until meat thermometer inserted in center registers 140°F.

5 Remove tenderloin from pan; cover with foil to keep warm. Add small amount of vegetable sauce to roasting pan; stir to loosen any browned bits. Bring remainder of vegetable sauce in saucepan to a boil, adding sauce from roasting pan. Cut tenderloin into slices. Serve with sauce.

NUTRITION INFORMATION PER SERVING: Calories 385 • Total Fat 16g • Saturated Fat 6g • Cholesterol 115mg • Sodium 350mg • Total Carbohydrate 4g • Dietary Fiber 1g • Sugars 2g • Protein 44g. DIETARY EXCHANGES: 6 Lean Meat • 0 Carb Choice.

cook's notes

Shorten your to-do list by serving the tenderloin with a rice side dish that starts with a boxed mix. Packaged salad greens round out the meal easily.

skillet chicken and winter vegetables

Caroling Party

Welcome the holidays by serenading neighbors with classic Yuletide favorites. Then, invite everyone over for a casual feast sure to chase the chill and warm the soul.

p. 115

p. 136

p. 134

p. 133

p. 126

sweet and spicy meatballs p. 142

pork chop skillet and confetti salsa

pork chop skillet and confetti salsa

READY IN: 30 Minutes ✱ SERVINGS: 5

Pork Chops

- 5 (4 oz.) boneless pork loin chops
- 1/2 teaspoon salt
- 1 cup water
- 1 can (14 oz.) chicken broth
- 1-1/2 cups uncooked regular long-grain white rice
- 1 cup Old El Paso® Thick 'n Chunky salsa

Confetti Salsa

- 1 can (11 oz.) Green Giant® Mexicorn® whole kernel corn, red and green peppers, drained
- 1 avocado, pitted, peeled and chopped
- 1 papaya, peeled, seeded and chopped
- 1 tablespoon olive or vegetable oil
- 4 teaspoons fresh lime juice
- Fresh cilantro, if desired

1 Heat 12-inch nonstick skillet or Dutch oven over medium-high heat until hot. Sprinkle pork chops with salt; add to skillet. Cook 1 to 2 minutes or just until the pork chops begin to brown, turning once.

2 Add water and broth. Bring to a boil. Stir in rice. Reduce heat to medium-low; cover and simmer 20 minutes or until pork is no longer pink in center, rice is tender and liquid is absorbed.

3 Meanwhile, in medium bowl, combine all confetti salsa ingredients; mix well. Stir salsa into rice mixture in skillet; cook 1 minute or until thoroughly heated.

4 To serve, spoon confetti salsa over the pork chops and rice. If desired, sprinkle individual servings with chopped fresh cilantro.

High Altitude (3500-6500 ft): Increase water to 1-1/4 cups; cover and simmer pork chops and rice 22 minutes.

NUTRITION INFORMATION PER SERVING: Calories 565 • Total Fat 18g • Saturated Fat 5g • Cholesterol 70mg • Sodium 1020mg • Total Carbohydrate 72g • Dietary Fiber 5g • Sugars 7g • Protein 34g. DIETARY EXCHANGES: 5 Starch • 5 Other Carbohydrate • 2-1/2 Lean Meat • 2 Fat.

Kitchen tip

The secret to extracting the most juice from citrus fruit is to start with room-temperature fruit. Then roll the fruit on the counter, pressing gently. One medium lime yields about 2 tablespoons of juice.

beef and vegetable chili

PREP TIME: 5 Minutes ✱ READY IN: 8 Hours 5 Minutes ✱ SERVINGS: 6

- 1 box (8.5 oz.) Slow Cooker Helper® beef stew
- 3-1/2 cups hot water
- 1 lb. lean beef stew meat (3/4-inch pieces)
- 1 can (16 oz.) red beans in chili sauce, undrained
- 1 can (14.5 oz.) diced tomatoes with zesty mild green chiles, undrained
- Cheddar cheese, if desired

1 In 3-1/2- to 4-quart slow cooker, mix vegetables plus sauce from box and hot water. Stir in remaining ingredients.

2 Cover; cook on Low heat setting 8 to 10 hours (or on High heat setting 4 to 5 hours). Stir stew before serving. Serve individual servings topped with cheese.

NUTRITION INFORMATION PER SERVING: Calories 350 • Total Fat 10g • Saturated 3.5g • Cholesterol 45mg • Sodium 1550mg • Total Carbohydrate 43g • Dietary Fiber 8g • Sugars 9g • Protein 24g.

special touch

Garnish each serving of this tasty pie with a sprinkle of coarsely chopped pecans and a little extra Parmesan cheese. Add a cluster of red or green grapes alongside for a bit of color. If you wish, try walnuts or hazelnuts instead of the pecans in the recipe and for the garnish.

warm chicken salad pie

PREP TIME: 15 Minutes ✱ READY IN: 55 Minutes ✱ SERVINGS: 8

CRUST

1 Pillsbury® Refrigerated Pie Crust (from 15-oz. pkg.), softened as directed on package

FILLING

2 cups cubed cooked chicken or turkey
2 cups chopped celery
2 cups frozen broccoli florets
1/2 cup chopped pecans
1 tablespoon instant minced onion
1/2 teaspoon dried tarragon leaves
1-1/2 cups mayonnaise
3 tablespoons dry white wine or water
1-1/2 teaspoons lemon juice
1/4 cup grated fresh Parmesan cheese (1 oz.)

1 Heat oven to 425°F. Place pie crust in 9-inch glass pie pan as directed on package for one-crust filled pie. Do not pick crust. Bake for 8 minutes.

2 Meanwhile, in large bowl, combine all filling ingredients except cheese; mix well. Remove partially baked crust from oven. Reduce oven temperature to 400°F. Sprinkle with cheese.

3 Spoon the filling into crust. Return to oven; bake at 400°F for 25 to 35 minutes or until it is golden brown.

NUTRITION INFORMATION PER SERVING: Calories 635 • Total Fat 49g • Saturated Fat 10g • Cholesterol 60mg • Sodium 470mg • Total Carbohydrate 18g • Dietary Fiber 2g • Sugars 3g • Protein 14g. DIETARY EXCHANGES: 1 Starch • 1 Vegetable • 1 High-Fat Meat • 9 Fat OR 1 Carbohydrate • 1 Vegetable • 1 High-Fat Meat • 9 Fat • 1 Carb Choice.

cook's notes

This recipe is a great way to use up your leftover ham. If you plan on purchasing the meat, order a chunk rather than slices of ham at the deli counter. Choose boiled ham if you prefer its mildness, or for a deeper flavor, buy baked or smoked ham.

ham and swiss crescent braid

PREP TIME: 25 Minutes ✱ READY IN: 1 Hour ✱ SERVINGS: 8

3/4 lb. cooked ham, chopped (2-1/4 cups)
1 cup Green Giant Select® frozen 100% broccoli florets, thawed
1 cup shredded Swiss cheese (4 oz.)
1 jar (4.5 oz.) Green Giant® sliced mushrooms, drained
1/2 cup mayonnaise or salad dressing
1 tablespoon honey mustard
2 cans (8 oz. each) Pillsbury® Refrigerated Crescent Dinner Rolls
1 egg white, beaten
2 tablespoons slivered almonds

1 Heat oven to 375°F. Spray cookie sheet with nonstick cooking spray. In large bowl, combine ham, broccoli, cheese, mushrooms, mayonnaise and mustard; mix well.

2 Unroll both cans of dough into 2 large rectangles. Place dough with long sides together on sprayed cookie sheet, forming 15x12-inch rectangle. Press edges and perforations to seal.

3 Spoon and spread ham mixture lengthwise in 6-inch-wide strip down center of dough. With scissors or sharp knife, make cuts 1-1/2 inches apart on long sides of dough to within 1/2 inch of filling. Twisting each strip once, alternately cross strips over filling. Tuck short ends under; press to seal. Brush dough with egg white. Sprinkle with almonds.

4 Bake for 28 to 33 minutes or until deep golden brown. Cool loaf for 5 minutes. Cut crosswise into slices.

NUTRITION INFORMATION PER SERVING: Calories 440 • Total Fat 29g • Saturated Fat 7g • Cholesterol 40mg • Sodium 1230mg • Total Carbohydrate 26g • Dietary Fiber 1g • Sugars 5g • Protein 18g. DIETARY EXCHANGES: 1-1/2 Starch • 2 Lean Meat • 4-1/2 Fat OR 1-1/2 Carbohydrate • 2 Lean Meat • 4-1/2 Fat • 2 Carb Choices.

chicken and artichoke pizza

PREP TIME: 15 Minutes ✱ READY IN: 35 Minutes ✱ SERVINGS: 8

- 1 can (10 oz.) Pillsbury® Refrigerated Pizza Crust
- 1/4 cup purchased creamy Caesar salad dressing
- 3 tablespoons grated Parmesan cheese
- 2 cups chopped cooked chicken or turkey
- 1 jar (6-1/2 oz.) marinated artichoke hearts, drained, coarsely chopped
- 1-1/2 cups shredded fontina cheese (6 oz.)
- 2 Italian plum tomatoes, seeded, chopped

1 Heat oven to 400°F. Lightly grease 12-inch pizza pan. Unroll dough; place in greased pan. Starting at center, press out dough to edge of pan.

2 Bake for 6 to 8 minutes or until crust begins to dry. Meanwhile, in small bowl, combine salad dressing and Parmesan cheese.

3 Remove partially baked crust from oven. Spread dressing mixture over crust. Top with chicken and artichokes. Sprinkle with fontina cheese. Top with tomatoes.

4 Return to oven; bake an additional 15 to 20 minutes or until crust is golden brown and cheese is melted.

NUTRITION INFORMATION PER SERVING: Calories 290 • Total Fat 14g • Saturated Fat 6g • Cholesterol 55mg • Sodium 610mg • Total Carbohydrate 21g • Dietary Fiber 1g • Sugars 3g. DIETARY EXCHANGES: 1-1/2 Starch • 2 Lean Meat • 1-1/2 Fat OR 1-1/2 Carbohydrate • 2 Lean Meat • 1-1/2 Fat • 1-1/2 Carb Choices.

cook's notes

If you don't have an "official" pizza pan, press the dough out to form a 13x9-inch rectangle on a lightly greased cookie sheet. You'll need to reduce the baking time slightly: In Step 2, bake the crust at 400°F for 5 to 7 minutes. After the toppings go onto the partially baked crust, continue baking for an additional 10 to 12 minutes.

creamy meatballs and potatoes

creamy meatballs and potatoes

PREP TIME: 25 Minutes ✱ READY IN: 25 Minutes ✱ SERVINGS: 4

- 2 cups refrigerated potato wedges (from 20-oz. bag)
- 1 can (10-3/4 oz.) condensed cream of onion soup
- 1/4 cup water
- 2 cups Green Giant® SELECT® frozen broccoli florets
- 24 frozen cooked meatballs (about 12 oz.), thawed
- 1/4 cup sour cream

1 In 12-inch nonstick skillet, stir together potatoes, soup and water. Heat to boiling. Reduce heat to low; simmer uncovered 5 minutes, stirring occasionally.

2 Stir in broccoli and meatballs. Simmer uncovered 10 to 15 minutes, stirring occasionally, until broccoli and potatoes are tender.

3 Stir in sour cream. Cook just until thoroughly heated, stirring occasionally.

NUTRITION INFORMATION PER SERVING: Calories 380 • Total Fat 18g • Saturated Fat 7g • Cholesterol 110mg • Sodium 1140mg • Total Carbohydrate 32g • Dietary Fiber 5g. DIETARY EXCHANGES: 1 Starch • 1/2 Other Carbohydrate • 1 Vegetable • 2-1/2 Medium-Fat Meat • 1 Fat.

cook's notes

Slice up apples or pears to serve with this easy dish. For an even heartier dish, bake a warm loaf of Pillsbury® refrigerated bread.

chipotle-black bean chili

READY IN: 20 Minutes ✱ SERVINGS: 6

- 1 large onion, chopped (1 cup)
- 4 garlic cloves, minced
- 3 cans (15 oz. each) black beans, drained, rinsed
- 1 can (28 oz.) whole tomatoes, undrained, cut up
- 1 can (14.5 oz.) diced tomatoes, undrained
- 2 chipotle chiles in adobo sauce (from 7- or 11-oz. can), finely chopped
- 1-1/2 teaspoons dried oregano leaves
- 3/4 teaspoon cumin

1 Spray nonstick Dutch oven with nonstick cooking spray. Heat over medium heat until hot. Add onion and garlic; cover and cook 4 minutes, stirring occasionally.

2 Add all remaining ingredients; mix well. Bring to a boil. Reduce heat; cover and simmer 8 to 10 minutes to blend flavors, stirring occasionally.

NUTRITION INFORMATION PER SERVING: Calories 310 • Total Fat 2g • Saturated Fat 0g • Cholesterol 0mg • Sodium 1170mg • Total Carbohydrate 68g • Dietary Fiber 16g • Sugars 12g • Protein 21g. DIETARY EXCHANGES: 3 Starch • 1 Vegetable • 1-1/2 Very Lean Meat • 3-1/2 Carb Choices.

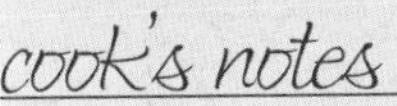

Set out bowls of shredded Cheddar cheese, sour cream, chopped green onions and chopped fresh tomatoes, and let everyone at the table personalize their own dish.

cook's notes

One teaspoon of dried basil can be used to flavor this pasta in place of the fresh basil. Add the dried basil with crushed red pepper; continue the recipe as directed.

tuscan-style pork 'n pasta

READY IN: 30 Minutes ✱ SERVINGS: 4

- 3/4 lb. pork tenderloin, cut into 1/2-inch pieces
- 1 package (1 lb.) Green Giant® Pasta Accents® garlic frozen vegetables with pasta
- 1/4 to 1/2 teaspoon crushed red pepper flakes
- 1 can (15.5 oz.) great northern beans, undrained
- 3 Italian plum tomatoes, seeded, chopped
- 1/4 cup grated fresh Parmesan cheese (1 oz.)
- 2 tablespoons chopped fresh basil or parsley

1 Spray large nonstick skillet with nonstick cooking spray. Heat over medium-high heat until hot. Add pork; cook 10 to 12 minutes or until browned, stirring frequently.

2 Add frozen vegetables with pasta and pepper flakes; mix well. Bring to a boil. Reduce heat to medium; cover and cook 7 to 8 minutes or until pork is no longer pink in center and vegetables are crisp-tender, stirring occasionally.

3 Add beans and tomatoes; cover and cook 1 minute or until thoroughly heated. Sprinkle with cheese and basil. Garnish with fresh sprig of basil, if desired.

NUTRITION INFORMATION PER SERVING: Calories 430 • Total Fat 12g • Saturated Fat 6g • Cholesterol 70mg • Sodium 580mg • Total Carbohydrate 52g • Dietary Fiber 9g • Sugars 5g • Protein 38g. DIETARY EXCHANGES: 3 Starch • 3 Other Carbohydrate • 1 Vegetable • 4 Lean Meat.

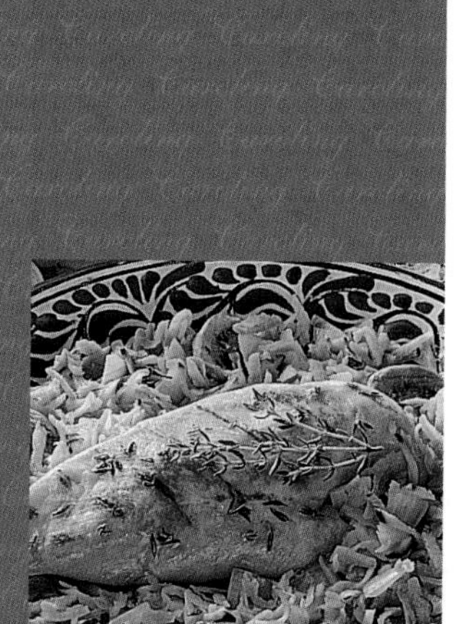

chicken breasts with veggie salsa

READY IN: 25 Minutes ✱ SERVINGS: 4

CHICKEN

- 1 tablespoon margarine or butter, softened
- 1 tablespoon honey
- 1 teaspoon chopped fresh thyme or 1/4 teaspoon dried thyme leaves
- 4 boneless skinless chicken breast halves

SALSA

- 1-1/2 cups shredded carrots
- 1-1/2 cups shredded zucchini
- 1 cup sliced fresh mushrooms
- 1 cup chopped onions
- 1 tablespoon margarine or butter
- 1/2 teaspoon chopped fresh thyme or 1/8 teaspoon dried thyme leaves
- 1/4 teaspoon salt
- 3 to 4 drops hot pepper sauce

1 Heat grill. In small bowl, combine 1 tablespoon margarine, honey and 1 teaspoon thyme; blend well.

2 When ready to grill, place chicken on gas grill over medium heat or on charcoal grill 4 to 6 inches from medium coals. Cook 8 to 10 minutes or until chicken is fork-tender and juices run clear, turning once and brushing with honey mixture during last 5 minutes of cooking.

3 In large skillet, combine all salsa ingredients. Cook and stir over medium-high heat 3 to 4 minutes or until vegetables are crisp-tender. Serve chicken over salsa.

NUTRITION INFORMATION PER SERVING: Calories 250 • Total Fat 9g • Saturated 2g • Cholesterol 75mg • Sodium 280mg • Total Carbohydrate 14g • Dietary Fiber 3g • Sugars 10g • Protein 29g. DIETARY EXCHANGES: 3 Vegetable • 3 Lean Meat.

tuscan-style pork 'n pasta

braided stuffed pizza bread

braided stuffed pizza bread

PREP TIME: 15 Minutes ✱ READY IN: 35 Minutes ✱ SERVINGS: 12

- 1 can (13.8 oz.) Pillsbury® Refrigerated Classic Pizza Crust
- 2 tablespoons gourmet spreadable cheese with garlic and herbs
- 3 oz. thinly sliced Canadian bacon
- 10 slices pepperoni
- 1 cup shredded mozzarella cheese (4 oz.)
- 2 tablespoons freshly grated Parmesan cheese
- 1 egg yolk
- 1 teaspoon water
- 1 to 2 teaspoons poppy seed
- Pizza sauce, if desired

1 Heat oven to 400°F. Spray cookie sheet with nonstick cooking spray. Unroll dough onto sprayed cookie sheet, forming 14x11-inch rectangle.

2 Spread garlic and herb cheese lengthwise down center 1/3 of rectangle to within 1/2 inch of short ends. Top with Canadian bacon, pepperoni, mozzarella and Parmesan cheese.

3 With scissors or sharp knife, make cuts 1 inch apart on long sides of dough to within 1/2 inch of filling. Alternately cross strips over filling. Fold ends under to seal.

4 In small bowl, combine egg yolk and water; mix well. Brush over dough; sprinkle with the poppy seed.

5 Bake for 11 to 16 minutes or until bread is golden brown. Cut bread into slices. Serve with the pizza sauce.

NUTRITION INFORMATION PER SERVING: Calories 160 • Total Fat 7g • Saturated Fat 3g • Cholesterol 35mg • Sodium 480mg • Total Carbohydrate 16g • Dietary Fiber 0g. DIETARY EXCHANGES: 1 Starch • 1/2 High-Fat Meat • 1/2 Fat.

cook's notes

One package of pizza-style Canadian bacon can be used for this recipe. Try hot and spicy pepperoni to fire up this pizza snack a bit. No poppy seed in the pantry? Use sesame seed.

cheesy bean dip

READY IN: 15 Minutes ✱ SERVINGS: 32

- 1 can (16 oz.) Old El Paso® refried beans
- 1 can (4.5 oz.) Old El Paso® chopped green chiles
- 2 cups shredded Mexican cheese blend (8 oz.)
- 1/2 medium red bell pepper, chopped
- 1 jalapeño chile, sliced, if desired
- Chopped fresh cilantro, if desired

1 In 9-inch microwavable pie plate, mix beans and green chiles; spread evenly. Cover with microwavable waxed paper. Microwave on High 2 minutes to 2 minutes 30 seconds or until dip is warm.

2 Uncover; sprinkle with cheese. Top with bell pepper and jalapeño chile; cover. Microwave on Medium 3 to 4 minutes longer or until cheese is almost melted. (Lift waxed paper slowly to allow steam to escape.) Pie plate will be hot; carefully remove from microwave oven. Let dip stand 2 minutes; uncover. Sprinkle with cilantro. Serve with tortilla chips.

NUTRITION INFORMATION PER SERVING: Calories 40 • Total Fat 2g • Saturated Fat 1g • Cholesterol 10mg • Sodium 105mg • Total Carbohydrate 3g • Dietary Fiber 0g. DIETARY EXCHANGE: 1/2 Medium-Fat Meat.

special touch

For entertaining, make the dip in a pretty fluted quiche dish or prepare it on a decorative, microwavable platter.

JUDITH A. HARPER
LOS ANGELES, CA
Bake-Off® Contest 10, 1958

snowcap brownies

PREP TIME: 30 Minutes ✷ READY IN: 2 Hours 10 Minutes ✷ SERVINGS: 24

BROWNIES

- 3/4 cup Pillsbury BEST® all-purpose flour
- 1 teaspoon baking powder
- 1/2 teaspoon salt
- 1/2 cup butter or margarine
- 2-1/2 oz. unsweetened baking chocolate
- 1-1/4 cups sugar
- 1 teaspoon vanilla
- 1/2 teaspoon red food color
- 2 whole eggs
- 1 egg yolk
- 1 cup chopped nuts

MERINGUE

- 1 egg white
- 1/2 cup sugar
- 1/2 teaspoon vanilla

1 Heat oven to 325°F. Generously grease a 15x10x1-inch baking pan with shortening or nonstick cooking spray.

2 In small bowl, stir together flour, baking powder and salt; set aside. In 2-quart saucepan, melt butter and chocolate over low heat, stirring frequently; cool 20 minutes. Stir in 1-1/4 cups sugar, 1 teaspoon vanilla and the food color. Add eggs and egg yolk; beat with spoon until well blended. Stir in flour mixture and nuts. Spread in pan.

3 In small bowl, beat egg white with electric mixer on high speed until stiff peaks form. Beat in 1/2 cup sugar and 1/2 teaspoon vanilla. Drop meringue by teaspoonfuls onto brownie batter. Draw tip of knife or metal spatula through batter lengthwise, then crosswise.

4 Bake 25 to 30 minutes or until meringue is light brown and edges are firm to the touch. Cool completely, about 1 hour.

HIGH ALTITUDE (3500-6500 FT): Bake 22 to 27 minutes.

NUTRITION INFORMATION PER SERVING: Calories 170 • Total Fat 9g • Saturated Fat 4g • Trans Fat 0g • Cholesterol 35mg • Sodium 105mg • Total Carbohydrate 19g • Dietary Fiber 0g • Sugars 15g • Protein 2g. DIETARY EXCHANGES: 1/2 Starch • 1 Other Carbohydrate • 1-1/2 Fat • Carb Choices 1.

cook's notes

Any pesto sauce works in this recipe. Eight ounces of dried fettuccine can be used in place of the refrigerated fettuccine.

fettuccine with beef and peppers

READY IN: 20 Minutes ✷ SERVINGS: 4

- 1 package (9 oz.) refrigerated fettuccine
- 1 lb. lean (at least 80%) ground beef
- 1 green bell pepper, cut into thin bite-sized strips
- 1 red bell pepper, cut into thin bite-sized strips
- 1/2 cup half-and-half
- 1/3 cup basil pesto
- 1/2 teaspoon salt
- 1/8 teaspoon pepper

1 Cook fettuccine as directed on package. Drain; cover to keep warm. In 12-inch skillet, cook ground beef over medium-high heat, stirring frequently, until thoroughly cooked; drain.

2 Add the green and red bell peppers to the skillet; cook and stir 4 to 6 minutes or until peppers are crisp-tender.

3 Add half-and-half, pesto, salt, pepper and cooked fettuccine. Reduce heat to medium; cook and stir 3 to 5 minutes or until thoroughly heated.

NUTRITION INFORMATION PER SERVING: Calories 530 • Total Fat 29g • Saturated Fat 9g • Cholesterol 85mg • Sodium 650mg • Total Carbohydrate 39g • Dietary Fiber 3g. DIETARY EXCHANGES: 2 Starch • 1 Vegetable • 3 Medium-Fat Meat • 2-1/2 Fat.

pasta skillet dinner

READY IN: 30 Minutes ✱ SERVINGS: 4

- 2 cups uncooked ziti pasta (7 oz.)
- 1 lb. lean (at least 80%) ground beef
- 1 jar (14 oz.) tomato pasta sauce (1-1/2 cups)
- 1/2 cup water
- 1/2 cup sour cream
- 1 cup shredded Cheddar cheese (4 oz.)

1 Cook pasta as directed on package; drain. Cover to keep warm. Meanwhile, in 10-inch skillet, cook ground beef over medium-high heat, stirring frequently, until thoroughly cooked; drain.

2 Stir in pasta sauce and water. Reduce heat to medium; simmer uncovered 5 minutes. Stir in cooked pasta.

3 In small bowl, mix sour cream and cheese. Spoon over pasta mixture. Reduce heat to low; cover and cook 6 to 8 minutes or until thoroughly heated.

NUTRITION INFORMATION PER SERVING: Calories 660 • Total Fat 32g • Saturated Fat 15g • Trans Fat 1g • Cholesterol 20mg • Sodium 920mg • Total Carbohydrate 58g • Dietary Fiber 4g • Sugars 9g • Protein 35g. DIETARY EXCHANGES: 3 Starch • 1 Other Carbohydrate • 3-1/2 Medium-Fat Meat • 2-1/2 Fat • 4 Carb Choices.

cook's notes

We call for ziti pasta in this recipe, but you could substitute rigatoni or penne pasta if you prefer. Serve this dish with a tossed green salad.

special touch

Dress up any dip by serving it in a glass or crystal bowl.

salsa and black bean dip

READY IN: 10 Minutes ✻ SERVINGS: 3

- 4 slices bacon, cooked, crumbled
- 1/2 cup chopped green onions
- 1 cup chunky-style salsa
- 1 can (15 oz.) black beans, drained
- Tortilla chips

1 In medium bowl, combine all of the ingredients; mix well. Cover dip; refrigerate 1 to 2 hours to blend flavors. Serve with tortilla chips.

NUTRITION INFORMATION PER SERVING: Calories 15 • Total Fat 0g • Saturated Fat 0g • Cholesterol 0mg • Sodium 65mg • Total Carbohydrate 3g • Dietary Fiber 1g • Sugars 0g • Protein 1g. DIETARY EXCHANGES: Free • 0 Carb Choice.

chicken waldorf pizza

READY IN: 30 Minutes ✱ SERVINGS: 6

- 1 can (13.8 oz.) Pillsbury® Refrigerated Classic Pizza Crust
- 1 cup chopped cooked chicken
- 1 cup chopped apple
- 1/2 cup sliced almonds, toasted
- 1/2 cup mayonnaise
- 1 teaspoon dried tarragon leaves
- 1/8 teaspoon salt
- 1/8 teaspoon pepper
- 2 cups shredded Swiss cheese (8 oz.)
- 2 teaspoons chopped green onions

1 Heat oven to 425°F. Lightly spray 14-inch pizza pan with nonstick cooking spray. Unroll dough; place in sprayed pan. Starting at center, press out dough with hands to edge of pan. Bake for 6 to 8 minutes or until crust begins to brown.

2 Meanwhile, in medium bowl, combine chicken, apple, almonds, mayonnaise, tarragon, salt and pepper; mix well.

3 Remove partially baked crust from oven. Spread chicken mixture evenly over the crust. Sprinkle with the cheese.

4 Return to oven; bake an additional 10 to 12 minutes or until cheese is melted and crust is deep golden brown. Sprinkle with green onions. Cut into 12 wedges.

NUTRITION INFORMATION PER SERVING: Calories 550 • Total Fat 33g • Saturated Fat 10g • Cholesterol 60mg • Sodium 720mg • Total Carbohydrate 38g • Dietary Fiber 2g • Protein 25g. DIETARY EXCHANGES: 1-1/2 Starch • 1 Other Carbohydrate • 2-1/2 High-Fat Meat • 2-1/2 Fat.

kitchen tip

A cookie sheet can be used in place of the 14-inch pizza pan. Spray the cookie sheet with nonstick cooking spray; press and shape the dough on the sheet into a 14-inch circle or square.

special touch

For an elegant yet easy garnish, top the manicotti with shavings of fresh Parmigiano-Reggiano cheese.

spinach pesto manicotti

PREP TIME: 35 Minutes ✳ READY IN: 1 Hour 15 Minutes ✳ SERVINGS: 6

- 8 oz. uncooked manicotti
- 1 lb. extra-lean ground beef
- 1 package (9 oz.) Green Giant® frozen spinach, thawed, squeezed to drain and chopped
- 1 cup mozzarella cheese, diced (4 oz.)
- 1/2 cup purchased pesto
- 1 egg
- 1 jar (26 to 28 oz.) tomato pasta sauce

1 Heat oven to 400°F. Spray 13x9-inch (3-quart) glass baking dish with nonstick cooking spray. Cook manicotti to desired doneness as directed on package. Drain; rinse with cold water to cool. Drain well.

2 Meanwhile, in large bowl, combine ground beef, spinach, cheese, pesto and egg. If desired, add salt and pepper; mix well. For easier stuffing, place beef mixture in resealable freezer plastic bag; seal bag. Cut hole in bottom corner of bag.

3 Fill each manicotti by squeezing beef mixture into manicotti; place in sprayed baking dish. Pour pasta sauce over manicotti. Cover with foil. Bake for 30 to 40 minutes or until filling is no longer pink in center.

HIGH ALTITUDE (3500-6500 FT): Bake 35 to 45 minutes.

NUTRITION INFORMATION PER SERVING: Calories 610 • Total Fat 29g • Saturated Fat 8g • Cholesterol 95mg • Sodium 1110mg • Total Carbohydrate 56g • Dietary Fiber 4g • Sugars 11 g • Protein 31 g. DIETARY EXCHANGES: 4 Starch • 4 Other Carbohydrate • 2-1/2 Medium-Fat Meat • 3 Fat.

baked chicken and biscuits

PREP TIME: 10 Minutes ✳ READY IN: 1 Hour 25 Minutes ✳ SERVINGS: 5

- 2-1/2 to 3 lb. cut-up frying chicken, skin removed
- 1 can (10-3/4 oz.) condensed cream of mushroom soup
- 1 container (8 oz.) sour cream
- 1/2 cup dry sherry or water
- 1 jar (4.5 oz.) whole mushrooms, drained
- 1 can (10 oz.) Pillsbury® Golden Layers™ refrigerated flaky biscuits
- Paprika
- Chopped fresh parsley, if desired

1 Heat oven to 350°F. Place chicken in 13x9-inch (3-quart) glass baking dish. In medium bowl, combine soup, sour cream and sherry; blend well. Stir in mushrooms. Pour over chicken.

2 Bake at 350°F for 45 to 55 minutes or until chicken is fork-tender and juices run clear. Remove chicken from oven.

3 Separate dough into 10 biscuits. Arrange over hot mixture around outer edges of dish. Sprinkle with paprika.

4 Return to oven; bake an additional 11 to 18 minutes or until biscuits are golden brown and bottoms are no longer doughy. Garnish with fresh parsley.

NUTRITION INFORMATION PER SERVING: Calories 520 • Total Fat 27g • Saturated Fat 10g • Cholesterol 110mg • Sodium 1310mg • Total Carbohydrate 37g • Dietary Fiber 2g • Sugars 12g • Protein 32g. DIETARY EXCHANGES: 2-1/2 Starch • 3-1/2 Medium-Fat Meat • 1 Fat OR 2-1/2 Carbohydrate • 3-1/2 Medium-Fat Meat • 1 Fat • 2-1/2 Carb Choices.

Kitchen tip

Curly parsley and flatleaf (or Italian) parsley can be used interchangeably in most recipes. You'll find that flatleaf parsley, however, has a stronger flavor but is not as readily available as the more decorative curly variety. Either type adds a fresh, vibrant touch to almost any entrée.

spinach pesto manicotti

secret-center cookie cups

secret-center cookie cups

PREP TIME: 55 Minutes ✱ READY IN: 1 Hour 10 Minutes ✱ SERVINGS: 36 Cookies

- 1 roll (16.5 oz.) refrigerated peanut butter cookie dough
- 36 miniature bars (about 1-inch square) chocolate-covered peanut, caramel and nougat candy, unwrapped
- 36 miniature paper or foil baking cups (1-1/4-inch diameter)
- 3/4 cup chocolate creamy ready-to-spread frosting (from 1-lb. container)

1 Heat oven to 375°F. For each cookie cup, wrap a heaping teaspoonful of cookie dough around 1 candy bar, enclosing it almost completely and forming ball. Place in paper baking cup; place cups 1 inch apart on ungreased cookie sheets.

2 Bake 8 to 12 minutes or until golden brown. Centers of cookies will sink slightly. Cool 1 minute; remove from cookie sheets. Cool completely, about 15 minutes.

3 Spoon chocolate frosting into a pastry bag with a star tip. Pipe the frosting on top of each of the cookie cup.

NUTRITION INFORMATION PER SERVING: Calories 120 • Total Fat 6g • Saturated Fat 2g • Trans Fat 1g • Cholesterol 0mg • Sodium 100mg • Total Carbohydrate 16g • Dietary Fiber 0g • Sugars 12g • Protein 2g. DIETARY EXCHANGES: 1/2 Starch • 1/2 Other Carbohydrate • 1 Fat • 1 Carb Choice.

Kitchen tip

Don't worry if you don't have a pastry bag. Just put the frosting in a resealable food-storage plastic bag and snip off a very small section of the corner (no more than 1/4 inch wide); squeeze the frosting onto your treats. Or, use a spoon to add dollops of frosting.

beef stew pot pie

PREP TIME: 40 Minutes ✱ READY IN: 1 Hour 20 Minutes ✱ SERVINGS: 6

- 1 package (15 oz.) Pillsbury® Refrigerated Pie Crusts, softened as directed on package
- 3/4 lb. boneless beef sirloin steak, cut into 1/2-inch cubes
- 2 small onions, cut into thin wedges
- 1-1/2 cups cubed (3/4 inch) peeled baking potatoes
- 3/4 cup cut (1x1/2x1/2 inch) carrot
- 1/2 cup frozen sweet peas
- 1 jar (4.5 oz.) whole mushrooms, drained
- 1 jar (12 oz.) brown gravy
- 2 tablespoons cornstarch
- 1/2 teaspoon dried thyme leaves
- 1/2 teaspoon salt
- 1/4 teaspoon pepper
- 1 egg yolk
- 2 teaspoons water
- 1 teaspoon sesame seed

1 Heat oven to 425°F. Prepare pie crusts as directed on package for two-crust pie using 9-inch glass pie pan.

2 In large nonstick skillet, cook beef and onions over medium-high heat for 4 to 6 minutes or until beef is browned, stirring frequently. Stir in potatoes, carrot, peas and mushrooms.

3 In small bowl, combine gravy, cornstarch, thyme, salt and pepper; mix well. Stir into beef mixture; cook until thoroughly heated. Pour mixture into crust-lined pan. Top with second crust; seal edges and flute. Cut small slits in several places in top crust.

4 In another small bowl, beat egg yolk and water until well blended. Brush top crust with egg mixture. Sprinkle with sesame seed.

5 Bake for 30 to 40 minutes or until crust is golden brown and filling is bubbly. Cover edge of crust with strips of foil after first 15 to 20 minutes of baking to prevent excessive browning. Let stand 10 minutes before serving.

NUTRITION INFORMATION PER SERVING: Calories 490 • Total Fat 23g • Saturated Fat 9g • Cholesterol 85mg • Sodium 880mg • Total Carbohydrate 53g • Dietary Fiber 3g • Sugars 5g • Protein 17g. DIETARY EXCHANGES: 3-1/2 Starch • 1 Lean Meat • 3-1/2 Fat OR 3-1/2 Carbohydrate • 1 Lean Meat • 3-1/2 Fat • 3-1/2 Carb Choices.

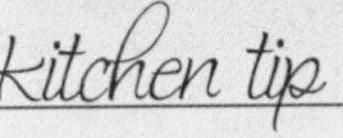

For the best results, store potatoes in a cool, dark place far from onions. They should never be stored in the refrigerator because that changes the flavor and texture and can make them turn dark when cooked.

cook's notes

To reduce the fat in each serving of this dip by about 4 grams, use light sour cream and light mayonnaise.

creamy spinach dip

PREP TIME: 20 Minutes ✻ READY IN: 2 Hours 20 Minutes ✻ SERVINGS: 28

- 1 package (10 oz.) Green Giant® frozen spinach
- 1 container (8 oz.) sour cream
- 1 cup mayonnaise
- 1/2 teaspoon celery salt
- 1/2 teaspoon dried dill
- 1/4 teaspoon onion salt
- 1/4 cup chopped green onions
- 1 can (8 oz.) water chestnuts, drained, finely chopped
- 1 jar (2 oz.) diced pimientos, drained
- Crackers or cut-up fresh vegetables

1 Cook spinach as directed on package. Cool slightly; squeeze to drain well. Meanwhile, in medium bowl, mix sour cream, mayonnaise, celery salt, dill and onion salt; blend well.

2 Stir in cooked spinach, onions, water chestnuts and pimientos. Cover; refrigerate at least 2 hours to blend flavors. Serve dip with crackers.

NUTRITION INFORMATION PER SERVING: Calories 120 • Total Fat 10g • Saturated Fat 2.5g • Trans Fat 0.5g • Cholesterol 10mg • Sodium 160mg • Total Carbohydrate 7g • Dietary Fiber 0g • Sugars 1g • Protein 1g. DIETARY EXCHANGES: 1/2 Starch • 2 Fat • 1/2 Carb Choice.

salmon burgers with lemon-dill sauce

READY IN: 25 Minutes ✻ SERVINGS: 4 Sandwiches

SAUCE

- 1/2 cup mayonnaise or salad dressing
- 1/4 cup chopped green onions
- 1 tablespoon chopped fresh dill or 1 teaspoon dried dill weed
- 2 teaspoons chopped fresh chives
- 1/4 teaspoon grated lemon peel
- 1 teaspoon lemon juice

BURGERS

- 1 can (7 oz.) salmon, drained, flaked
- 1/2 cup shredded zucchini
- 2 tablespoons unseasoned dry bread crumbs
- 2 tablespoons chopped green onions
- 1/2 teaspoon salt
- 1/4 teaspoon pepper
- 1 egg, beaten
- 4 lettuce leaves
- 4 sourdough English muffins, split, toasted

1 In small bowl, combine all sauce ingredients; mix well. Cover; refrigerate 1 hour.

2 Meanwhile, in medium bowl, combine salmon, zucchini, bread crumbs, 2 tablespoons green onions, salt, pepper and egg; mix well. Shape mixture into four 3- to 4-inch patties.

3 Spray large nonstick skillet with nonstick cooking spray. Add patties; cook over medium-high heat for 5 to 8 minutes or until firm and golden brown, turning once.

4 To serve, layer lettuce, burgers and sauce on bottom halves of English muffins. Cover with top halves of muffins.

NUTRITION INFORMATION PER SERVING: Calories 440 • Total Fat 28g • Saturated Fat 5g • Cholesterol 90mg • Sodium 970mg • Total Carbohydrate 31g • Dietary Fiber 2g • Sugars 9g • Protein 16g. DIETARY EXCHANGES: 2 Starch • 1 Lean Meat • 4 Fat OR 2 Carbohydrate • 1 Lean Meat • 4 Fat.

cook's notes

To broil burgers, place on oiled broiler pan; broil 4 to 6 inches from heat using recipe times as a guide, turning once.

creamy spinach dip

cheese and roasted pepper calzones

READY IN: 25 Minutes ✷ SERVINGS: 5

- 1 can (10.2 oz.) Pillsbury® Grands!® Refrigerated Buttermilk Biscuits (5 biscuits)
- 1/2 cup shredded Swiss cheese (2 oz.)
- 1/2 cup shredded Cheddar cheese (2 oz.)
- 1/4 cup grated Parmesan cheese
- 1/3 cup roasted red bell pepper (from a jar), cut into strips

1 Heat oven to 375°F. Separate dough into 5 biscuits. Press or roll each to form 5-1/2-inch round. Sprinkle all cheeses evenly onto biscuits. Top each with pepper strips.

2 Fold half of biscuit over filling; seal edges. Press edges firmly with fork to seal. Cut 3 slits in top of each for steam to escape. Place on ungreased cookie sheet. Bake for 12 to 15 minutes or until deep golden brown.

NUTRITION INFORMATION PER SERVING: Calories 315 • Total Fat 17g • Saturated Fat 8g • Cholesterol 25mg • Sodium 890mg • Total Carbohydrate 29g • Dietary Fiber 1g • Sugars 9g • Protein 12g. DIETARY EXCHANGES: 1-1/2 Starch • 1/2 Fruit • 1 High-Fat Meat • 1-1/2 Fat OR 2 Carbohydrate • 1 High-Fat Meat • 1-1/2 Fat • 2 Carb Choices.

kitchen tip

To roast your own bell peppers, broil or grill them. As the skin on the side near the heat blackens, turn the peppers to expose a new side. When the peppers are completely blackened, remove them from the heat. When they're cool enough to handle, peel off the blackened skin to reveal sweet roasted pepper.

crafty crescent lasagna

cook's notes

This is a nice homestyle dish to serve on a cool evening. If you need to substitute for the poultry seasoning, use 1/8 teaspoon ground sage and a dash of ground thyme. No thyme? Use all ground sage, and it will still be tasty.

baked pork chops with biscuit stuffin'

PREP TIME: 20 Minutes ✱ READY IN: 1 Hour 15 Minutes ✱ SERVINGS: 6

- 1 tablespoon oil
- 6 (1/2 inch thick) pork loin chops
- 1 can (10-3/4 oz.) condensed cream of chicken soup
- 1 cup chopped celery
- 1 cup chopped onions
- 1 egg
- 1/4 teaspoon pepper
- 1/8 teaspoon poultry seasoning
- 1 can (7.5 oz.) Pillsbury® Refrigerated Biscuits

1. Heat oven to 350°F. Heat oil in large skillet over medium heat until hot. Add pork chops; cook until browned on both sides. Place pork chops in an ungreased 13x9-inch pan.
2. In medium bowl, combine the cream of chicken soup, celery, onions, egg, pepper and poultry seasoning; mix well.
3. Separate dough into 10 biscuits; cut each into 8 pieces. Stir biscuit pieces into soup mixture. Spoon over pork chops.
4. Bake for 45 to 55 minutes or until the biscuit pieces are golden brown and no longer doughy in the center.

NUTRITION INFORMATION PER SERVING: Calories 340 • Total Fat 17g • Saturated Fat 5g • Cholesterol 110mg • Sodium 860mg • Total Carbohydrate 23g • Dietary Fiber 1g • Sugars 7g • Protein 24g. DIETARY EXCHANGES: 1-1/2 Starch • 3 Medium-Fat Meat OR 1-1/2 Carbohydrate • 3 Medium-Fat Meat • 1-1/2 Carb Choices.

kitchen tip

Cold pack cheese foods come in little plastic containers. Look for them in the dairy case near the other cheese products.

three-cheese party wheel

READY IN: 15 Minutes ✱ SERVINGS: 20

- 1 container (8 oz.) Swiss almond cold pack cheese food
- 1 container (8 oz.) sharp Cheddar cold pack cheese food
- 1 container (8 oz.) chives and onion cream cheese spread
- 1/4 cup sliced almonds, toasted if desired
- 1/4 cup finely chopped fresh parsley
- 1 package (9.75 oz.) assorted crackers

1. On sheet of waxed paper, spread Swiss almond cheese into a 5-inch round, about 1/2 inch thick with small metal spatula, smooth side and top.
2. Evenly spread Cheddar cheese over Swiss cheese; smooth side and top. Evenly spread cream cheese spread over top; smooth side and top to even layers. Sprinkle almonds over top; press into cheese lightly.
3. Press parsley into side of cheese wheel. Serve immediately, or wrap in waxed paper and refrigerate until serving time. To serve, place cheese wheel on serving plate; arrange assorted crackers around cheese.

NUTRITION INFORMATION PER SERVING: Calories 180 • Total Fat 12g • Saturated Fat 7g • Cholesterol 30mg • Sodium 350mg • Total Carbohydrate 12g • Dietary Fiber 0g. DIETARY EXCHANGES: 1 Starch • 1/2 High-Fat Meat • 1-1/2 Fat.

spicy sausage and potato squares

PREP TIME: 10 Minutes ✱ READY IN: 1 Hour 35 Minutes ✱ SERVINGS: 6

- 1 lb. bulk Italian sausage
- 4 cups frozen potatoes O'Brien with onions and peppers (from 28-oz. bag), thawed
- 1-1/2 cups shredded Colby-Monterey Jack cheese (6 oz.)
- 1 box (9 oz.) Green Giant® frozen asparagus cuts, thawed
- 4 eggs
- 3/4 cup milk
- 2 tablespoons shredded Parmesan cheese (1/2 oz.)

1 Heat oven to 350°F. Spray 8-inch square (2-quart) glass baking dish with nonstick cooking spray. In 8-inch skillet, cook sausage over medium heat 8 to 10 minutes, stirring occasionally, until no longer pink.

2 In baking dish, layer half of the thawed potatoes, half of the Colby-Monterey Jack cheese, the cooked sausage, thawed asparagus, remaining potatoes and cheese.

3 In medium bowl, beat eggs and milk until well blended. Pour evenly over potato mixture. Cover tightly with foil; bake 1 hour.

4 Uncover dish; sprinkle with Parmesan cheese. Bake uncovered 15 to 20 minutes longer or until knife inserted in center comes out clean. Let stand about 5 minutes before serving.

NUTRITION INFORMATION PER SERVING: Calories 480 • Total Fat 28g • Saturated Fat 12g • Trans Fat 0g • Cholesterol 215mg • Sodium 810mg • Total Carbohydrate 29g • Dietary Fiber 3g • Sugars 3g • Protein 28g. DIETARY EXCHANGES: 2 Starch • 3 High-Fat Meat • 1/2 Fat • 2 Carb Choices.

Kitchen tip

You can use frozen broccoli, thawed, instead of the asparagus. Also, if you have Cheddar cheese on hand, go ahead and substitute it for the Colby-Monterey Jack cheese.

cheesy crescent nachos

cheesy crescent nachos

PREP TIME: 15 Minutes ✱ READY IN: 45 Minutes ✱ SERVINGS: 24

- 1 can (8 oz.) Pillsbury® Refrigerated Crescent Dinner Rolls
- 3 tablespoons cornmeal
- 1 can (4.5 oz.) Old El Paso® chopped green chiles, drained
- 1 cup shredded Cheddar cheese (4 oz.)
- 1 cup shredded mozzarella or Monterey Jack cheese (4 oz.)
- Old El Paso® Thick 'n Chunky salsa or taco sauce, if desired

1 Heat oven to 350°F. Separate dough into 4 rectangles. Coat both sides of each rectangle with cornmeal. Place in ungreased 13x9-inch pan; press over bottom and 1/2 inch up sides to form crust. Press edges and perforations to seal. Sprinkle with any remaining cornmeal. Top evenly with chiles, Cheddar and mozzarella cheese.

2 Bake for 24 to 28 minutes or until crust is golden brown. Cool 5 minutes. Cut into triangles or squares. Serve warm with salsa.

NUTRITION INFORMATION PER SERVING: Calories 70 • Total Fat 4g • Saturated Fat 2g • Cholesterol 10mg • Sodium 190mg • Total Carbohydrate 6g • Dietary Fiber 0g. DIETARY EXCHANGE: 1/2 High-Fat Meat.

special touch

Chopped green onions are a colorful, crunchy topping for the salsa.

meatball stew with dill biscuits

PREP TIME: 30 Minutes ✱ READY IN: 50 Minutes ✱ SERVINGS: 5

Meatballs

- 1 egg, beaten
- 1/4 cup milk
- 1/4 cup Italian-style dry bread crumbs
- 1/2 teaspoon salt
- 1/4 teaspoon pepper
- 1 lb. lean ground beef

Stew

- 1 can (10-3/4 oz.) condensed tomato soup
- 1-1/4 cups water
- 2 tablespoons Worcestershire sauce
- 1 package (1 lb.) frozen mixed vegetables

Biscuits

- 1 can (12 oz.) Pillsbury® Golden Layers™ Refrigerated Flaky Biscuits
- 1 tablespoon margarine or butter, melted
- 1 tablespoon cornmeal
- 3/4 teaspoon dried dill weed

1 Heat oven to 425°F. Spray 13x9-inch pan with nonstick cooking spray. In large bowl, combine all meatball ingredients; mix well. Shape mixture into 36 meatballs; place in sprayed pan.

2 Bake for 12 to 15 minutes or until meatballs are thoroughly cooked. Reduce the oven temperature to 400°F.

3 Meanwhile, in large ovenproof skillet, combine all stew ingredients; mix well. Cook over medium heat for 10 to 12 minutes or until mixture comes to a boil, stirring occasionally.

4 Drain meatballs; add to stew. Separate dough into 10 biscuits. Dip 1 side of each biscuit in melted margarine; place margarine side up over stew. In small bowl, combine cornmeal and dill; mix well. Sprinkle over biscuits.

5 Bake at 400°F for 13 to 16 minutes or until the biscuits are golden brown and bottoms are no longer doughy.

NUTRITION INFORMATION PER SERVING: Calories 560 • Total Fat 26g • Saturated Fat 8g • Cholesterol 100mg • Sodium 1550mg • Total Carbohydrate 54g • Dietary Fiber 4g • Sugars 9g • Protein 27g. DIETARY EXCHANGES: 3 Starch • 1/2 Fruit • 2-1/2 Medium-Fat Meat • 2-1/2 Fat OR 3-1/2 Carbohydrate • 2-1/2 Medium-Fat Meat • 2-1/2 Fat • 3-1/2 Carb Choices.

cook's notes

To save time, use frozen cooked meatballs instead of making them from scratch. About half of a 16-ounce package will give you 36 frozen meatballs. This will vary a little bit with different brands of meatballs. Heat the meatballs as directed on the package.

cook's note

Chicken strips for stir-fry conveniently save prep and cleanup time. Look for packages of chicken strips in the grocery store's poultry section.

spicy herbed chicken and orzo

PREP TIME: 10 Minutes ✱ READY IN: 35 Minutes ✱ SERVINGS: 5

- 1 tablespoon olive or vegetable oil
- 1 lb. uncooked chicken breast strips for stir-fry
- 1 cup uncooked orzo or rosamarina pasta (7 oz.)
- 2 cans (14.5 oz. each) stewed tomatoes, undrained, cut up
- 1 box (9 oz.) frozen baby lima beans, thawed
- 1 teaspoon garlic salt
- 1 teaspoon dried basil leaves
- 1/2 teaspoon hot pepper sauce

1 In 12-inch skillet, heat oil over medium-high heat. Cook chicken in oil 3 minutes, stirring frequently.

2 Stir in all remaining ingredients. Bring to a boil. Reduce heat; cover and simmer 20 to 25 minutes or until liquid is absorbed and orzo is tender, stirring occasionally.

NUTRITION INFORMATION PER SERVING: Calories 370 • Total Fat 7g • Saturated Fat 1g • Cholesterol 55mg • Sodium 740mg • Total Carbohydrate 53g • Dietary Fiber 6g • Protein 30g. DIETARY EXCHANGES: 3 Fruit • 1 Vegetable • 2-1/2 Very Lean Meat • 1 Fat.

easy cheesy beef and bow ties

READY IN: 20 Minutes ✱ SERVINGS: 4

- 2-1/2 cups uncooked bow tie (farfalle) pasta (6 oz.)
- 1 lb. lean (at least 80%) ground beef
- 1/2 cup chopped green onions (8 medium)
- 1 can (10-3/4 oz.) condensed Cheddar cheese soup
- 1 cup Old El Paso® Thick 'n Chunky salsa
- 1-1/2 cups shredded American-Cheddar cheese blend (6 oz.)

1 Cook and drain pasta as directed on package. Meanwhile, in 12-inch nonstick skillet, cook ground beef over medium-high heat, stirring frequently, until thoroughly cooked; drain.

2 Reserve 2 tablespoons onions for garnish. Stir the remaining onions, soup and salsa into beef. Heat to boiling. Reduce heat to medium-low; cook 5 minutes.

3 Stir in cooked pasta; cook 3 to 5 minutes, stirring occasionally, until thoroughly heated. Sprinkle with cheese; cook just until melted. Sprinkle with reserved 2 tablespoons onions.

NUTRITION INFORMATION PER SERVING: Calories 660 • Total Fat 33g • Saturated Fat 16g • Cholesterol 120mg • Sodium 2000mg • Total Carbohydrate 50g • Dietary Fiber 2g • Protein 39g. DIETARY EXCHANGES: 3 Starch • 1/2 Other Carbohydrate • 4 High-Fat Meat.

cook's notes

You can use the same amount of rotini or penne pasta instead of the bow ties. Use medium or hot salsa for spicier flavor. Cook the pasta ahead of time and toss it with 1 to 2 teaspoons of oil in a resealable plastic bag. Refrigerate until it's time to add it to the skillet.

special touch

For a pretty presentation, use fresh rosemary sprigs and yellow bell pepper stars.

sweet and spicy meatballs

PREP TIME: 15 Minutes ✱ READY IN: 50 Minutes ✱ SERVINGS: 18

Meatballs

- 3/4 lb. lean (at least 80%) ground beef
- 3/4 lb. ground pork
- 1/3 cup Progresso® plain bread crumbs
- 1/3 cup finely chopped onion
- 1/3 cup finely chopped red bell pepper
- 3/4 teaspoon garlic powder
- 3/4 teaspoon salt
- 1/2 teaspoon ground coriander
- 1/4 teaspoon pepper
- 1 egg, slightly beaten

Sauce

- 1 cup red or amber hot jalapeño jelly
- 2/3 cup apple juice
- 2 tablespoons cornstarch
- 1 teaspoon salt
- 1/2 teaspoon ground ginger
- 1/2 teaspoon garlic powder

1 Heat oven to 375°F. Line 15x10x1-inch pan with foil; grease foil. In large bowl, mix all meatball ingredients until well blended. Shape into 1-1/4-inch meatballs. Place in pan. Bake 25 to 30 minutes or until browned and thoroughly cooked in center.

2 In large saucepan, mix all sauce ingredients. Cook over medium heat 2 to 3 minutes or until thickened, stirring constantly.

3 Add meatballs to sauce; stir to coat. Cook over medium-low heat 5 to 7 minutes or until thoroughly heated, stirring occasionally.

NUTRITION INFORMATION PER SERVING: Calories 140 • Total Fat 5g • Saturated Fat 2g • Cholesterol 35mg • Sodium 270mg • Total Carbohydrate 16g • Dietary Fiber 0g. DIETARY EXCHANGES: 1 Other Carbohydrate • 1 Medium-Fat Meat.

crunchy biscuit chicken casserole

PREP TIME: 15 Minutes ✱ READY IN: 45 Minutes ✱ SERVINGS: 6

- 2 cans (5 oz. each) chunk chicken or 2 cups cubed cooked chicken
- 1 can (10-3/4 oz.) condensed cream of chicken soup
- 1 can (8.25 oz.) half-inch diagonal-cut green beans, drained
- 1 jar (2.5 oz.) sliced mushrooms, undrained
- 1 cup shredded Cheddar or American cheese (4 oz.)
- 1/2 cup mayonnaise or salad dressing
- 1 teaspoon lemon juice
- 1 can (16.3 oz.) Pillsbury® Grands!® Refrigerated Buttermilk Biscuits
- 1 to 2 tablespoons margarine or butter, melted
- 1/4 to 1/2 cup crushed Cheddar cheese flavor or seasoned croutons

1 Heat oven to 375°F. In medium saucepan, combine chicken, soup, green beans, mushrooms, cheese, mayonnaise and lemon juice. Bring to a boil, stirring occasionally. Pour hot chicken mixture into ungreased 13x9-inch (3-quart) glass baking dish.

2 Separate dough into 8 biscuits. Arrange over hot chicken mixture in dish. Brush each biscuit with margarine. Sprinkle with crushed croutons.

3 Bake at 375°F for 23 to 27 minutes or until biscuits are deep golden brown and bottoms are no longer doughy.

NUTRITION INFORMATION PER SERVING: Calories 630 • Total Fat 42g • Saturated Fat 12g • Cholesterol 65mg • Sodium 1920mg • Total Carbohydrate 41g • Dietary Fiber 2g • Sugars 8g • Protein 23g. DIETARY EXCHANGES: 2-1/2 Starch • 2 Medium-Fat Meat • 6 Fat OR 2-1/2 Carbohydrate • 2 Medium-Fat Meat • 6 Fat • 3 Carb Choices.

cook's notes

Out of cream of chicken soup? You can still make this family favorite using any canned cream soup you might have on hand–and you might discover a great new flavor combination! Why not try cream of broccoli, cream of mushroom, cream of asparagus or even cream of celery?

sweet and spicy meatballs

chicken cacciatore with biscuits

chicken cacciatore with biscuits

PREP TIME: 25 Minutes ✱ READY IN: 1 Hour 30 Minutes ✱ SERVINGS: 5

- 2-1/2 to 3 lb. cut-up frying chicken
- 1/2 medium green bell pepper, cut into strips
- 2 cups whole fresh mushrooms
- 1 jar (28 to 30 oz.) tomato pasta sauce
- 1/4 cup chopped onion
- 1 teaspoon dried oregano leaves, crushed
- 1 can (12 oz.) Pillsbury® Golden Layers™ Refrigerated Buttermilk Biscuits
- 1 tablespoon margarine or butter, melted
- 2 tablespoons grated Parmesan cheese

1 Heat oven to 375°F. Spray large nonstick skillet with nonstick cooking spray. Heat over medium-high heat until hot. Add chicken pieces; cook until browned on all sides. Place browned chicken in ungreased 13x9-inch (3-quart) glass baking dish. Top with bell pepper and mushrooms.

2 In small bowl, combine pasta sauce, onion and oregano; mix well. Pour over chicken; spread evenly around edges of baking dish. Cover with foil. Bake for 45 minutes.

3 Remove chicken from oven; uncover. Separate dough into 10 biscuits. Arrange over hot mixture around outer edges of dish. Brush biscuits with margarine. Sprinkle with Parmesan cheese.

4 Return to oven; bake an additional 14 to 20 minutes or until biscuits are deep golden brown, and chicken is fork-tender and juices run clear.

NUTRITION INFORMATION PER SERVING: Calories 590 • Total Fat 29g • Saturated Fat 7g • Cholesterol 95mg • Sodium 1570mg • Total Carbohydrate 45g • Dietary Fiber 4g • Sugars 4g • Protein 37g. DIETARY EXCHANGES: 3 Starch • 4 Lean Meat • 3 Fat OR 3 Carbohydrate • 4 Lean Meat • 3 Fat • 3 Carb Choices.

cook's notes

Cacciatore is simply the Italian word for "hunter" and refers to dishes prepared "hunter style" with mushrooms, tomatoes, onions and herbs. Serve this tasty version of the classic chicken dish with cut green beans and spaghetti topped with a generous sprinkle of shredded Parmesan cheese.

chili casserole with cheesy crust

PREP TIME: 35 Minutes ✱ READY IN: 1 Hour ✱ SERVINGS: 6

- 1 can (10 oz.) Pillsbury® Refrigerated Pizza Crust
- 1 package (8 oz.) string cheese
- 1 cup chopped onions
- 1 cup chopped green bell pepper
- 1 can (15 oz.) southwestern chili beans with cumin and cayenne in chili sauce, undrained
- 1 can (14.5 oz.) diced tomatoes, undrained
- 1 can (6 oz.) tomato paste
- 1/2 cup frozen whole kernel corn
- 1 cup shredded Cheddar cheese (4 oz.)

1 Heat oven to 425°F. Grease 13x9-inch pan. Unroll dough; place in greased pan. Starting at center, press out dough over bottom and 1-1/2 inches up sides.

2 Place string cheese, end to end, on dough around edges of pan, cutting to fit if necessary. Reserve any remaining cheese. Fold edge of dough over cheese; pinch to seal under cheese. Bake for 10 minutes. Remove partially baked crust from oven. Reduce oven temperature to 375°F.

3 Meanwhile, spray large skillet with nonstick cooking spray. Heat over medium-high heat until hot. Add onions and bell pepper; cook 5 to 7 minutes or until tender, stirring occasionally.

4 Add beans, tomatoes, tomato paste and corn; mix well. Bring to a boil. Reduce heat to medium; cook 6 to 8 minutes or until slightly thickened.

5 Spoon bean mixture evenly into partially baked crust. Chop any reserved string cheese. Sprinkle string cheese and Cheddar cheese over top.

6 Return to oven; bake at 375°F for an additional 15 to 25 minutes or until crust is deep golden brown and cheese is melted. Let stand about 5 minutes before serving.

NUTRITION INFORMATION PER SERVING: Calories 430 • Total Fat 15g • Saturated Fat 9g • Cholesterol 40mg • Sodium 1290mg • Total Carbohydrate 50g • Dietary Fiber 6g • Sugars 8g • Protein 24g. DIETARY EXCHANGES: 2-1/2 Starch • 2 Vegetable • 1-1/2 High-Fat Meat • 1/2 Fat OR 2-1/2 Carbohydrate • 2 Vegetable • 1-1/2 High-Fat Meat • 1/2 Fat • 3 Carb Choices.

Nonstick cooking spray is vegetable oil in a pressurized can that allows the oil to be dispersed in a much finer layer than you could achieve by pouring oil from the bottle. If you like, you can make your own sprayer. Just purchase a spray bottle at a specialty kitchen store and fill it with your favorite vegetable oil, and you're in business!

Christmas Breakfast

Rejoice with an eye-opening brunch of heartwarming specialties. Golden breads, satisfying egg bakes and so much more make Christmas morning deliciously memorable.

p. 165

p. 157

p. 170

p. 149

p. 166

cream cheese french toast bake p. 169

creamy swiss eggs on biscuits

chocolate-hazelnut breakfast ring

wild rice and ham country tart

wild rice and ham country tart

PREP TIME: 30 Minutes ✱ READY IN: 1 Hour 5 Minutes ✱ SERVINGS: 8

- 1 Pillsbury® Refrigerated Pie Crust (from 15-oz. package), softened as directed on package
- 1 cup diced cooked ham
- 1/2 cup cooked wild rice
- 1/3 cup finely chopped red bell pepper
- 1/4 cup thinly sliced green onion tops
- 1 jar (4.5 oz.) Green Giant® sliced mushrooms, well drained
- 3 eggs
- 1 container (8 oz.) sour cream
- 1 tablespoon country-style Dijon mustard
- 1/2 teaspoon salt
- 1/8 teaspoon pepper
- 2 cups shredded Swiss cheese (8 oz.)
- 8 pecan halves, if desired

1 Heat oven to 450°F. Place pie crust in 10-inch tart pan with removable bottom or 9-inch pie pan as directed on package for one-crust filled pie. Press in bottom and up sides of pan. Trim edges if necessary. Do not prick crust. Bake for 9 to 11 minutes or until crust is light golden brown. Remove from oven. Reduce heat to 400°F.

2 In medium bowl, combine ham, wild rice, bell pepper, onions and mushrooms; mix well. Beat eggs in small bowl until well blended. Add sour cream, mustard, salt and pepper; blend well.

3 Sprinkle 1 cup of the cheese over bottom of baked crust. Spread ham mixture over cheese. Pour egg mixture over ham mixture. Sprinkle with remaining 1 cup cheese.

4 Bake at 400°F for 30 to 35 minutes or until knife inserted in center comes out clean, arranging the pecan halves on top of tart during last 10 minutes of baking time. Let stand 10 minutes before serving.

High Altitude (3500-6500 ft): Add 1 tablespoon all-purpose flour to ham mixture.

NUTRITION INFORMATION PER SERVING: Calories 360 • Total Fat 24g • Saturated Fat 13g • Trans Fat 0g • Cholesterol 140mg • Sodium 770mg • Total Carbohydrate 19g • Dietary Fiber 0g • Sugars 3g • Protein 17g. DIETARY EXCHANGES: 1 Starch • 1 Other Carbohydrate • 2 High-Fat Meat • 1-1/2 Fat • Carbohydrate Choices.

cook's notes

This recipe calls for 1 cup or about 6 ounces of ham. From the deli, order ham sliced 1/4 inch thick; these slices can be easily diced.

citrus crescent swirls

PREP TIME: 15 Minutes ✱ READY IN: 30 Minutes ✱ SERVINGS: 24

- 1/2 cup firmly packed brown sugar
- 2 tablespoons butter or margarine
- 1 tablespoon grated orange peel
- 3 tablespoons orange juice
- 2 cans (8 oz.) Pillsbury® Refrigerated Crescent Dinner Rolls

1 Heat oven to 375°F. Spray 12-1/2-inch pizza pan with nonstick cooking spray. In small saucepan, combine brown sugar, butter, orange peel and juice; mix well. Cook over medium heat until bubbly, stirring constantly. Set aside.

2 Remove dough from each can, keeping dough in 1 piece; do not unroll. Cut each roll into 12 slices. Arrange the slices cut side down in the sprayed pan. Spoon brown sugar mixture evenly over slices.

3 Bake for 13 to 15 minutes or until golden brown. Remove rolls from pan with pancake turner. Serve warm.

NUTRITION INFORMATION PER SERVING: Calories 100 • Total Fat 5g • Saturated Fat 1g • Cholesterol 0mg • Sodium 160mg • Total Carbohydrate 12g • Dietary Fiber 0g • Sugars 6g • Protein 1g. DIETARY EXCHANGES: 1/2 Starch • 1/2 Fruit • 1 Fat OR 1 Carbohydrate • 1 Fat • 1 Carb Choice.

cook's notes

If you're expecting company and want to have these rolls ready to go, they can be made up to 4 hours ahead. Just prepare them as directed, cover with plastic wrap and refrigerate. When you're ready to bake them, remove the wrap and bake as directed.

Millicent Caplan
Tamarac, Florida
Bake-Off® Contest 29, 1980
Grand Prize Winner

italian zucchini crescent pie

PREP TIME: 30 Minutes ✷ READY IN: 55 Minutes ✷ SERVINGS: 6

- 2 tablespoons butter or margarine
- 4 cups thinly sliced zucchini
- 1 cup chopped onions
- 2 tablespoons dried parsley flakes
- 1/2 teaspoon salt
- 1/2 teaspoon pepper
- 1/4 teaspoon garlic powder
- 1/4 teaspoon dried basil leaves
- 1/4 teaspoon dried oregano leaves
- 2 eggs, well beaten
- 2 cups shredded Muenster or mozzarella cheese (8 oz.)
- 1 can (8 oz.) Pillsbury® Refrigerated Crescent Dinner Rolls
- 2 teaspoons prepared mustard

1 Heat oven to 375°F. Melt butter in 12-inch skillet over medium-high heat. Add zucchini and onions; cook and stir 6 to 8 minutes or until tender. Stir in the parsley flakes, salt, pepper, garlic powder, basil and oregano.

2 In large bowl, combine eggs and shredded cheese; mix well. Stir egg mixture into the cooked vegetable mixture.

3 Separate dough into 8 triangles. Place in ungreased 10-inch pie pan or 11-inch quiche pan; press over bottom and up sides to form crust. Firmly press perforations to seal. Spread crust with mustard. Pour egg mixture evenly into crust-lined pan.

4 Bake for 18 to 22 minutes or until knife inserted near center comes out clean. Cover edge of crust with strips of foil during last 10 minutes of baking if necessary to prevent excessive browning. Let stand 10 minutes before serving.

NUTRITION INFORMATION PER SERVING: Calories 370 • Total Fat 25g • Saturated Fat 10g • Cholesterol 105mg • Sodium 790mg • Total Carbohydrate 21g • Dietary Fiber 2g • Sugars 7g • Protein 15g. DIETARY EXCHANGES: 1 Starch • 1 Other Carbohydrate • 1 Vegetable • 1-1/2 High-Fat Meat • 2-1/2 Fat.

cheesy smoked sausage breakfast cups

READY IN: 30 Minutes ✷ SERVINGS: 10

- 1 can (12 oz.) Pillsbury® Golden Layers™ Refrigerated Buttermilk or Flaky Biscuits
- 4 eggs, beaten
- 4 oz. cocktail-sized smoked link sausages (about 13), cut into small pieces
- 2/3 cup finely shredded Cheddar cheese (2-1/2 oz.)

1 Spray 10 muffin cups with nonstick cooking spray, or line cups with foil baking cups and spray with cooking spray.

2 Separate dough into 10 biscuits. Place 1 biscuit in each sprayed cup; firmly press in bottom and up sides.

3 Spray large nonstick skillet with cooking spray. Heat over medium heat until hot. Add eggs; cook until almost set but still moist, stirring occasionally. Stir in sausage pieces.

4 Divide egg mixture evenly into biscuit-lined cups. Top each with 1 tablespoon cheese. Bake at 400°F for 11 to 13 minutes or until edges are light golden brown.

NUTRITION INFORMATION PER SERVING: Calories 480 • Total Fat 35g • Saturated Fat 19g • Cholesterol 170mg • Sodium 970mg • Total Carbohydrate 15g • Dietary Fiber 0g • Sugars 3g • Protein 25g. DIETARY EXCHANGES: 1 Starch • 3 High-Fat Meat • 2 Fat OR 1 Carbohydrate • 3 High-Fat Meat • 2 Fat • 1 Carb Choice.

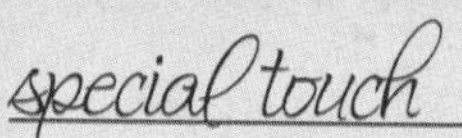

Add a splash of color to the finished cups by garnishing each serving with snipped fresh chives or diced roasted red peppers.

italian zucchini crescent pie

chocolate chip cinnamon roll coffee cake

chocolate chip cinnamon roll coffee cake

PREP TIME: 10 Minutes ✷ READY IN: 55 Minutes ✷ SERVINGS: 16

- 1/2 cup butter or margarine, softened
- 2 cans (12.4 oz.) Pillsbury® Refrigerated Cinnamon Rolls with Icing
- 1 package (3.4 oz.) vanilla pudding and pie filling mix (not instant)
- 1/2 cup firmly packed brown sugar
- 1/4 cup miniature semisweet chocolate chips

1 Heat oven to 375°F. Using 1 tablespoon of the butter, generously grease 12-cup fluted tube pan. Place remaining butter in small microwavable bowl. Microwave on High for 1 minute or until melted when stirred.

2 Separate both cans of dough into 16 rolls; cut each in half crosswise. Place half of roll pieces in greased pan. Sprinkle with half of the pudding mix and half of the brown sugar. Drizzle with half of the melted butter. Repeat layering with remaining roll pieces, pudding mix, brown sugar and melted butter. Sprinkle with chocolate chips.

3 Bake for 24 to 28 minutes or until rolls are deep golden brown and dough appears done when slightly pulled apart. Cool in the pan 2 minutes. Invert onto a serving platter. Cool 15 minutes.

4 Remove lid from icing. Microwave icing on High for 10 to 15 seconds or until of drizzling consistency. Drizzle over warm coffee cake. Cut into wedges. Serve warm.

NUTRITION INFORMATION PER SERVING: Calories 260 • Total Fat 12g • Saturated Fat 3g • Cholesterol 9mg • Sodium 460mg • Total Carbohydrate 35g • Dietary Fiber 1g • Sugars 19g • Protein 3g. DIETARY EXCHANGES: 1 Starch • 1 Fruit • 2-1/2 Fat OR 2 Carbohydrate • 2-1/2 Fat • 2 Carb Choices.

kitchen tip

Melting or softening butter or margarine in the microwave is easy. Place it in a bowl that is microwavable and be sure to cover the dish with a piece of waxed paper to prevent any spattering.

cherry pistachio scones

PREP TIME: 35 Minutes ✷ READY IN: 1 Hour 10 Minutes ✷ SERVINGS: 12 Scones

- 2 cups all-purpose flour
- 2 tablespoons sugar
- 3 teaspoons baking powder
- 3/4 teaspoon ground cinnamon
- 1/2 cup butter
- 3/4 cup chopped drained maraschino cherries
- 1/2 cup chopped shelled pistachio nuts
- 1/2 cup milk
- 1 egg, separated
- 4 teaspoons coarse white sparkling sugar or granulated sugar

1 Heat oven to 375°F. Line cookie sheet with parchment paper or lightly grease cookie sheet with shortening. In large bowl, mix flour, 2 tablespoons sugar, the baking powder and cinnamon. With pastry blender or fork, cut in butter until mixture resembles coarse crumbs. Stir in cherries and pistachios.

2 In small bowl, blend the milk and egg yolk. Add to flour mixture. Stir just until dry ingredients are moistened.

3 On lightly floured surface, gently knead dough several times. Divide dough in half; place on cookie sheet. Pat each half into 6-inch round. Cut each round into 6 wedges; do not separate.

4 In small bowl, beat egg white. Brush top of each round with egg white; sprinkle with coarse sugar. Bake 17 to 22 minutes or until golden brown. Cool 10 minutes before serving.

NUTRITION INFORMATION PER SERVING: Calories 220 • Total Fat 11g • Saturated Fat 5g • Trans Fat 0g • Cholesterol 40mg • Sodium 190mg • Total Carbohydrate 26g • Dietary Fiber 2g • Sugars 8g • Protein 4g. DIETARY EXCHANGES: 1/2 Starch • 1-1/2 Other Carbohydrate • 2 Fat • Carbohydrate Choices 2.

cook's notes

Pistachio nuts are available in their natural tan shell, or in a dyed red shell. Don't use the red pistachios for this recipe because the red dye bleeds in-to the dough.

quick corn and mushroom brunch squares

PREP TIME: 20 Minutes ✱ READY IN: 1 Hour ✱ SERVINGS: 2

HELEN HUBER
Conroe, Texas
Bake-Off® Contest 33, 1988

- 2 cans (8 oz.) Pillsbury® Refrigerated Crescent Dinner Rolls
- 2 cups chopped cooked ham
- 1-1/2 cups shredded Monterey Jack cheese (6 oz.)
- 1-1/2 cups shredded Swiss cheese (6 oz.)
- 1 can (11 oz.) Green Giant® Mexicorn® whole kernel corn, red and green peppers, drained
- 1 jar (4.5 oz.) Green Giant® sliced mushrooms, drained
- 6 eggs
- 1 cup milk
- 1/2 teaspoon salt, if desired
- 1/4 to 1/2 teaspoon pepper

1 Heat oven to 375°F. Unroll both cans of dough into 4 long rectangles. Place crosswise in ungreased 15x10x1-inch baking pan; press firmly over bottom and 3/4 inch up sides to form crust. Press edges and perforations to seal.

2 Sprinkle ham, Monterey Jack cheese, Swiss cheese, corn and mushrooms evenly over crust. In medium bowl, beat eggs, milk, salt and pepper until well blended. Pour evenly over ham, cheeses and vegetables.

3 Bake for 35 to 40 minutes or until crust is deep golden brown, egg mixture is set and knife inserted in center comes out clean. Cool 5 minutes. Cut into squares.

HIGH ALTITUDE (3500-6500 FT): Bake 37 to 42 minutes.

NUTRITION INFORMATION PER SERVING: Calories 350 • Total Fat 19g • Saturated Fat 8g • Trans Fat 0g • Cholesterol 145mg • Sodium 1060mg • Total Carbohydrate 25g • Dietary Fiber 1g • Sugars 7g • Protein 20g. DIETARY EXCHANGES: 1-1/2 Starch • 1-1/2 Other Carbohydrate • 2 Medium-Fat Meat • 2 Fat.

make-ahead scrambled eggs

READY IN: 40 Minutes ✱ SERVINGS: 12

- 8 slices bacon
- 3 cups sliced fresh mushrooms (from an 8-oz. pkg.)
- 3 tablespoons butter or margarine
- 16 eggs
- 1 cup half-and-half or milk
- 1/2 teaspoon salt
- 1/4 teaspoon pepper
- 1 can (10-3/4 oz.) condensed cream of mushroom soup
- 2 tablespoons chopped fresh chives
- 4 Italian plum tomatoes, quartered, sliced
- 2 cups shredded Cheddar cheese (8 oz.)

1 In 12-inch nonstick skillet, cook bacon until crisp. Drain on paper towels. Crumble bacon; set aside. Reserve 1 tablespoon bacon drippings in skillet. Add mushrooms to drippings; cook 4 to 5 minutes or until tender, stirring frequently. Remove from skillet; set aside. Wipe skillet clean with paper towel.

2 Melt butter in same skillet over medium heat. Beat eggs in large bowl. Add half-and-half, salt and pepper; beat well. Add egg mixture to skillet; cook over medium heat until firm but still moist, stirring occasionally. Stir in soup and chives.

3 Place half of egg mixture in 3-1/2- to 4-quart slow cooker. Top with half of each of the cooked mushrooms, tomatoes, cheese and crumbled bacon. Repeat layers. Serve immediately, or cover and keep warm on Low setting for up to 4 hours.

NUTRITION INFORMATION PER SERVING: Calories 280 • Total Fat 22g • Saturated Fat 11g • Cholesterol 320mg • Sodium 570mg • Total Carbohydrate 5g • Dietary Fiber 0g • Sugars 3g • Protein 16g. DIETARY EXCHANGES: 2-1/2 High-Fat Meat • 1/2 Fat • 0 Carb Choice.

special touch

Scrambled eggs from a slow cooker? Bet you didn't even know it was possible. Before serving, sprinkle a few chopped fresh chives and diced plum tomato pieces on top. An additional sprinkle of cheese never hurts, either.

three cheese and egg crescent pie

PREP TIME: 15 Minutes ✱ READY IN: 1 Hour 10 Minutes ✱ SERVINGS: 6

- 1 can (8 oz.) Pillsbury® Refrigerated Crescent Dinner Rolls
- 6 eggs
- 1-1/2 cups shredded sharp Cheddar cheese (6 oz.)
- 1/2 cup cottage cheese
- 1/4 cup chive and onion cream cheese spread (from 8-oz. container)
- 1/4 cup all-purpose flour
- 1/2 teaspoon baking powder
- 1 Italian plum tomato, thinly sliced

1 Heat oven to 350°F. Separate dough into 8 triangles. Place triangles in ungreased 9-inch glass pie pan; press over bottom and up sides to form crust. Turn outside edges under; flute if desired.

2 Beat eggs in large bowl. Add all remaining ingredients except tomato; mix well. Pour egg mixture into crust-lined pan. Bake for 20 minutes.

3 Remove pie from oven. Top with tomato slices. If necessary, cover edge of crust with strips of foil to prevent excessive browning.

4 Return pie to oven; bake an additional 19 to 28 minutes or until knife inserted near center comes out clean. Let stand 5 minutes. Cut into wedges.

NUTRITION INFORMATION PER SERVING: Calories 390 • Total Fat 24g • Saturated Fat 11g • Cholesterol 255mg • Sodium 840mg • Total Carbohydrate 24g • Dietary Fiber 0g • Sugars 8g • Protein 20g. DIETARY EXCHANGES: 1 Starch • 1/2 Fruit • 2-1/2 High-Fat Meat • 1 Fat OR 1-1/2 Carbohydrate • 2-1/2 High-Fat Meat • 1 Fat • 1-1/2 Carb Choices.

For a creative finish, sprinkle sliced ripe olives on top of the pie with the tomato. How many designs can you think of? Try arranging the olives and tomatoes in alternating stripes, for example, or concentric circles.

cook's notes

If you don't have the roasted red bell peppers, use a drained 2-ounce jar of diced pimientos instead.

potato frittata

READY IN: 25 Minutes ✱ SERVINGS: 4

- 6 eggs
- 1/3 cup milk
- 1/2 teaspoon salt
- Dash black pepper
- 1/4 cup chopped roasted red bell peppers (from a jar)
- 2 tablespoons chopped fresh chives
- 2 tablespoons vegetable oil
- 3 cups frozen southern-style hash brown potatoes (from 32-oz. bag)

1 In medium bowl, beat eggs, milk, salt and black pepper with wire whisk until well blended. Stir in roasted peppers and chives; set aside.

2 In 12-inch nonstick skillet, heat oil over medium-high heat. Add potatoes; cook 4 to 5 minutes, stirring frequently, until thawed.

3 Reduce heat to medium-low. Stir egg mixture; pour over potatoes in skillet. Cover; cook 8 to 10 minutes or until eggs are set, lifting edges occasionally to allow uncooked egg mixture to flow to bottom of skillet. Cut into 8 wedges to serve.

NUTRITION INFORMATION PER SERVING: Calories 320 • Total Fat 15g • Saturated Fat 3.5g • Trans Fat 0g • Cholesterol 320mg • Sodium 430mg • Total Carbohydrate 33g • Dietary Fiber 3g • Sugars 4g • Protein 13g. DIETARY EXCHANGES: 2 Starch • 1 Medium-Fat Meat • 2 Fat.

JANELLE SMITH
Bunker Hill, West Virginia
Bake-Off® Contest 30, 1982

whole wheat-applesauce bars

PREP TIME: 25 Minutes ✱ READY IN: 1 Hour 50 Minutes ✱ SERVINGS: 24

BARS

- 3/4 cup Pillsbury BEST® all-purpose flour
- 3/4 cup Pillsbury BEST® whole wheat flour
- 1 teaspoon baking powder
- 1/4 teaspoon baking soda
- 1/4 teaspoon salt
- 1/4 teaspoon ground cinnamon
- 1/2 cup granulated sugar
- 1/4 cup butter or margarine, softened
- 1/4 cup molasses
- 1 egg
- 1/2 cup applesauce
- 1/4 cup sour cream
- 1/2 cup chopped walnuts

FROSTING

- 1 cup powdered sugar
- 2 tablespoons butter or margarine, softened
- 1-1/2 oz. cream cheese (from 3-oz. package), softened
- 1-1/2 teaspoons milk
- 1/2 teaspoon vanilla
- 1/4 cup finely chopped walnuts

1 Heat oven to 350°F. Grease 13x9-inch pan with shortening or cooking spray. In small bowl, stir together flours, baking powder, baking soda, salt and cinnamon; set aside.

2 In large bowl, beat granulated sugar, brown sugar, 1/2 cup butter and the molasses with electric mixer on medium speed until light and fluffy. Beat in egg. Beat in applesauce and sour cream. On low speed, gradually beat in flour mixture until well blended. Stir in 1/2 cup walnuts. Spread evenly in pan.

3 Bake 20 to 25 minutes or until toothpick inserted in center comes out clean. Cool completely, about 1 hour.

4 In small bowl, beat all frosting ingredients except 1/4 cup walnuts on medium speed until smooth and creamy. Spread frosting over bars. Sprinkle with walnuts. For bars, cut into 6 rows by 4 rows. Store in refrigerator.

NUTRITION INFORMATION PER SERVING: Calories 170 • Total Fat 9g • Saturated Fat 4g • Trans Fat 0g • Cholesterol 25mg • Sodium 105mg • Total Carbohydrate 22g • Dietary Fiber 0g • Sugars 14g • Protein 2g. DIETARY EXCHANGES: 1/2 Starch • 1-1/2 Other Carbohydrate • 1/2 Fat • 1-1/2 Carb Choices.

potato frittata

apple-cheddar strata

microwave caramel sticky buns

READY IN: 15 Minutes ✱ SERVINGS: 5 rolls

TOPPING

- 1/4 cup butter or margarine
- 1/2 cup firmly packed brown sugar
- 2 tablespoons light corn syrup
- 2 tablespoons whipping cream

BUNS

- 2 tablespoons butter or margarine
- 1/3 cup firmly packed brown sugar
- 1/2 teaspoon cinnamon
- 1 can (10.2 oz.) Pillsbury® Grands!® Refrigerated Buttermilk Biscuits (5 biscuits)

1. Place 1/4 cup butter in 9-inch microwavable pie pan. Microwave on High for 40 to 60 seconds. Add all remaining topping ingredients; mix well. Microwave on High for 1 minute; stir.

2. In shallow microwavable dish, melt 2 tablespoons butter in microwave on High for 20 to 30 seconds. In another shallow dish, combine 1/3 cup brown sugar and cinnamon; mix well.

3. Separate dough into 5 biscuits. Dip biscuits in melted butter to coat all sides; dip in brown sugar mixture, coating well. Arrange biscuits in a circle over the topping in pie pan, leaving center open.

4. Microwave on High for 4 to 6 minutes or until biscuits are no longer doughy in center. Cool 30 seconds; invert onto serving plate. Serve warm.

NUTRITION INFORMATION PER SERVING: Calories 510 • Total Fat 24g • Saturated Fat 8g • Cholesterol 20mg • Sodium 860mg • Total Carbohydrate 70g • Dietary Fiber 1g • Sugars 47g • Protein 4g. DIETARY EXCHANGES: 2 Starch • 2-1/2 Fruit • 4-1/2 Fat OR 4-1/2 Carbohydrate • 4-1/2 Fat • 4-1/2 Carb Choices.

cook's notes

Because these ooey, gooey rolls are cooked in the microwave, the cooking time is critical. Be sure to cook them just until they are no longer doughy as the recipe directs. If they are microwaved for too long, they will become tough and the caramel may harden.

cream cheese french toast bake

cream cheese french toast bake

PREP TIME: 30 Minutes ✳ READY IN: 9 Hours ✳ SERVINGS: 6

- 1 loaf (1 lb.) French bread (about 18 inches long), cut into 24 (3/4-inch-thick) slices
- 1 container (8 oz.) pineapple cream cheese
- 4 eggs
- 1 cup milk
- 3/4 cup sugar
- 1/4 teaspoon salt
- 1/4 teaspoon ground cinnamon
- 1 quart (4 cups) fresh strawberries
- 2 tablespoons amaretto, if desired
- 2 tablespoons butter or margarine, melted

1 Spray 13x9-inch (3-quart) glass baking dish with cooking spray. Spread about 1 tablespoon cream cheese on each of 12 slices of bread. Top with remaining bread slices to make 12 sandwiches. Place sandwiches in baking dish to cover bottom.

2 In medium bowl, beat eggs, milk, 1/4 cup of the sugar, the salt and cinnamon with wire whisk until well blended. Pour over bread in baking dish. Let stand 5 minutes. Turn sandwiches over. Cover; refrigerate 8 hours or overnight.

3 Chop 1 cup of the strawberries; refrigerate remaining berries. In nonmetal bowl, gently stir chopped strawberries, remaining 1/2 cup sugar and the amaretto to mix. Cover; refrigerate 8 hours or overnight.

4 Heat oven to 400°F. Drizzle melted butter over bread in dish; bake uncovered 25 to 30 minutes or until golden brown.

5 Meanwhile, slice remaining strawberries; stir into chilled strawberry mixture. Serve French toast with strawberry topping.

HIGH ALTITUDE (3500-6500 FT): In step 4, heat oven to 425°F.

NUTRITION INFORMATION PER SERVING: Calories 560 • Total Fat 22g • Saturated Fat 11g • Cholesterol 185mg • Sodium 740mg • Total Carbohydrate 79g • Dietary Fiber 4g. DIETARY EXCHANGES: 2-1/2 Starch • 2-1/2 Other Carbohydrate • 1 Medium-Fat Meat • 3 Fat.

cook's notes

Serve the French toast with bacon or pork sausage patties, fresh fragrant coffee and apple juice.

grands!® sunrise sandwiches

READY IN: 30 Minutes ✳ SERVINGS: 8 sandwiches

- 1 can (16.3 oz.) Pillsbury® Grands!® Refrigerated Buttermilk Biscuits
- 1 tablespoon butter or margarine
- 1/4 cup chopped green bell pepper
- 1/4 cup chopped onion
- 8 eggs
- 1/4 teaspoon salt
- 1/8 teaspoon pepper
- 8 slices (2/3 oz.) American pasterized process cheese food
- 8 slices bacon, crisply cooked, cut in half

1 Bake biscuits as directed on can. Keep warm. Meanwhile, melt butter in medium skillet over medium heat. Add bell pepper and onion; cook and stir 2 minutes or until tender.

2 In small bowl, combine eggs, salt and pepper; beat well. Add to mixture in skillet; cook until egg mixture is thoroughly cooked and set but still moist, stirring occasionally.

3 Split warm biscuits. Spoon egg mixture evenly onto bottom half of each biscuit. Top each with 1 slice of cheese, 2 bacon halves and top half of biscuit.

NUTRITION INFORMATION PER SERVING: Calories 380 • Total Fat 24g • Saturated Fat 9g • Cholesterol 235mg • Sodium 1090mg • Total Carbohydrate 25g • Dietary Fiber 1g • Sugars 6g • Protein 16g. DIETARY EXCHANGES: 1-1/2 Starch • 1-1/2 High-Fat Meat • 2-1/2 Fat OR 1-1/2 Carbohydrate • 1-1/2 High-Fat Meat • 2-1/2 Fat • 1-1/2 Carb Choices.

kitchen tip

Store your eggs in their original carton on the refrigerator shelf, not in the refrigerator door. While built-in egg compartments on the door might seem handy, they unfortunately can subject eggs to too many temperature fluctuations in the refrigerator.

kitchen tip

Refrigerated dough is easy to handle when it is very cold. Have all other ingredients ready to go before removing the dough from the refrigerator.

quick swedish tea ring

PREP TIME: 25 Minutes ✱ READY IN: 45 Minutes ✱ SERVINGS: 12

- 1 can (11 oz.) Pillsbury® Refrigerated Crusty French Loaf
- 3 tablespoons butter, softened
- 2 tablespoons sugar
- 1 tablespoon cinnamon
- 1/2 cup powdered sugar
- 1 to 1-1/2 teaspoons milk
- 8 pecan halves
- 4 candied red cherries, halved
- 2 candied green cherries, cut into slivers

1 Heat oven to 375°F. Line cookie sheet with parchment paper or lightly grease cookie sheet. Unroll dough onto lightly floured surface. Press dough to form 15x12-inch rectangle.

2 Spread 2 tablespoons of the butter over dough to edge of short sides and to within 1/2 inch of long sides. In small bowl, mix sugar and cinnamon; sprinkle evenly over butter.

3 Starting with 1 long side, roll up dough; pinch edge to seal. Shape dough into ring, seam side down, on paper-lined cookie sheet; pinch ends to seal. With kitchen scissors, cut ring at 1-inch intervals from outside almost through to center. Twist each section so cut edge is up.

4 Bake at 375°F for 15 to 20 minutes or until golden brown. Remove tea ring from cookie sheet; place on serving platter. Cool 10 minutes.

5 In small bowl, blend powdered sugar, remaining 1 tablespoon butter and enough milk for desired spreading consistency. Spread over warm tea ring. Decorate with pecans and cherries.

NUTRITION INFORMATION PER SERVING: Calories 130 • Total Fat 4g • Saturated Fat 2g • Cholesterol 10mg • Sodium 180mg • Total Carbohydrate 21g • Dietary Fiber 0g • Sugars 10g • Protein 2g. DIETARY EXCHANGES: 1/2 Starch • 1 Other Carbohydrate • 1 Fat • 1-1/2 Carb Choices.

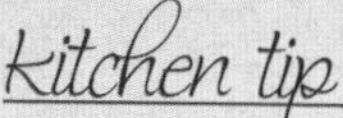

Because you are using a nonstick skillet to cook the eggs in this recipe, very little butter or margarine is needed. To prolong the life of a nonstick pan, use only wooden or plastic utensils and don't store anything in the pan. If you must nest pans for storage, protect the surface with a kitchen towel or double layers of paper towels before stacking the next pan on top.

denver scrambled egg pizzas

READY IN: 25 Minutes ✱ SERVINGS: 4 Pizzas

- 1 can (10 oz.) Pillsbury® Refrigerated Pizza Crust
- 1 tablespoon butter or margarine
- 1 cup frozen bell pepper and onion stir-fry
- 8 eggs
- 2 tablespoons milk
- 1/4 teaspoon salt
- 1/2 cup chopped cooked ham
- 2 to 3 tablespoons creamy mustard-mayonnaise sauce

1 Heat oven to 400°F. Lightly spray large cookie sheet with nonstick cooking spray. Unroll dough. Cut dough into 4 equal pieces; place on sprayed cookie sheet. Press out each piece of dough to form 6x5-inch rectangle. With fingers, create slight rim on edge of each dough rectangle. Bake at 400°F for 11 to 15 minutes or until golden brown.

2 Meanwhile, melt butter in large nonstick skillet over medium heat. Add bell pepper and onion stir-fry; cook 3 to 5 minutes or until tender, stirring occasionally.

3 In medium bowl, combine eggs, milk, salt and ham; beat well. Add mixture to skillet; cook 4 to 5 minutes or until egg mixture is thoroughly cooked and set but still moist, stirring occasionally.

4 Spread each baked crust with mustard-mayonnaise sauce. Spoon egg mixture evenly over sauce. Serve warm.

NUTRITION INFORMATION PER SERVING: Calories 410 • Total Fat 18g • Saturated Fat 6g • Cholesterol 435mg • Sodium 1230mg • Total Carbohydrate 39g • Dietary Fiber 1g • Sugars 7g • Protein 23g. DIETARY EXCHANGES: 2 Starch • 1/2 Fruit • 2-1/2 Medium-Fat Meat • 1 Fat OR 2-1/2 Carbohydrate • 2-1/2 Medium-Fat Meat • 1 Fat • 2-1/2 Carb Choices.

quick swedish tea ring

Heartwarming Gifts

Smiles will abound when friends receive a present made in your very own kitchen. Brownies, coffee cakes, muffins and more make gift giving deliciously rewarding.

p. 183

p. 175

p. 176

p. 180

p. 188

white fudge cookie cutter gifts p. 178

christmas candy brownie mix

christmas candy brownie mix

PREP TIME: 15 Minutes ✱ READY IN: 1 Hour 25 Minutes ✱ SERVINGS: 16 Brownies

- 1 cup red and green candy-coated chocolate candies
- 1/2 cup plus 2 tablespoons all-purpose flour
- 1 teaspoon salt
- 1/3 cup unsweetened baking cocoa
- 1/2 cup all-purpose flour
- 2/3 cup packed brown sugar
- 2/3 cup granulated sugar
- 1/2 cup coarsely chopped walnuts
- 2/3 cup vegetable oil
- 1 teaspoon vanilla
- 3 eggs

1 Place 2 tablespoons of the chocolate candies in small resealable food storage plastic bag; seal. In 1-quart glass jar, layer in order the 1/2 cup plus 2 tablespoons flour, salt, remaining chocolate candies, cocoa, 1/2 cup flour, brown sugar, granulated sugar and walnuts. Place candies in bag on top of the walnuts. Cover tightly. If desired, cover lid with 7- to 8-inch square of fabric tied with ribbon or raffia. Attach tag with recipe and baking directions.

2 To make brownies, heat oven to 350°F. Grease 8- or 9-inch square pan. Set aside candies in plastic bag. In large bowl, mix contents of jar with oil, vanilla and eggs. (If brown sugar has become slightly firm, break up with fork.) With spoon beat about 30 strokes until well blended. Spoon and spread in pan. Sprinkle candies from bag over top.

3 Bake 35 to 40 minutes or until set. Cool completely, about 45 minutes. For brownies, cut into 4 rows by 4 rows.

HIGH ALTITUDE (3500-6500 FT): Bake 38 to 43 minutes.

NUTRITION INFORMATION PER SERVING: Calories 290 • Total Fat 16g • Saturated Fat 3.5g • Trans Fat 0g • Cholesterol 40mg • Sodium 170mg • Total Carbohydrate 35g • Dietary Fiber 1g • Sugars 25g • Protein 4g. DIETARY EXCHANGES: 1/2 Starch • 2 Other Carbohydrate • 3 Fat • 2 Carb Choices.

kitchen tip

For easy clean-up, line the pan with foil and spray with cooking spray. Lift brownies from pan with foil for easy cutting and serving.

quick 'n easy herb flatbread

READY IN: 25 Minutes ✱ SERVINGS: 9

- 1 can (10 oz.) Pillsbury® Refrigerated Pizza Crust
- 1 tablespoon olive or vegetable oil
- 1/2 to 1 teaspoon dried basil leaves
- 1/2 to 1 teaspoon dried rosemary leaves, crushed
- 1/2 teaspoon minced garlic
- 1/8 teaspoon salt
- 1 small tomato
- 1/4 cup shredded fresh Parmesan cheese (1 oz.)

1 Heat oven to 425°F. Spray cookie sheet with nonstick cooking spray. Unroll dough; place on sprayed cookie sheet. Starting at center, press out dough to form 12x8-inch rectangle.

2 In small bowl, combine oil, basil, rosemary and garlic; mix well. Brush over dough. Sprinkle with salt. Chop tomato; place in shallow bowl. With back of spoon, crush tomato. Spread tomato over the dough.

3 Bake for 5 to 9 minutes or until edges are light golden brown. Sprinkle with cheese. Bake an additional 2 to 3 minutes or until cheese is melted and edges are golden brown. Cut into squares. Serve warm.

NUTRITION INFORMATION PER SERVING: Calories 100 • Total Fat 3g • Saturated Fat 1g • Cholesterol 2mg • Sodium 290mg • Total Carbohydrate 15g • Dietary Fiber 1g • Sugars 2g • Protein 4g. DIETARY EXCHANGES: 1 Starch • 1/2 Fat OR 1 Carbohydrate • 1/2 Fat • 1 Carb Choice.

special touch

Personalize the flatbread with a sprinkling of chopped green or red bell pepper or even sliced ripe olives.

special touch

Stacked in a pretty tin, these bars make a tasty change-of-pace gift from classic cookie platters.

treasure chest bars

PREP TIME: 30 Minutes ✱ READY IN: 2 Hours ✱ SERVINGS: 48 Bars

Bars

- 2 cups all-purpose flour
- 1/2 cup granulated sugar
- 1/2 cup packed brown sugar
- 1 teaspoons baking powder
- Dash salt
- 1/2 cup butter, softened
- 3/4 cup milk
- 1 teaspoon vanilla
- 2 eggs
- 3 bars (1.55 oz. each) milk chocolate candy, cut into small pieces
- 1 cup maraschino cherries, drained, halved
- 1 cup coarsely chopped mixed nuts

Frosting

- 1/4 cup butter (do not use margarine)
- 2 cups powdered sugar
- 1/2 teaspoon vanilla
- 2 to 3 tablespoons milk

1 Heat oven to 350°F. Grease 15x10x1-inch pan with shortening or nonstick cooking spray. In large bowl, beat all bar ingredients except chocolate candy, cherries and nuts with electric mixer on medium speed 2 minutes, scraping bowl occasionally, until smooth. With spoon, stir in chocolate candy, cherries and nuts. Spread evenly in pan.

2 Bake 25 to 30 minutes or until light golden brown. Meanwhile, in 1-quart saucepan, heat 1/4 cup butter over medium heat, stirring constantly, until light golden brown. Remove from heat. Stir in powdered sugar and 1 teaspoon vanilla. Stir in 2 to 3 tablespoons milk until frosting is smooth and spreadable.

3 Quickly spread frosting over warm bars. Cool completely in pan on cooling rack, about 1 hour. For bars, cut into 8 rows by 6 rows.

NUTRITION INFORMATION PER SERVING: Calories 130 • Total Fat 6g • Saturated Fat 2.5g • Trans Fat 0g • Cholesterol 15mg • Sodium 60mg • Total Carbohydrate 17g • Dietary Fiber 0g • Sugars 12g • Protein 2g. DIETARY EXCHANGES: 1 Starch • 1 Fat • 1 Carb Choice.

fido's favorite treats

PREP TIME: 20 Minutes ✱ READY IN: 1 Hour 20 Minutes ✱ SERVINGS: 42 Dog Biscuits

- 1 cup rolled oats
- 1/3 cup butter or margarine
- 1 cup boiling water
- 3/4 cup cornmeal
- 1 tablespoon sugar
- 1 to 2 teaspoons chicken or beef-flavored instant bouillon
- 1/2 cup milk
- 1 cup shredded Cheddar cheese (4 oz.)
- 1 egg, beaten
- 2 to 3 cups all-purpose or whole wheat flour

1 Heat oven to 325°F. Grease cookie sheets. In large bowl, combine rolled oats, butter and boiling water; mix well. Let stand 10 minutes.

2 Stir in cornmeal, sugar, bouillon, milk, cheese and egg; mix well. Add flour 1 cup at a time, mixing well after each addition to form a stiff dough.

3 On floured surface, knead in remaining flour until dough is smooth and no longer sticky, 3 to 4 minutes. Roll or pat dough to 1/2-inch thickness. Cut with bone-shaped cookie cutter; place 1 inch apart on greased cookie sheets.

4 Bake for 35 to 45 minutes or until golden brown. Remove from cookie sheets. Cool 15 minutes or until completely cooled. Store in loosely covered container.

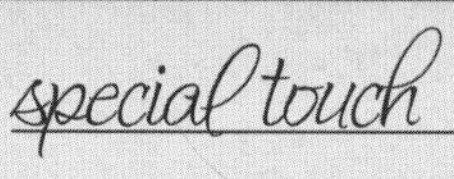

Give these canine snacks to your favorite dog owner. Include a bone-shaped cutter and a copy of the recipe.

treasure chest bars

white fudge cookie cutter gifts

white fudge cookie cutter gifts

PREP TIME: 25 Minutes ✱ READY IN: 1 Hour 25 Minutes ✱ SERVINGS: 20 (5 Gifts)

- 1 package (12 oz.) white vanilla chips (2 cups)
- 1 can (16 oz.) vanilla frosting
- 1/2 teaspoon cherry extract
- Decorator frosting
- Colored sugar
- Candies

1 Line large cookie sheet with foil. Spray foil with nonstick cooking spray. Generously spray hollow metal 6-inch cookie cutters; place on sprayed foil-lined cookie sheet.

2 Melt white vanilla chips in medium saucepan over low heat, stirring frequently until smooth. Remove from heat. Stir in frosting and cherry extract.

3 Fill each cookie cutter with 1/2 cup melted mixture. Refrigerate about 1 hour or until firm. Decorate as desired.

4 Wrap each filled cookie cutter gift with cellophane or plastic wrap; tie with ribbon. Store in the refrigerator.

NUTRITION INFORMATION PER SERVING: Calories 190 • Total Fat 9g • Saturated Fat 6g • Cholesterol 5mg • Sodium 15mg • Total Carbohydrate 26g • Dietary Fiber 0g. DIETARY EXCHANGES: 2 Fruit • 2 Other Carbohydrate • 2 Fat.

Kitchen tip

To enjoy this treat, you can eat the fudge with a spoon or, to loosen the fudge filling, run a thin-bladed knife along the inside edge of the cookie cutter and slip out the fudge. The cookie cutter can then be washed to use again.

mocha streusel coffeecake

PREP TIME: 25 Minutes ✱ READY IN: 2 Hours 30 Minutes ✱ SERVINGS: 12

Streusel

- 1/3 cup packed brown sugar
- 2 tablespoons all-purpose flour
- 1 tablespoon instant coffee granules or crystals
- 4 oz. semisweet baking chocolate, cut into 1-inch pieces
- 1/2 cup pecan pieces

Coffee Cake

- 1 cup granulated sugar
- 1 cup butter or margarine, softened
- 3 eggs
- 1/2 teaspoon almond extract
- 2-3/4 cups all-purpose flour
- 2 teaspoons baking powder
- 1 teaspoon ground cinnamon
- 1/4 teaspoon baking soda
- 1/4 teaspoon salt
- 1 container (8 oz.) plain yogurt

1 Heat oven to 350°F. Spray angel food (tube cake) pan with nonstick cooking spray. In food processor bowl with metal blade, place brown sugar, 2 tablespoons flour and the instant coffee. Cover; process with on-and-off pulses until mixed. Add chocolate; pulse to finely chop. Add pecans; pulse to chop. Set aside.

2 In large bowl, beat granulated sugar and butter with electric mixer on medium speed until fluffy. Beat in 1 egg at a time until well blended. Add almond extract; mix well.

3 In small bowl, mix 2-3/4 cups flour, the baking powder, cinnamon, baking soda and salt. Add half of flour mixture to sugar-egg mixture; beat with electric mixer on low speed just until combined. Add yogurt; blend well. Add remaining flour mixture; mix well.

4 Spoon half of batter into pan, spreading evenly. Sprinkle with half of streusel mixture. Top with remaining batter and remaining streusel mixture.

5 Bake 55 to 65 minutes or until toothpick inserted in center comes out clean. Cool upright in pan on cooling rack 1 hour. Remove cake from pan. Serve warm or cool.

High Altitude (3500-6500 ft): Increase flour in coffee cake to 3 cups.

NUTRITION INFORMATION PER SERVING: Calories 450 • Total Fat 23g • Saturated Fat 12g • Trans Fat 1g • Cholesterol 95mg • Sodium 300mg • Total Carbohydrate 54g • Dietary Fiber 2g • Sugars 29g • Protein 7g. DIETARY EXCHANGES: 2 Starch • 1-1/2 Other Carbohydrate • 4-1/2 Fat • 3-1/2 Carb Choices.

cook's notes

Swap out the almond extract for vanilla or even rum if you would like.

Kitchen tip

The zucchini in this recipe makes the bread very moist, so it stays fresh for several days.

pineapple zucchini bread

PREP TIME: 20 Minutes ✱ READY IN: 2 Hours ✱ SERVINGS: 12

Bread

- 1 cup packed brown sugar
- 1/2 cup butter or margarine, softened
- 1 cup shredded zucchini (1 small)
- 1 can (8 oz.) crushed pineapple in juice, undrained, reserving 1 tablespoon liquid
- 2 eggs, slightly beaten
- 2 cups all-purpose flour
- 1 teaspoon baking soda
- 1 teaspoon ground cinnamon
- 1/4 teaspoon salt
- 1/4 teaspoon ground allspice
- 1/2 cup chopped walnuts or pecans

Glaze

- 1/2 cup powdered sugar
- Reserved 1 tablespoon pineapple liquid
- 1 teaspoon corn syrup
- 1/4 teaspoon ground cinnamon

1 Heat oven to 350°F. Grease and flour bottom only of 9x5-inch loaf pan. In large bowl with electric mixer, beat brown sugar and butter on medium speed until light and fluffy. With spoon, stir in zucchini, pineapple and eggs. Stir in flour, baking soda, 1 teaspoon cinnamon, the salt and allspice until well blended. Fold in walnuts. Spread evenly in pan.

2 Bake 60 to 70 minutes or until toothpick inserted in center comes out clean. Cool 10 minutes; remove from pan to cooling rack. Cool 30 minutes.

3 In small bowl, mix all glaze ingredients until smooth; spoon over warm loaf. Cool completely, about 1 hour. Store in refrigerator.

High Altitude (3500-6500 ft): Heat oven to 375°F. Bake 55 to 65 minutes.

NUTRITION INFORMATION PER SERVING: Calories 300 • Total Fat 12g • Saturated Fat 5g • Cholesterol 55mg • Sodium 230mg • Total Carbohydrate 43g • Dietary Fiber 1g • Sugars 26g • Protein 4g. DIETARY EXCHANGES: 1 Starch • 2 Other Carbohydrate • 2 Fat.

soft pesto pretzels

PREP TIME: 20 Minutes ✱ READY IN: 40 Minutes ✱ SERVINGS:12 Pretzels

- 1 can (11 oz.) Pillsbury® Refrigerated Breadsticks
- 1 tablespoon purchased pesto
- 1 egg white
- 2 teaspoons grated Parmesan-Romano cheese blend

1 Heat oven to 375°F. Line cookie sheet with parchment paper or use ungreased cookie sheet. Separate dough into 12 breadsticks. With finger, firmly press dough to make indentation lengthwise down center of each breadstick.

2 Spoon 1/4 teaspoon pesto into each indentation. Fold dough lengthwise over pesto; press edges to seal.

3 Twist and stretch each breadstick to form 22-inch rope. Shape each rope into pretzel shape; tuck ends under and press to seal. Place on paper-lined cookie sheet. Beat egg white in small bowl until foamy. Brush over pretzels. Sprinkle with cheese. Bake for 12 to 18 minutes or until golden brown. Serve warm.

NUTRITION INFORMATION PER SERVING: Calories 80 • Total Fat 2g • Saturated Fat 1g • Cholesterol 0mg • Sodium 210mg • Total Carbohydrate 12g • Dietary Fiber 0g • Sugars 2g • Protein 2g. DIETARY EXCHANGES: 1 Starch OR 1 Carbohydrate • 1 Carb Choice.

pineapple zucchini bread

cook's notes

When baking these muffins, check for doneness at the minimum baking time. They're light in color when they are done baking.

granola streusel cranberry muffin mix

PREP TIME: 10 Minutes ✱ READY IN: 30 Minutes ✱ SERVINGS: 12 Muffins

Muffin Mix

- 2 cups all-purpose flour
- 3/4 cup sweetened dried cranberries
- 1/2 cup sugar
- 1/2 cup nonfat dry milk
- 3 teaspoons baking powder
- 1/2 teaspoon pumpkin pie spice
- 1/2 teaspoon salt

Streusel Mix

- 2 Nature Valley® Oats 'n Honey crunchy granola bars (1 pouch from 8.9-oz. box), finely crushed (about 1/3 cup)
- 2 tablespoons sugar

To Make Muffins:

- 3/4 cup water
- 1/3 cup vegetable oil
- 1 egg, slightly beaten
- 2 tablespoons butter or margarine, melted

1 In large bowl, mix Muffin Mix ingredients. Spoon into jar with lid or resealable food-storage plastic bag; cover jar or seal bag. In another jar or bag, mix Streusel Mix ingredients; cover or seal.

2 To make muffins, heat oven to 375°F. Line 12 regular-size muffin cups with paper baking cups or spray bottoms only of muffin cups with nonstick cooking spray. In large bowl, mix Muffin Mix, water, oil and egg just until dry ingredients are moistened. Spoon batter evenly into muffin cups.

3 In small bowl, mix Streusel Mix with melted butter. Sprinkle mixture evenly over batter in cups; press in lightly.

4 Bake 14 to 18 minutes or until toothpick inserted in center comes out clean. Remove from muffin cups; serve warm.

NUTRITION INFORMATION PER SERVING: Calories: 250 • Total Fat 9g • Saturated Fat 2g • Trans Fat 0g • Cholesterol 25mg • Sodium 270mg • Total Carbohydrate 37g • Dietary Fiber 1g • Sugars 19g • Protein 4g. DIETARY EXCHANGES: 1-1/2 Starch • 1 Other Carbohydrate • 1-1/2 Fat • 2-1/2 Carb Choices.

honey-sage whipped butter

READY IN: 5 Minutes ✱ SERVINGS: 8

- 2 tablespoons finely chopped fresh sage
- 2 tablespoons honey
- 1/2 cup butter, softened

1 In small microwavable bowl, combine chopped sage and honey; mix well. Microwave on High for 15 seconds. Cool 2 minutes.

2 Beat butter in small bowl with electric mixer at medium speed until fluffy. Add honey mixture; beat well. Store in refrigerator for up to 2 weeks or freeze for 1 month.

NUTRITION INFORMATION PER SERVING: Calories 120 • Total Fat 12g • Saturated Fat 7g • Cholesterol 30mg • Sodium 75mg • Total Carbohydrate 4g • Dietary Fiber 0g • Sugars 4g; Protein 0g. DIETARY EXCHANGES: 2-1/2 Fat • 0 Carb Choice.

special touch

This makes a cute gift when paired with bee-themed kitchen accessories. Look for bee napkins, butter spreaders and appetizer plates at specialty and kitchen supply stores.

crispy chocolate treats in a jar

READY IN: 10 Minutes ✱ YIELD: 20 cookies

- 2/3 cup miniature candy-coated semisweet chocolate baking bits
- 1 cup Wheat Chex® cereal
- 1/2 cup raisins
- 1/2 cup peanuts
- 1/3 cup butterscotch chips

1 Place 1/3 cup of the baking bits in resealable food storage plastic bag or wrap in sheet of plastic wrap. Place in bottom of a 1-quart glass jar with a cover, hiding zipper section underneath bag.

2 Layer with 1/2 cup of the cereal squares, the raisins, peanuts, remaining 1/2 cup cereal squares, remaining 1/3 cup baking bits and the butterscotch chips. Press down gently while layering to make sure all ingredients fit. Cover; decorate as desired. Write directions (see Step 3) on decorative card; attach to container.

3 To make treats, line cookie sheets with waxed paper. Place 1/4 cup creamy peanut butter in medium saucepan. Spoon in butterscotch chips and top layer of baking bits. Cook over low heat, stirring constantly until melted. Remove from heat. Stir in remaining contents of jar except for baking bits in plastic bag. Drop mixture by rounded tablespoonfuls onto waxed paper-lined cookie sheets. Sprinkle remaining baking bits in bag evenly over top of cookies. Refrigerate about 10 minutes or until set.

NUTRITION INFORMATION PER SERVING: Calories 70 • Total Fat 4g • Saturated Fat 1g • Cholesterol 0mg • Sodium 60mg • Total Carbohydrate 7g • Dietary Fiber 1g • Sugars 3g • Protein 2g. DIETARY EXCHANGES: 1/2 Starch • 1/2 Fat • 1/2 Carb Choice.

special touch

The jars make great gifts for teachers. Assembling them with kids is half the fun.

elegant party mix

READY IN: 10 Minutes ✱ SERVINGS: 32

- 2 cups coarsely cut dried mangoes
- 1 cup dried pineapple chunks, each cut in half
- 1 cup dried red tart cherries
- 1 cup dried banana chips
- 1 cup chocolate-covered raisins
- 1 cup yogurt-covered pretzels
- 1/2 cup salted shelled pistachios
- 1 jar (3.25 oz.) macadamia nuts

1 In a large container, combine all of the ingredients; mix well. Spoon the mix into decorative food storage containers.

NUTRITION INFORMATION PER SERVING: Calories 130 • Total Fat 5g • Saturated Fat 2g • Cholesterol 0mg • Sodium 40mg • Total Carbohydrate 20g • Dietary Fiber 2g. DIETARY EXCHANGES: 1/2 Starch • 1/2 Fruit • 1 Fat.

kitchen tip

Look for dried fruit chips in the produce department.

Kitchen tip

Chop maraschino cherries easily by snipping them with a kitchen scissors. Drain on paper towels to dry.

candy cane coffee cake

PREP TIME: 20 Minutes ✷ READY IN: 1 Hour 15 Minutes ✷ SERVINGS: 12

Coffee Cake

- 1 package (3 oz.) cream cheese, softened
- 2 tablespoons granulated sugar
- 1 teaspoon almond extract
- 1/4 cup sliced almonds
- 1/4 cup chopped maraschino cherries, well drained
- 1 can (8 oz.) Pillsbury® Refrigerated Crescent Dinner Rolls

Glaze

- 1/2 cup powdered sugar
- 2 teaspoons milk

1. Heat oven to 375°F. Grease cookie sheet with shortening. In small bowl, beat cream cheese and granulated sugar until light and fluffy. Stir in almond extract, almonds and cherries; set aside.
2. Unroll dough onto cookie sheet; press into 13x7-inch rectangle, firmly pressing perforations to seal. Spoon cream cheese mixture down center 1/3 of rectangle.
3. On each long side of dough rectangle, make cuts 1 inch apart to edge of filling. Fold opposite strips of dough over filling and cross in center to form a braided appearance; seal ends. Curve one end to form candy cane shape.
4. Bake 18 to 22 minutes or until golden brown. Remove from cookie sheet; place on wire rack. Cool completely, about 30 minutes.
5. In small bowl, mix glaze ingredients until smooth; drizzle over coffee cake. If desired, garnish with additional sliced almonds and cherries. Store in refrigerator.

NUTRITION INFORMATION PER SERVING: Calories: 135 • Total Fat 6g • Saturated 2g • Cholesterol 10mg • Sodium • 250mg • Total Carbohydrates 18g • Dietary Fiber 0g • Sugars 11 g • Protein 2g. DIETARY EXCHANGES: 1 Starch • 1 Fat • 1 Carb Choice.

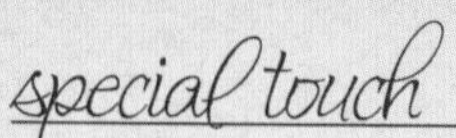

Serve the bread with 1/4 cup softened butter that you've seasoned with 1/2 teaspoon dried basil or oregano leaves.

savory biscuit monkey bread

PREP TIME: 15 Minutes ✷ READY IN: 55 Minutes ✷ SERVINGS: 10

- 1/4 cup butter or margarine, melted
- 1/2 teaspoon dry mustard
- 1 garlic clove, minced, or 1/4 teaspoon garlic powder
- 1 can (12 oz.) Pillsbury® Golden Layers™ Refrigerated Buttermilk Biscuits
- 1/4 cup grated Parmesan cheese

1. Heat oven to 400°F. In small bowl, combine butter, dry mustard and garlic; mix well. Coat bottom of 8- or 9-inch round cake pan with 2 tablespoons of the butter mixture.
2. Separate dough into 10 biscuits; cut each into quarters. Arrange biscuit pieces evenly in prepared pan. Drizzle reserved butter mixture over biscuit pieces. Sprinkle with cheese.
3. Bake for 30 to 40 minutes or until golden brown. Invert bread onto wire rack; invert again onto serving plate. Serve warm.

NUTRITION INFORMATION PER SERVING: Calories 235 • Total Fat 13g • Saturated Fat 3g • Cholesterol 0mg • Sodium 710mg • Total Carbohydrate 25g • Dietary Fiber 1g • Sugars 7g • Protein 5g. DIETARY EXCHANGES: 1-1/2 Starch • 2-1/2 Fat OR 1-1/2 Carbohydrate • 2-1/2 Fat.

candy cane coffee cake

apple-ginger scones

apple-ginger scones

PREP TIME: 30 Minutes ✳ READY IN: 50 Minutes ✳ SERVINGS: 8

Scones

- 2 cups all-purpose flour
- 1/3 cup sugar
- 3 teaspoons baking powder
- 1/2 teaspoon salt
- 6 tablespoons butter, cut into pieces
- 1/2 cup finely chopped, peeled apple
- 1/4 cup finely chopped crystallized ginger
- 1 egg
- 1/2 cup whipping cream
- 1/2 teaspoon grated lemon peel

Glaze

- 3/4 cup powdered sugar
- 2 tablespoons fresh lemon juice

1 Heat oven to 400°F. Spray cookie sheet with nonstick cooking spray. In medium bowl, combine flour, sugar, baking powder and salt; mix well. With pastry blender or fork, cut in butter until mixture resembles coarse crumbs. Stir in apple and ginger.

2 Beat egg in small bowl. Stir in the cream and the lemon peel. Add to dry ingredients; stir just until moistened.

3 On floured surface, gently knead dough 5 or 6 times. Place dough on sprayed cookie sheet; press to form 8-inch round, about 1 inch thick. Cut into 8 wedges; separate wedges slightly.

4 Bake at 400°F for 15 to 20 minutes or until light golden brown and center is set. In small bowl, combine powdered sugar and lemon juice; blend well. Drizzle the warm scones with the glaze. Serve warm.

High Altitude (3500-6500 ft): Decrease baking powder to 1-1/2 teaspoons. Bake as directed above.

NUTRITION INFORMATION PER SERVING: Calories 350 • Total Fat 15g • Saturated Fat 9g • Cholesterol 70mg • Sodium 420mg • Total Carbohydrate 50g • Dietary Fiber 1g. DIETARY EXCHANGES: 1-1/2 Starch • 2 Fruit • 3-1/2 Other Carbohydrate • 2-1/2 Fat.

Kitchen tip

Scones are a traditional Scottish quick bread. Originally scones were made with oats, cut into wedges and baked on a hot griddle. Contemporary scone recipes, both savory and sweet, are mixed with flour and baked in the oven. Whether cut into classic wedges or with a shaped cutter, scones are welcome at breakfast-, tea- or snack-time.

smoky snack mix

PREP TIME: 5 Minutes ✳ READY IN: 2 Hours 35 Minutes ✳ SERVINGS: 34

- 4 cups bite-size squares crisp corn cereal
- 3 cups whole almonds
- 1 bag (10 to 12 oz.) oyster crackers
- 1 box (9.5 to 10 oz.) bite-size cheese crackers
- 1/2 cup butter or margarine, melted
- 2 tablespoons liquid smoke
- 1 tablespoon Worcestershire sauce
- 1 teaspoon seasoned salt

1 In 6-quart slow cooker, place cereal, almonds, oyster crackers and cheese crackers. In a bowl, mix remaining ingredients until well blended. Pour butter mixture over cereal mixture; toss to coat.

2 Cook uncovered on High setting 2-1/2 hours, stirring thoroughly every 30 minutes. To serve warm, unplug slow cooker. Serve with large spoon.

NUTRITION INFORMATION PER SERVING: Calories 200 • Total Fat 12g • Saturated Fat 3g • Trans Fat 1g • Cholesterol 10mg • Sodium 270mg • Total Carbohydrate 17g • Dietary Fiber 2g • Sugars 3g • Protein 5g. DIETARY EXCHANGES: 1/2 Starch • 1/2 Other Carbohydrate • 1/2 High-Fat Meat • 1-1/2 Fat • 1 Carb Choice.

special touch

When giving jars of the muffin mix, don't forget to jot down the recipe and include it! You'll find the no-fuss recipe for Tropical Fruit Muffins below.

tropical fruit muffin mix

READY IN: 15 Minutes ✱ SERVINGS: 2 Jars of Muffin Mix

CONTAINERS
- 2 (1 quart) wide-mouth canning jars with lids
- 2 small resealable food storage plastic bags

MUFFIN MIX
- 3-3/4 cups all-purpose flour
- 1/2 cup sugar
- 5 teaspoons baking powder
- 1 teaspoon salt
- 1-1/4 cups butter-flavor or regular shortening
- 2/3 cup diced dried mangoes
- 2/3 cup diced dried pineapple

STREUSEL TOPPING MIX
- 1/3 cup all-purpose flour
- 1/3 cup sugar
- 1/4 cup finely chopped macadamia nuts

1 In large bowl, combine flour, sugar, baking powder and salt; mix well. With pastry blender, cut in shortening until mixture resembles coarse crumbs. Spoon half of flour mixture (about 3 cups) into each jar. Layer 1/3 cup mango and 1/3 cup pineapple in each jar.

2 In small bowl, combine all streusel topping ingredients; mix well. Spoon half of topping (about 1/3 cup) into each plastic bag; seal bags. Place on top of fruit layers in jars. Seal jars with lids. Include Tropical Fruit Muffins recipe. (See recipe below.)

NUTRITION INFORMATION PER SERVING: Not possible to calculate because recipe variables.

tropical fruit muffins

READY IN: 30 Minutes ✱ SERVINGS: 12 Muffins

- 1 jar Tropical Muffin Mix (recipe above)
- 3 tablespoons butter or margarine, softened
- 3/4 cup milk
- 1 egg

1 Heat oven to 400°F. Line 12 muffin cups with paper baking cups. Pour contents of small plastic bag from jar into medium bowl. Add butter; mix with fork until crumbly. Set aside for the streusel topping.

2 Pour contents of jar into large bowl; mix well. In small bowl, combine milk and egg; beat well. Pour over flour mixture; mix with fork just until dry ingredients are moistened.

3 Spoon batter evenly into paper-lined muffin cups, filling each about 3/4 full. Top each evenly with streusel topping mixture. Bake for 15 to 20 minutes or until a toothpick inserted in the center comes out clean. Serve muffins warm.

NUTRITION INFORMATION PER SERVING: Calories 280 • Total Fat 16g • Saturated Fat 5g • Cholesterol 25mg • Sodium 230mg • Total Carbohydrate 30g • Dietary Fiber 1g • Sugars 12g • Protein 4g. DIETARY EXCHANGES: 1-1/2 Starch • 1/2 Other Carbohydrate • 3 Fat • 2 Carb Choices.

olive focaccia with roasted bell pepper dip

READY IN: 35 Minutes ✱ SERVINGS: 16

Focaccia

- 3 tablespoons olive oil
- 1 can (1 lb. 1.4 oz.) Pillsbury® Refrigerated White Homestyle Loaf
- 1/4 cup coarsely chopped, pitted kalamata olives
- 1 teaspoon dried rosemary leaves, crushed
- 1/2 teaspoon dried oregano leaves

Dip

- 1 container (8 oz.) light cream cheese with roasted garlic
- 1 jar (7.25 oz.) roasted red bell peppers drained

1 Heat oven to 400°F. Grease bottom only of 15x10x1-inch baking pan with 1 tablespoon of the olive oil. Remove dough from can; carefully unroll dough. Cut in half crosswise. Place side by side in greased pan.

2 With fingertips, make indentations over both halves. Evenly brush the remaining 2 tablespoons of the oil on each half of dough. Sprinkle with olives; press lightly into dough. Sprinkle evenly with rosemary and oregano.

3 Bake for 15 to 20 minutes or until golden brown. Remove focaccia from pan; place on wire rack. Cool 5 minutes.

4 Meanwhile, in food processor bowl with metal blade, combine cream cheese and roasted peppers; process until smooth. Place in small serving bowl.

5 Cut each focaccia in half lengthwise; cut each half crosswise into 8 strips. Place strips on serving platter with dip.

NUTRITION INFORMATION PER SERVING: Calories 160 • Total Fat 8g • Saturated Fat 3g • Cholesterol 10mg • Sodium 290mg • Total Carbohydrate 16g • Dietary Fiber 1g • Sugars 2g • Protein 4g. DIETARY EXCHANGES: 1 Starch • 1-1/2 Fat OR 1 Carbohydrate • 1-1/2 Fat.

cook's notes

To save time, prepare the focaccia the day before and simply reheat it before serving. To warm the focaccia, simply wrap it in foil and bake at 375°F for 4 to 6 minutes.

Holiday Cookie Exchange

Glad tidings are bound to be had when friends gather to share a little good cheer...as well as platters of cookies, bars and other must-try treasures.

p. 227

p. 204

p. 235

p. 198

p. 236

holiday moments p. 214

chocolate ganache meringues

salted peanut chews

moonbeam cookies

moonbeam cookies

READY IN: 1 Hour ✱ SERVINGS: 36 Cookies

- 1 roll (16.5 oz.) Pillsbury® Create 'n Bake® Refrigerated Sugar Cookies
- 1 cup coconut
- 1/2 cup lemon curd (from 10-oz. jar) or lemon pie filling
- 2 oz. vanilla-flavored candy coating or almond bark, chopped, or 1/3 cup white vanilla chips

1 Heat oven to 350°F. Break up cookie dough into large bowl. Stir in coconut. Shape dough into 1-inch balls. Place 2 inches apart on ungreased cookie sheets.

2 With thumb or handle of wooden spoon, make indentation in center of each cookie. Spoon about 1/2 teaspoon lemon curd into each indentation.

3 Bake for 10 to 13 minutes or until edges are light golden brown. Immediately remove from cookie sheets; place on wire racks. Cool 5 minutes.

4 Microwave candy coating in small microwavable bowl on Medium for 2 minutes. Stir until smooth. Drizzle over cookies.

NUTRITION INFORMATION PER SERVING: Calories 90 • Total Fat 4g • Saturated Fat 2g • Cholesterol 10mg • Sodium 55mg • Total Carbohydrate 13g • Dietary Fiber 0g. DIETARY EXCHANGES: 1 Other Carbohydrate • 1 Fat.

Kitchen tip

Lemon curd is traditionally served at tea with scones, strawberry jam and clotted cream. It also makes a tasty pie and tart filling.

chocolate-covered cherry cookies

READY IN: 1 Hour 5 Minutes ✱ SERVINGS: 36 Cookies

Cookies

- 1/2 cup granulated sugar
- 3/4 cup butter, softened
- 1 teaspoon vanilla
- 1 egg yolk
- 1-1/2 cups all-purpose flour
- 1/4 cup unsweetened cocoa

Filling

- 1/4 cup butter, softened
- 1 tablespoon brandy or 1/2 teaspoon brandy extract
- 1 cup powdered sugar

Topping

- 36 maraschino cherries with stems, drained on paper towels
- 1/2 cup semisweet chocolate chips
- 1 teaspoon vegetable oil

1 Heat oven to 375°F. In large bowl, combine granulated sugar, 3/4 cup butter, the vanilla and egg yolk; beat until light and fluffy. Add flour and cocoa; beat until well mixed.

2 Shape rounded teaspoonfuls of dough into 1-inch balls; place 1 inch apart on ungreased cookie sheets. With index finger, make indentation in center of each cookie.

3 Bake for 7 to 9 minutes or until set. Immediately remove from cookie sheets. Cool 10 minutes or until completely cooled.

4 Meanwhile, in medium bowl, combine all filling ingredients; beat until smooth. Spoon about 1/2 teaspoon filling into center of each cooled cookie. Press cherry into filling.

5 In small saucepan, melt chocolate chips with oil over low heat, stirring constantly. Spoon or drizzle melted chocolate over cherry on each cookie. Let stand until chocolate is set.

NUTRITION INFORMATION PER SERVING: Calories 110 • Total Fat 6g • Saturated Fat 4g • Cholesterol 20mg • Sodium 35mg • Total Carbohydrate 13g • Dietary Fiber 0g • Sugars 9g • Protein 1g. DIETARY EXCHANGES: 1 Fat • 1 Other Carbohydrate • 1 Carb Choice.

special touch

For contrast, try spooning or drizzling melted white chocolate or almond bark over the cherries.

special touch

It's easy to create an assortment of pretty cookies. Purchase a variety of decorative cookie stamps at a cookware store. Or flatten the dough balls with interesting kitchen finds; try a fork, a meat mallet, crinkle vegetable cutter or the bottom of a fancy cut-glass cup.

cardamom print sandwich cookies

PREP TIME: 20 Minutes ✱ READY IN: 1 Hour 50 Minutes ✱ SERVINGS: 24 Cookies

COOKIES

- 1 cup firmly packed brown sugar
- 1 cup butter, softened
- 1 egg
- 2 cups all-purpose flour
- 1 teaspoon cardamom
- 1 teaspoon cinnamon
- 1/4 cup sugar

FILLING

- 2 tablespoons butter
- 1-1/4 cups powdered sugar
- 1/2 teaspoon vanilla
- 4 to 5 teaspoons milk

1 In large bowl, combine brown sugar and 1 cup butter; beat until light and fluffy. Add egg; blend well. Add flour, cardamom and cinnamon; mix well. If necessary, cover with plastic wrap; refrigerate 1 hour for easier handling.

2 Heat oven to 350°F. Shape dough into 1-inch balls; roll in sugar. Place 2 inches apart on ungreased cookie sheets. For each cookie, dip bottom of glass that has textured base in sugar; flatten dough ball to form 1-1/2-inch round.

3 Bake for 6 to 10 minutes or until firm to the touch. Immediately remove from cookie sheets. Cool 15 minutes or until completely cooled.

4 Melt 2 tablespoons butter in medium saucepan over medium heat; cook until light golden brown. Remove from heat. Stir in all remaining filling ingredients, adding enough milk for desired spreading consistency. For each sandwich cookie, spread about 1 teaspoon filling between 2 cooled cookies.

HIGH ALTITUDE (3500-6500 FT): Bake at 350°F for 8 to 12 minutes.

NUTRITION INFORMATION PER SERVING: Calories 190 • Total Fat 9g • Saturated Fat 5g • Cholesterol 30mg • Sodium 95mg • Total Carbohydrate 25g • Dietary Fiber 0g. DIETARY EXCHANGES: 1/2 Starch • 1 Fruit • 1-1/2 Other Carbohydrate • 2 Fat.

cook's notes

For easier cutting of the bars, line the baking pan with foil so it extends over the edges. After baking and cooling the bars, simply use the foil to lift the bars out of the pan.

chocolate toffee bars

PREP TIME: 20 Minutes ✱ READY IN: 1 Hour 35 Minutes ✱ SERVINGS: 36 Bars

CRUST

- 1 cup all-purpose flour
- 1/2 cup firmly packed brown sugar
- 1/2 cup butter, softened

TOPPING

- 1 cup firmly packed brown sugar
- 2 tablespoons all-purpose flour
- 1 teaspoon baking powder
- 2 eggs
- 1 package (6 oz.) semisweet chocolate chips (1 cup)
- 1/2 cup chopped nuts

1 Heat oven to 350°F. In small bowl, combine all crust ingredients; blend well. Press in bottom of ungreased 13x9-inch pan. Bake for 8 to 10 minutes or until lightly browned. Cool 5 minutes or until slightly cooled. Increase oven temperature to 375°F.

2 Meanwhile, in medium bowl, combine 1 cup brown sugar, 2 tablespoons flour, baking powder and eggs; blend well. Stir in chocolate chips and nuts. Pour topping evenly over crust, spreading slightly if necessary.

3 Bake at 375°F for 13 to 18 minutes or until deep golden brown and center is set. Cool 1 hour or until completely cooled. Cut into bars.

NUTRITION INFORMATION PER SERVING: Calories 110 • Total Fat 5g • Saturated Fat 3g • Cholesterol 20mg • Sodium 45mg • Total Carbohydrate 15g • Dietary Fiber 0g. DIETARY EXCHANGES: 1 Fruit • 1 Other Carbohydrate • 1 Fat.

cardamom print sandwich cookies

cook's notes

Add color to your tray of cookies by using a variety of jams or preserves as fillings for these gems. We used strawberry and apricot.

quick 'n nutty jam gems

READY IN: 1 Hour 20 Minutes ✱ SERVINGS: 48 Cookies

- 1 roll (16.5 oz.) Pillsbury® Create 'n Bake® Refrigerated Sugar Cookies
- 3/4 cup finely chopped peanuts
- 1/3 cup strawberry or favorite flavor jam or preserves

1 Heat oven to 350°F. Cut cookie dough into 24 slices; cut each slice in half crosswise. Shape dough into balls and roll in peanuts; place 2 inches apart on ungreased cookie sheets.

2 Bake 12 to 14 minutes or until edges are golden brown. Immediately, with back of measuring teaspoon, make indentation in each baked cookie. Fill each indentation with heaping 1/4 teaspoon jam. Remove from cookie sheets.

NUTRITION INFORMATION PER SERVING: Calories 60 • Total Fat 3g • Saturated Fat 0.5g • Cholesterol 0mg • Sodium 40mg • Total Carbohydrate 8g • Dietary Fiber 0g. DIETARY EXCHANGES: 1/2 Starch • 1/2 Fat.

snow-capped cocoa crinkles

READY IN: 1 Hour ✱ SERVINGS: 32 Cookies

1 roll (16.5 oz.) Pillsbury® Create 'n Bake® Refrigerated Sugar Cookies
1/2 cup unsweetened baking cocoa
2 teaspoons vanilla
1/2 cup powdered sugar
4 teaspoons red sugar
4 teaspoons green sugar

1 Heat oven to 325°F. In large bowl, break up cookie dough. Stir or knead in cocoa and vanilla until well blended. Divide dough in half; wrap each half in plastic wrap. Freeze 10 minutes.

2 Meanwhile, in small bowl, mix 1/4 cup of the powdered sugar and both red and green sugars; set aside.

3 Shape half of dough into 1-inch balls and roll in remaining 1/4 cup powdered sugar; place on ungreased cookie sheets. Repeat with remaining half of dough.

4 Bake 9 to 12 minutes or until set. Immediately remove from cookie sheets. Roll cookies again in red and green powdered sugar mixture; place on wire racks to cool.

HIGH ALTITUDE (3500-6500 FT): Heat oven to 350°F. Continue and bake as directed above.

NUTRITION INFORMATION PER SERVING: Calories 80 • Total Fat 3g • Saturated Fat 1g • Cholesterol 5mg • Sodium 50mg • Total Carbohydrate 13g • Dietary Fiber 0g. DIETARY EXCHANGES: 1 Other Carbohydrate • 1/2 Fat.

special touch

Children enjoy remembering their teachers during the holidays with homemade treats like these. Encourage the kids to be resourceful by packaging the goodies in recycled shortening cans, coffee cans or potato chip containers. Have the kids clean the containers and decorate them with festive gift wrap or paper illustrated with their own designs.

brown sugar oatmeal cookies

chocolate macaroon crescent bars

PREP TIME: 15 Minutes ✱ READY IN: 1 Hour 50 Minutes ✱ SERVINGS: 36 Bars

- 1 can (8 oz.) Pillsbury® Refrigerated Crescent Dinner Rolls
- 2 cups coconut
- 1 can (14 oz.) sweetened condensed milk (not evaporated)
- 1/8 to 1/4 teaspoon almond extract
- 1 package (6 oz.) semisweet chocolate chips (1 cup)
- 2 tablespoons peanut butter
- 1/2 cup chopped almonds, if desired

1 Heat oven to 375°F. Spray 13x9-inch pan with nonstick cooking spray. Unroll dough into 2 long rectangles. Place in sprayed pan; press over bottom and 1/2 inch up sides to form crust. Press edges and perforations to seal. Sprinkle coconut over crust.

2 In medium bowl, combine condensed milk and almond extract; mix well. Drizzle over coconut. Bake for 16 to 20 minutes or until golden brown. Cool 15 minutes.

3 Melt chocolate chips in small saucepan over low heat, stirring frequently. Stir in peanut butter. Spread chocolate mixture over bars. Sprinkle with almonds. Refrigerate 1 hour or until chocolate is set. Cut into bars.

NUTRITION INFORMATION PER SERVING: Calories 125 • Total Fat 6g • Saturated Fat 3g • Cholesterol 5mg • Sodium 110mg • Total Carbohydrate 16g • Dietary Fiber 0g. DIETARY EXCHANGES: 1 Starch • 1 Other Carbohydrate • 1 Fat.

special touch

These bars are ideal for serving as part of a cookie sampler tray. Cut smaller squares and place each little square in a colored foil cup before arranging them on the tray.

raspberry jam strips

maple-walnut pie bars

cook's notes

Feel free to top the warm candy coating with toasted coconut flakes or chopped nuts.

nutty chocolate-pretzel bars

PREP TIME: 20 Minutes ✱ READY IN: 1 Hour 30 Minutes ✱ SERVINGS: 36 Bars

- 1 can (10 oz.) deluxe salted mixed nuts (coarsely chop Brazil nuts)
- 1 roll (16.5 oz.) Pillsbury® Create 'n Bake® Refrigerated Sugar Cookies
- 1 cup toffee bits
- 1-1/2 cups milk chocolate chips
- 1/3 cup butterscotch chips
- 1/3 cup creamy peanut butter
- 1 cup coarsely chopped salted pretzels
- 1 oz. vanilla-flavored candy coating or almond bark, chopped

1 Heat oven to 375°F. Spray 13x9-inch pan with nonstick cooking spray. Spread nuts evenly in pan. Cut cookie dough into 1/2-inch-thick slices; arrange slices over nuts. With floured fingers, press dough evenly in pan to form crust. Sprinkle toffee bits evenly over crust; press in lightly. Bake 20 to 25 minutes or until golden brown. Cool on wire rack 30 minutes.

2 In large microwavable bowl, microwave chocolate chips and butterscotch chips on High 1-1/2 to 2 minutes or until melted, stirring every 30 seconds until smooth. Stir in peanut butter until well blended. Fold in pretzels. Spread mixture evenly over cooled baked crust.

3 In small microwavable bowl, microwave candy coating on High 30 to 60 seconds or until melted, stirring every 15 seconds until smooth. Drizzle over bars. Refrigerate until chocolate is set, about 15 minutes. Cut into bars.

NUTRITION INFORMATION PER SERVING: Calories 210 • Total Fat 13g • Saturated Fat 4.5g • Cholesterol 10mg • Sodium 130mg • Total Carbohydrate 20g • Dietary Fiber 1g. DIETARY EXCHANGES: 1/2 Starch • 1 Other Carbohydrate • 2-1/2 Fat.

chocolate-glazed peppermint cookies

READY IN: 45 Minutes ✱ SERVINGS: 36 Cookies

Cookies

1 package (18 oz.) Pillsbury® Refrigerated Sugar Cookies, well chilled

3 tablespoons finely crushed hard peppermint candy

Glaze

1/2 cup semisweet chocolate chips

1-1/2 teaspoons shortening

1 Heat oven to 350°F. Cut cookie dough into 1/4-inch slices. Place slices 2 inches apart on ungreased cookie sheets. Sprinkle 1/4 teaspoon peppermint candy in center of each slice.

2 Bake for 7 to 11 minutes or until light golden brown. Cool 1 minute; remove from cookie sheets. Cool 15 minutes or until completely cooled.

3 In small saucepan, melt chocolate chips and shortening over low heat, stirring constantly. Drizzle glaze over cooled cookies. Let stand until set.

NUTRITION INFORMATION PER SERVING: Calories 80 • Total Fat 3g • Saturated Fat 1g • Cholesterol 2mg • Sodium 65mg • Total Carbohydrate 12g • Dietary Fiber 0g • Sugars 0g • Protein 1g. DIETARY EXCHANGES: 1/2 Starch • 1/2 Fat OR 1/2 Carbohydrate • 1/2 Fat.

Kitchen tip

Slice chilled cookie dough with a serrated knife, sawing gently back and forth rather than pushing the knife smoothly through the dough. Give the roll of dough a slight turn after cutting each cookie to prevent the roll from flattening too much.

candy bar-oatmeal cookies

holiday moments

festive two-in-one bars

sugar-and-spice shortbread sticks

tropical oatmeal cookies

white chocolate macaroons

almond gingers

reindeer spice cookies

cook's notes

To keep your fingers from getting sticky, use a small plastic bag, mitten-style, to grease the pan and to press the mixture into the pan. Or, spray your hands with nonstick cooking spray before pressing the mixture in the pan.

fruit and nut snack bars

PREP TIME: 20 Minutes ✱ READY IN: 50 Minutes ✱ SERVINGS: 36 Bars

Snack Mix

- 4 cups Cheerios® cereal
- 1/2 cup chopped dried apricots
- 1/2 cup raisins
- 1/2 cup shelled sunflower seeds
- 1/2 cup salted peanuts
- 1/2 cup flaked coconut

Syrup

- 3/4 cup firmly packed brown sugar
- 1/2 cup corn syrup
- 1/4 cup peanut butter
- 1 teaspoon vanilla extract

1 Grease 13x9-inch pan with nonstick cooking spray. In large bowl, combine all snack mix ingredients; mix well. Set aside.

2 In medium saucepan, combine all syrup ingredients except vanilla. Cook over medium-high heat until mixture comes to a boil, stirring constantly. Boil 1 minute. Remove from the heat. Stir in vanilla extract.

3 Pour syrup over snack mix; toss to coat. Press mixture firmly in greased pan. Cool 30 minutes or until completely cooled. Cut into bars. Store in tightly covered container.

NUTRITION INFORMATION PER SERVING: Calories 105 • Total Fat 4g • Saturated Fat 1g • Cholesterol 0mg • Sodium 70mg • Total Carbohydrate 15g • Dietary Fiber 1g. DIETARY EXCHANGES: 1/2 Starch • 1/2 Other Carbohydrate • 1 Fat.

maple leaf cream wafers

peanut butter sandwich chippers

easy caramel-filled chocolate chip cookies

PREP TIME: 40 Minutes ✱ SERVINGS: 12 Cookies

- 1 package (16 oz.) Pillsbury® Big Deluxe Classics® Refrigerated Chocolate Chip Cookies (12 cookies)
- 12 chewy chocolate-coated caramel candies, unwrapped
- 1/4 cup milk chocolate chips
- 1/2 teaspoon shortening

1 Heat oven to 350°F. For each cookie, shape 1 unbaked cookie around 1 caramel candy, covering the candy completely.

2 Place the cookies, with the thickest part of the dough down, 2-1/2 inches apart on ungreased large cookie sheet.

3 Bake for 12 to 15 minutes or until golden brown. Cool 2 minutes. Remove from cookie sheet; place on wire racks. Cool 15 minutes or until completely cooled.

4 In small microwavable bowl, combine chocolate chips and shortening. Microwave on High for 30 seconds. Stir; continue microwaving, stirring every 10 seconds, until chocolate is melted and can be stirred smooth. Drizzle chocolate over cooled cookies. Let stand until the chocolate is completely set before storing.

NUTRITION INFORMATION PER SERVING: Calories 250 • Total Fat 12g • Saturated Fat 5g • Cholesterol 10mg • Sodium 140mg • Total Carbohydrate 31g • Dietary Fiber 1g. DIETARY EXCHANGES: 1/2 Starch • 1-1/2 Other Carbohydrate • 2-1/2 Fat.

cook's notes

Some candy may melt out and stick onto the cookie sheet during baking. If this occurs, cool the cookies before removing them from the sheet. Worried about sticky cookies? Just line the cookie sheet with parchment paper.

cook's notes

Six ounces of white chocolate baking bar may be used in place of the white chocolate chunks; coarsely chop the bar before adding it to the dough.

cashew-white chocolate drops

READY IN: 40 Minutes ✱ SERVINGS: 36 Cookies

- 3/4 cup firmly packed brown sugar
- 1/2 cup sugar
- 1 cup butter, softened
- 2 teaspoons milk
- 1 teaspoon vanilla
- 1 egg
- 2 cups all-purpose flour
- 1 teaspoon baking soda
- 1 cup coarsely chopped cashew halves and pieces
- 1 cup white chocolate chunks (from 12-oz. pkg.)

1 Heat oven to 375°F. In large bowl, combine brown sugar, sugar and butter; beat until light and fluffy. Add milk, vanilla and egg; blend well. Add flour and baking soda; mix well. Stir in cashews and chocolate chunks.

2 Drop dough by rounded tablespoonfuls 2 inches apart onto ungreased cookie sheets. Bake for 8 to 10 minutes or until light golden brown. Cool 1 minute; remove from cookie sheets.

HIGH ALTITUDE (3500-6500 FT): Decrease butter to 3/4 cup. Bake as directed above.

NUTRITION INFORMATION PER SERVING: Calories 160 • Total Fat [illegible] Saturated Fat 5g • Cholesterol 20mg • Sodium 100mg • Total Carbohydrate 18g • Dietary Fiber 0g. DIETARY EXCHANGES: [illegible]

cook's notes

Cookie monsters of all ages love this recipe. Moms like the big batch, perfect for bake sales, scout meetings and parties.

monster cookies

READY IN: 1 Hour 15 Minutes ✱ SERVINGS: 48 Cookies

- 1 cup sugar
- 1 cup firmly packed brown sugar
- 1 cup peanut butter
- 1/2 cup butter, softened
- 3 eggs
- 4-1/2 cups quick-cooking rolled oats
- 2 teaspoons baking soda
- 1 package (6 oz.) semisweet chocolate chips (1 cup)
- 1 cup candy-coated chocolate pieces
- 1 cup chopped peanuts
- 1/2 cup raisins

1 Heat oven to 350°F. In large bowl, combine sugar, brown sugar, peanut butter and butter; beat until light and fluffy. Add eggs, 1 at a time, beating well after each addition. Add oats and baking soda; mix well. Stir in chocolate chips, chocolate pieces, peanuts and raisins.

2 Drop dough by heaping tablespoonfuls 2-1/2 inches apart onto ungreased cookie sheets. Bake for 11 to 14 minutes or until light golden brown. Cool 2 minutes; remove from cookie sheets.

HIGH ALTITUDE (3500-6500 FT): Add 1/4 cup water with eggs; add 1/4 cup all-purpose flour with oats. Bake at 350°F for 13 to 16 minutes.

NUTRITION INFORMATION PER SERVING: Calories 185 • Total Fat 9g • Saturated Fat 3g • Cholesterol 20mg • Sodium 115mg • Total Carbohydrate 22g • Dietary Fiber 1g. DIETARY EXCHANGES: 1-1/2 Starch • 1-1/2 Fat.

chocolate-peanut butter cookie bars

PREP TIME: 15 Minutes ✷ READY IN: 1 Hour 55 Minutes ✷ SERVINGS: 24 Bars

- 1 roll (16.5 oz.) Pillsbury® Create 'n Bake® Refrigerated Chocolate Chip Cookies
- 3 cups powdered sugar
- 1 cup peanut butter
- 2 tablespoons butter or margarine, softened
- 1/4 cup water
- 1 cup milk chocolate chips, melted
- 24 pecan halves, if desired

1 Heat oven to 350°F. Cut cookie dough in half crosswise. Cut each section in half lengthwise. With floured fingers, press dough in bottom of ungreased 9-inch square pan. Bake for 16 to 24 minutes or until golden brown. Cool 15 minutes.

2 In medium bowl, combine powdered sugar, peanut butter, butter and water; mix well. (If necessary, add additional water 1 teaspoon at a time up to 1 tablespoon until mixture is smooth.) Drop spoonfuls of mixture over baked cookie crust; press evenly to cover crust.

3 Spread melted chocolate chips over peanut butter mixture. If desired, decoratively swirl chocolate with fork. Garnish with pecan halves. Refrigerate 1 hour or until chocolate is set. Cut into bars.

NUTRITION INFORMATION PER SERVING: Calories 260 • Total Fat 13g • Saturated Fat 4g • Cholesterol 5mg • Sodium 120mg • Total Carbohydrate 33g • Dietary Fiber 1g. DIETARY EXCHANGES: 1 Starch • 1 Other Carbohydrate • 2-1/2 Fat.

kitchen tip

Use an offset or angled metal spatula to perfectly and evenly spread the frosting on the bars. Look for offset spatulas in kitchenware stores.

guess again candy crunch

READY IN: 35 Minutes ✷ SERVINGS: 50 Pieces

- 1/2 cup white chocolate candy melts for candy making
- 1/2 cup extra-crunchy or creamy peanut butter
- 1 cup Progresso® plain bread crumbs
- 1 cup light or dark chocolate candy melts for candy making
- 1/4 cup dry-roasted peanuts, finely chopped

1 Line large cookie sheet with waxed paper. In small microwavable bowl, combine white chocolate candy melts and peanut butter. Microwave on Medium for 2 minutes. Stir mixture until smooth.

2 Add bread crumbs; mix well. Place on waxed paper-lined cookie sheet. Place another sheet of waxed paper over mixture; pat or roll to form 11x7-inch rectangle (1/4-inch thick). Remove top sheet of waxed paper.

3 Place 1/2 cup of the light chocolate candy melts in small microwavable bowl. Microwave on Medium for 2 minutes. Stir until smooth. Spread evenly over peanut butter layer on cookie sheet. Sprinkle with 2 tablespoons of the peanuts. Refrigerate 10 minutes to set chocolate.

4 Meanwhile, place remaining 1/2 cup light chocolate candy melts in same small microwavable bowl. Microwave on Medium for 2 minutes. Stir until smooth.

5 Remove candy from refrigerator. Turn candy over on cookie sheet; remove waxed paper. Spread light chocolate over candy. Immediately sprinkle with remaining 2 tablespoons peanuts. Refrigerate 10 minutes or until set. Break or cut candy into small pieces.

High Altitude (3500-6500 ft): Watch candy closely during microwaving to avoid scorching or burning.

NUTRITION INFORMATION PER SERVING: Calories 65 • Total Fat 4g • Saturated Fat 1g • Cholesterol 0mg • Sodium 40mg • Total Carbohydrate 6g • Dietary Fiber 0g. DIETARY EXCHANGE: 1 Fat.

cook's notes

Chopped vanilla-flavored and chocolate-flavored candy coating or white vanilla chips and semisweet chocolate chips can be substituted for the white and light chocolate candy melts for candy making.

Merry Kitchen Creations

Deck the halls with this cute collection of shaped cookies, creative cakes and other fun bites. Each adorable idea is sure to delight the child in everyone.

p. 264

p. 267

p. 251

p. 248

p. 260

holiday cereal bears p. 255

santa's reindeer cookies

santa's reindeer cookies

READY IN: 1 Hour ✱ SERVINGS: 48 Cookies

- 1 roll (18 oz.) refrigerated sugar cookies, well chilled
- 4 tablespoons all-purpose flour
- 1/3 cup vanilla ready-to-spread frosting (from 16-oz. can)
- 4 cups (108) small pretzel twists
- 14 candied red or green cherries, cut into quarters, or spice drop candies
- 1/3 cup raisins

1 Heat oven to 350°F. Cut cookie dough in half; unwrap one half and refrigerate remaining half of dough until needed. Coat sides of dough with 2 tablespoons of the flour.

2 Roll out dough to form 9-inch square, using additional flour as needed to prevent sticking. Cut square into 4 (2-1/4-inch) strips; cut each strip into 6 equal triangles. Place on ungreased cookie sheet.

3 Bake at 350°F for 6 to 8 minutes or until light golden brown. Cool 1 minute; remove from cookie sheet. Cool 10 minutes or until completely cooled. Repeat with remaining half of dough and flour.

4 Spread frosting over cookies. Press pretzels into top 2 corners of each cookie to resemble antlers. Place cherry piece at bottom to resemble nose. Place raisins on frosting for eyes. Let stand until frosting is set before storing.

NUTRITION INFORMATION PER SERVING: Calories 130 • Total Fat 4g • Saturated Fat 3g • Cholesterol 0mg • Sodium 230mg • Total Carbohydrate 22g • Dietary Fiber 1g • Sugars 10g • Protein 2g. DIETARY EXCHANGES: 1 Starch • 1 Fat • 1/2 Other Carbohydrate • 1-1/2 Carb Choices.

cook's note

Ready-to-spread chocolate frosting can be used in place of the vanilla frosting, and chocolate chips or white vanilla chips can be used instead of the raisins. Or, mix and match so each cookie has a unique look.

santa claus cake

PREP TIME: 50 Minutes ✱ READY IN: 2 Hours 15 Minutes ✱ SERVINGS: 12

Cake

- 1 box (1 lb. 2.25 oz.) yellow cake mix with pudding
- 1-1/4 cups water
- 1/3 cup vegetable oil
- 3 eggs

Frosting and Decorations

- 1 large marshmallow
- 1 container (1 lb.) creamy ready-to-spread vanilla frosting
- 1/2 cup flaked coconut
- 1 to 2 tablespoons red sugar
- 1 teaspooon red edible glitter
- 1 large green gumdrop, halved
- 1 miniature marshmallow
- 3 strands pull-apart red licorice twists

1 Heat oven to 350°F (if using dark or nonstick pans, heat oven to 325°F). Generously grease 13x9-inch pan with shortening; lightly flour. In large bowl, beat cake mix, water, oil and eggs with electric mixer on low speed 30 seconds or until blended. Beat on medium speed 2 minutes, scraping bowl occasionally.

2 Bake 29 to 34 minutes or until toothpick inserted in center comes out clean. Cool 15 minutes. Carefully remove cake from pan. Cool completely.

3 From bottom of pan, cut two 6-1/4-inch triangles. Cover 22x12-inch piece of heavy cardboard with foil. Cut and assemble cake pieces on cardboard, placing cut triangles at the top for the hat.

4 Frost large marshmallow with vanilla frosting; dip in coconut. Set aside. Frost assembled cake with remaining vanilla frosting. Sprinkle red sugar on cake for top of hat; sprinkle red edible glitter on top of red sugar. Sprinkle coconut on cake for border of hat and beard.

5 Place large coconut-coated marshmallow on top of hat for tassel. Place gumdrop halves, sugar-side-up, on cake for eyes, mini marshmallow for nose and red licorice twists for mouth. Sprinkle red sugar on cake for cheeks.

NUTRITION INFORMATION PER SERVING: Calories 450 • Total Fat 20g • Saturated Fat 6g • Trans Fat 4g • Cholesterol 55mg • Sodium 400mg • Total Carbohydrate 65g • Dietary Fiber 0g • Sugars 46g • Protein 3g. DIETARY EXCHANGES: 1/2 Starch • 4 Other Carbohydrate • 4 Fat 4 Carb Choices.

cook's notes

Express your own "Santa-artistry" by using miniature marshmallows instead of coconut for the hat border and beard—or try something completely different.

cook's notes

If you have gingerbread dough left over, follow the directions on the cookie package for cut-out cookies. You could decorate them at the same time you do the carolers.

caroling kids

PREP TIME: 2 Hours ✱ READY IN: 2 Hours 20 Minutes ✱ SERVINGS: 20 Cookies

- 1 roll (16.5 oz.) Pillsbury® Create 'n Bake® Refrigerated Sugar Cookies
- 1/4 roll (from 16.5-oz. size) Pillsbury® Create 'n Bake® Refrigerated Gingerbread Cookies
- Round or flower-shaped candy sprinkles
- Miniature candy-coated baking bits
- Drinking straw
- Red sugar
- Red and green decorating gel (or other colors as desired)

1 Heat oven to 350°F. Remove half of sugar cookie dough from wrapper; refrigerate remaining dough until needed. Cut half of dough into 15 (about 1/4-inch-thick) slices. Leave 10 slices whole to resemble carolers' heads; place 2 inches apart on ungreased large cookie sheet.

2 Cut remaining 5 slices in half crosswise to make collars and hats (see photo). For collars, cut half slice into 2 pieces and attach under head. For hats, shape half slice of dough with fingers into hat shape; do not attach at this point.

3 Place small portions of gingerbread dough into garlic press. Press to make long, short and medium hair; attach to heads gently. Add hats to top of heads as desired.

4 Place candy sprinkles (blue or green) on face for eyes. With drinking straw, poke hole for mouth. If desired, shape small pieces of gingerbread dough for earmuffs. Sprinkle red sugar on cheeks to resemble blush. Repeat with remaining dough.

5 Bake 11 to 13 minutes or until light golden brown. Cool 1 minute; carefully remove from cookie sheet and place on wire racks. If necessary, re-poke hole for mouth. Cool completely, about 20 minutes. Decorate hats, collars and faces with decorating gel.

HIGH ALTITUDE (3500-6500 FT): Bake at 350°F 13 to 15 minutes. Continue as directed above.

NUTRITION INFORMATION PER SERVING: Calories 210 • Total Fat 10g • Saturated Fat 2.5g • Cholesterol 15mg • Sodium 150mg • Total Carbohydrate 28g • Dietary Fiber 0g. DIETARY EXCHANGES: 2 Other Carbohydrate • 2 Fat.

special touch

These ornaments are great gifts that your children can make themselves for the special people in their lives. Use these edible decorations as party favors for children's holiday parties.

kiddy pop ornaments

READY IN: 15 Minutes ✱ SERVINGS: Varies

- Assorted small candies
- Suckers with looped handles, unwrapped
- Vanilla frosting (from 16-oz. can)

1 To make ornaments, attach candies to suckers using frosting. Let stand until dry. Place on tree using looped handles of suckers as hangers.

NUTRITION INFORMATION PER SERVING: Not possible to calculate because of recipe variables.

caroling kids

candy clay

candy clay

PREP TIME: 15 Minutes ✻ READY IN: 1 Hour 45 Minutes ✻ SERVINGS: 12 Candies

- 10 oz. vanilla-flavored candy coating or almond bark, cut into pieces
- 1/3 cup light corn syrup
- 4 food colors
- 2 teaspoons assorted small candies

1 Line 8-inch square pan with foil; spray foil with nonstick cooking spray. Place candy coating in medium microwavable bowl. Microwave on High for 1 minute. Stir; continue to microwave in 15-second increments until coating can be stirred smooth.

2 Add corn syrup; blend well. Spread candy-coating mixture evenly in sprayed foil-lined pan. Let stand at room temperature for 20 to 60 minutes or until dough is firm enough to handle.

3 Spray inside of 4 food storage plastic bags with nonstick cooking spray. Divide dough into 4 sections. Squeeze each section with hands until workable. To color each section, place dough in sprayed bag. Add food color as desired (about 1/8 teaspoon for 1/4 of dough); knead dough until color is well blended. Turn bag inside out; scrape out dough. Let stand 15 to 30 minutes before sculpting.

4 Cut each section of clay into 3 pieces. Sculpt clay as desired. Decorate with small candies. Candy clay will harden when exposed to air. (Store unused clay in sealed plastic bag. Before sculpting, knead with hands to soften or microwave several seconds.)

NUTRITION INFORMATION PER SERVING: Calories 165 • Total Fat 8g • Saturated Fat 5g • Cholesterol 5mg • Sodium 35mg • Total Carbohydrate 22g • Dietary Fiber 0g • Sugars 19g • Protein 1g. DIETARY EXCHANGES: 1/2 Starch • 2 Fat • 1/2 Other Carbohydrate • 1 Carb Choice.

special touch

Try rolling the dough in edible glitter or decorative sugar. Not only does it make the dough easier to shape, but it also adds a festive touch.

easy santa cookies

PREP TIME:1 Hour ✻ READY IN: 2 Hours ✻ SERVINGS: 34 Cookies

COOKIES
- 1 roll (16.5 oz.) refrigerated sugar cookies

FROSTING
- 2 cups powdered sugar
- 2 tablespoons butter or margarine, softened
- 2 to 3 tablespoons milk
- 2 to 3 drops red food color

DECORATIONS
- 68 semisweet chocolate chips (about 1/4 cup)
- 34 red cinnamon candies
- 2/3 cup coconut
- 34 miniature marshmallows

1 Freeze cookie dough at least 1 hour. Heat oven to 350°F. Cut frozen dough into 1/4-inch slices. (Return dough to freezer if it becomes too soft to cut.) Place slices 3 inches apart on ungreased cookie sheets. Bake 8 to 12 minutes or until golden brown. Cool 2 minutes; remove from cookie sheets. Cool completely.

2 Meanwhile, in small bowl, beat powdered sugar, butter and enough milk for desired spreading consistency until smooth. In another small bowl, place half of frosting. Add red food color; stir until blended.

3 Frost cooled cookies with red and white frosting. Use small amount of frosting to attach chocolate chips for eyes and cinnamon candy for nose. Gently press coconut into white frosting for beard. Press marshmallow into red frosting for tassel on cap. Let stand until frosting is set. Store between sheets of waxed paper in tightly covered container.

NUTRITION INFORMATION PER SERVING: Calories 110 • Total Fat 4g • Saturated Fat 2g • Trans Fat 0.5g • Cholesterol 5mg • Sodium 45mg • Total Carbohydrate 18g • Dietary Fiber 0g • Sugars 13g • Protein 0g. DIETARY EXCHANGES: 1 Other Carbohydrate • 1 Fat • 1 Carb Choice.

special touch

For a great stocking stuffer, make Santa Cookie Pops: insert a wooden stick with rounded ends or cookie stick halfway into each cookie before baking. Wrap finished "pops" with colored plastic wrap, leaving the stick unwrapped, and tie.

cook's notes

To avoid breaking a candy bar during assembly, insert a toothpick completely through a gumdrop. Place the gumdrop on a candy bar and continue pressing the toothpick through the candy bar.

candy train

READY IN: 1 Hour ✱ SERVINGS: Vary

- Fun-size candy bars, unwrapped
- Candy bar miniatures, unwrapped
- Chocolate frosting (from 16-oz. can)
- Bite-sized round buttery crackers and/or bite-sized creme-filled sandwich cookies, separated
- Frilly-topped toothpicks
- Assorted candies

1 For each engine, attach candy bar miniature to top of fun-size candy bar with frosting. Attach bite-sized crackers and cookie halves to sides as wheels. To form smokestack, attach 1 candy, wide end up, to top with toothpick.

2 For coal car or log car, with frosting, attach crackers to fun-size bar. With frosting, attach candies for cargo or pretzel sticks for logs. Let stand until frosting is set.

NUTRITION INFORMATION PER SERVING: Not possible to calculate because of recipe variables.

holiday biscuit cutouts

PREP TIME: 15 Minutes ✱ READY IN: 35 Minutes ✱ SERVINGS: 12 Biscuits

- 2-1/4 cups all-purpose flour
- 2 teaspoons baking powder
- 1/2 teaspoon baking soda
- 1/4 teaspoon salt
- 1/2 lb. bulk pork sausage, cooked, crumbled and well drained
- 2 tablespoons butter or margarine
- 1/4 cup finely chopped pecans
- 3/4 to 1 cup buttermilk
- 2 tablespoons milk

1 Heat oven to 400°F. Grease cookie sheet with shortening. In large bowl, mix flour, baking powder, baking soda and salt. Using fork or pastry blender, cut in sausage, butter and pecans until mixture resembles fine crumbs. Stir in buttermilk, adding enough to form soft dough.

2 Turn dough out onto well-floured surface; knead dough 5 to 6 times. On lightly floured surface, roll out dough to 1/2-inch thickness. Cut with floured 3-inch holiday cookie cutter or 3-inch biscuit cutter. Place biscuits 2 inches apart on cookie sheet; brush with milk.

3 Bake 15 to 20 minutes or until light golden brown. Immediately remove from cookie sheet. Cool slightly on cooling rack.

NUTRITION INFORMATION PER SERVING: Calories 160 • Total Fat 7g • Saturated Fat 2.5g • Trans Fat 0g • Cholesterol 15mg • Sodium 280mg • Total Carbohydrate 19g • Dietary Fiber 0g • Sugars 1g • Protein 5g. DIETARY EXCHANGES: 1/2 Starch • 1 Other Carbohydrate • 1/2 High-Fat Meat • 1/2 Fat.

kitchen tip

To substitute for buttermilk, use 2-1/4 to 3 teaspoons vinegar or lemon juice plus milk to make 3/4 to 1 cup.

candy train

peppermint-bark hearts

peppermint-bark hearts

PREP TIME: 20 Minutes ✱ READY IN: 50 Minutes ✱ SERVINGS: 9 Candy Hearts

- 18 (2-1/2-inch) peppermint candy canes, unwrapped
- 5 oz. vanilla-flavored candy coating or almond bark, chopped
- 2 teaspoons crushed peppermint candy canes

1 Line cookie sheet with waxed paper. Arrange candy canes on waxed paper in groups of 2 with ends touching to form heart shapes.

2 Place candy coating in 2-cup microwavable measuring cup. Microwave on Medium for 2 to 3 minutes, stirring once halfway through cooking time. Stir until melted and smooth.

3 Spoon or pipe candy coating into centers of hearts to fill spaces. Sprinkle with crushed candy canes. Cool 30 minutes or until set.

NUTRITION INFORMATION: Calories 110 • Total Fat 5g • Saturated Fat 3g • Cholesterol 5mg • Sodium 15mg • Total Carbohydrate 15g • Dietary Fiber 0g • Sugars 16g • Protein 1g. DIETARY EXCHANGES: 1 Fat • 1 Other Carbohydrate • 1 Carb Choice.

cook's notes

Chocolate-flavored candy coating can be used instead of vanilla-flavored candy coating. Or make two batches—one of each!

holiday cereal bears

PREP TIME: 30 Minutes ✱ READY IN: 1 Hour ✱ SERVINGS: 7 Bears

- 1/4 cup butter or margarine
- 1 package (10 oz.) regular marshmallows
- 6 Cups Nestlé Nesquik™ cereal
- 1 tablespoon chocolate chips
- 7 small candy hearts
- 7 miniature red candy-coated chocolate baking bits
- 14 miniature blue candy-coated chocolate baking bits
- 21 miniature green candy-coated chocolate baking bits
- Red chewy fruit snack rolls (from 4.5-oz. package)

1 Melt butter in Dutch oven over medium-low heat. Add marshmallows; cook until marshmallows are melted, stirring frequently. Stir in cereal until well coated. Cool 5 minutes.

2 Meanwhile, line large cookie sheet with waxed paper; spray paper with nonstick cooking spray. Spray inside of 5- to 6-inch open bear cookie cutter. Place sprayed cookie cutter on sprayed waxed paper. Generously butter or spray hands and fingers.

3 Press cereal mixture into cookie cutter, packing tightly. Remove cookie cutter; place in different spot on waxed paper. Continue forming bears until all mixture is used. If necessary, respray cookie cutter.

4 Place chocolate chips in small microwave-safe bowl. Microwave on High for 30 seconds; stir until melted and smooth. If necessary, microwave an additional 20 seconds. Attach candy heart to each bear with small amount of melted chocolate.

5 With melted chocolate, attach red baking bits for noses, blue baking bits for eyes and green baking bits for buttons. Cut strips of chewy fruit snack rolls and tie around neck of each bear. Let stand 30 minutes to set. Wrap each bear in plastic wrap or cellophane.

NUTRITION INFORMATION PER SERVING: Calories 365 • Calories from Fat 90 • Total Fat 10g • Saturated Fat 5g • Cholesterol 20mg • Sodium 290mg • Total Carbohydrate 67g • Dietary Fiber 1g • Sugars 41g • Protein 2g. DIETARY EXCHANGES: 1 Starch • 3-1/2 Other Carbohydrate • 2 Fat • 4-1/2 Carb Choices.

cook's notes

Can't find heart-shaped candies? Make gumdrop hearts: Flatten small red gumdrops with a rolling pin and use a tiny heart-shaped cookie cutter or the tip of a knife to shape the small hearts.

cook's notes

If your children don't like coconut, just decorate the hat brims with mini marshmallows instead.

elf hat cookies

PREP TIME: 1 Hour ✱ READY IN: 1 Hour ✱ SERVINGS: 16 Cookies

- 1 roll (18 oz.) Pillsbury® Refrigerated Sugar Cookies
- 1 can (16 oz.) creamy white ready-to-spread frosting
- 1/2 teaspoon red food color
- 1/2 teaspoon green food color
- 1/3 cup coconut, if desired
- Miniature marshmallows and/or small gumdrops

1 Heat oven to 350°F. Cut cookie dough in half lengthwise to make 2 long pieces; refrigerate one half until ready to use. On floured surface, roll half of dough into 8x5-1/2-inch rectangle (use edge of ruler to make sides straight).

2 With sharp knife, cut dough rectangle crosswise into 4 (5-1/2x2-inch) rectangles. Cut each small rectangle diagonally into 2 triangles; place triangles 2 inches apart on ungreased large cookie sheet. Bend tops of triangles as desired to resemble stocking caps.

3 Bake 7 to 11 minutes or until edges are light golden brown. Cool 1 minute; remove from cookie sheet. Cool completely, about 15 minutes. Repeat with remaining half of dough.

4 Divide frosting into 3 small bowls. Leaving 1 portion white, stir red and green food color into remaining portions. Frost each cookie with about 1 tablespoon red or green frosting. Frost about 1 inch of short side of each triangle with about 1-1/2 teaspoons white frosting for hat brim. Sprinkle brims with coconut. Place marshmallows on ends of hats for tassels. Let stand until set before storing.

High Altitude (3500-6500 ft): In Step 3, bake 9 to 13 minutes.

NUTRITION INFORMATION PER SERVING: Calories 260 • Total Fat 10g • Saturated Fat 5g • Cholesterol 10mg • Sodium 85mg • Total Carbohydrate 41g • Dietary Fiber 0g • Sugars 31g • Protein 1g. DIETARY EXCHANGES: 3 Other Carbohydrate • 2 Fat • 3 Carb Choices.

cook's notes

Help children roll the dough and make the penguins. Then, when they are cooled, set up the table with all of the decorations. Decorate one penguin as an example, then let kids decorate their own.

penguin cuties

READY IN: 1 Hour 50 Minutes ✱ SERVINGS: 16 Cookies

- 1 roll (16.5 oz.) Pillsbury® Create 'n Bake® Refrigerated Sugar Cookies
- Fluffy white whipped ready-to-spread frosting (from 12-oz. can)
- Orange decorating gel
- Black decorating gel
- Any red and/or green chewy fruit snack in three-foot rolls, if desired
- Red and/or green decorating gel, if desired

1 Heat oven to 350°F. Remove half of cookie dough from wrapper; refrigerate remaining dough until needed. Shape dough into 8 large (1-inch) balls, 24 medium (3/4-inch) balls and 16 small (1/2-inch) balls.

2 On ungreased cookie sheet, to make each penguin, press 1 large ball to form oval 1/4 inch thick for body. Place 1 medium ball on one end to resemble head, pressing to 1/4-inch thickness. Roll 2 medium balls into ropes; attach to sides of body. Flatten 2 small balls to resemble feet; attach to body. Repeat with remaining half of dough.

3 Bake 11 to 14 minutes or until edges are golden brown. Cool 1 minute; carefully remove from cookie sheet and place on wire racks. Cool completely, about 20 minutes.

4 Spread fluffy white frosting on cooled cookies. Use orange gel to outline feet and make beak on head. Use black gel to outline penguin face and decorate body. Cut chewy fruit snack to make scarf for around neck or use decorating gel to make bow tie.

High Altitude (3500-6500 ft): Bake at 350°F 13 to 16 minutes. Continue as directed above.

NUTRITION INFORMATION PER SERVING: Calories 270 • Total Fat 8g • Sodium 110mg • Total Carbohydrate 48g • Dietary Fiber 0g.

elf hat cookies

"gingerbread boy" chocolate cake

"gingerbread boy" chocolate cake

PREP TIME: 55 Minutes ✱ READY IN: 2 Hours ✱ SERVINGS: 16

Cake

- 1 box (1 lb. 2.25 oz.) German chocolate cake mix with pudding
- 1-1/4 cups water
- 1/2 cup vegetable oil
- 3 eggs
- 1 cup semisweet chocolate chips (16 oz.)

Frosting and Decorations

- 1 container (1 lb.) vanilla creamy ready-to-spread frosting
- 1 container (1 lb.) chocolate creamy ready-to-spread frosting
- 3 large red gumdrops
- 2 milk chocolate stars

1 Heat oven to 350°F (if using dark or nonstick pans, heat oven to 325°F). Grease bottom of 13x9-inch pan with shortening; line with waxed paper. Grease waxed paper with shortening; lightly flour. Generously grease 5-inch round ovenproof bowl that holds at least 1 cup with shortening; lightly flour.

2 In large bowl, beat cake mix, water, oil and eggs with electric mixer on low speed 30 seconds or until moistened. Beat on medium speed 2 minutes, scraping bowl occasionally. Pour 1/2 cup batter into greased and floured bowl; pour remaining batter into pan. Sprinkle 2 tablespoons of the chocolate chips on batter in bowl; sprinkle remaining chips on batter in pan.

3 Bake bowl 17 to 22 minutes and pan 27 to 35 minutes or until cake springs back when touched lightly in center.

4 Cool cakes in bowl and pan 10 minutes. Invert cakes onto cooling rack; remove waxed paper. Cool completely, about 30 minutes. To easily cut and shape cake shapes, chill it thoroughly in refrigerator or freezer before cutting it in step 6. Invert onto flat serving tray or foil-covered cardboard, about 20x14 inches.

5 Spoon 1/2 cup of the vanilla frosting into resealable food-storage plastic bag. Seal bag; set aside. In medium bowl, blend remaining vanilla frosting and the chocolate frosting.

6 Using serrated knife, cut cake into body as shown in photo. Spread cut edge of neck with frosting; attach round cake for head. Spread thin layer of frosting over all cut areas. Spread remaining frosting evenly over cake. Cut off small corner of bag with vanilla frosting. Pipe frosting onto cake and decorate as shown in photo.

NUTRITION INFORMATION PER SERVING: Calories 520 • Total Fat 25g • Saturated Fat 7g • Cholesterol 40mg • Sodium 420mg • Total Carbohydrate 69g • Dietary Fiber 1g • Sugars 53g • Protein 3g. DIETARY EXCHANGES: 1 Starch • 3-1/2 Other Carbohydrate • 5 Fat.

Kitchen tip

Decorated like a gingerbread boy, this cake isn't a spice cake. It's really chocolate, and who doesn't like chocolate? A small, snack-size resealable food-storage plastic bag works great for piping frosting. Put the frosting in the bag and snip a tiny opening in one bottom corner to pipe the frosting.

holiday pinwheels

PREP TIME: 1 Hour ✱ READY IN: 2 Hours ✱ SERVINGS: 32 Cookies

- 1 roll (18 oz.) Pillsbury® Refrigerated Sugar Cookies
- 1/2 cup all-purpose flour
- 3 tablespoons red sugar
- 3 tablespoons green sugar

1 Remove cookie dough from wrapper; cut roll in half crosswise. Sprinkle 1/4 cup of the flour onto work surface. Roll out half of dough into 12x7-inch rectangle. Repeat with remaining half of dough and 1/4 cup flour.

2 Sprinkle 1 rectangle evenly with red sugar; sprinkle green sugar evenly over second rectangle. Starting with one short side of each rectangle, roll up. Wrap rolls in waxed paper; refrigerate at least 1 hour for easier handling. Heat oven to 350°F. Cut each roll into 16 slices; place 1 inch apart on ungreased cookie sheets. Bake 10 to 13 minutes or until edges are light golden brown. Cool 1 minute; remove from sheets.

NUTRITION INFORMATION PER SERVING: Calories 80 • Total Fat 3g • Saturated Fat 1g • Cholesterol 4mg • Sodium 55mg • Total Carbohydrate 13g • Dietary Figer 0g • Sugars 70g • Protein 1g. DIETARY EXCHANGES: 1/2 Starch • 1/2 Fruit • 1/2 Fat.

Kitchen tip

Keep dough well chilled for easy handling. If dough becomes too warm, it is difficult to shape.

chocolate-dipped heart cookies

READY IN: 1 Hour ✱ SERVINGS: 24 Cookies

- 1 roll (16.5 oz.) Pillsbury® Create 'n Bake® Refrigerated Sugar Cookies, well chilled
- 1/4 to 1/2 cup all-purpose flour
- 1-1/2 cups semisweet chocolate chips
- 1 tablespoon shortening
- Candy sprinkles, if desired

1 Heat oven to 350°F. Remove half of cookie dough from wrapper; refrigerate remaining dough until needed.

2 Sprinkle about 3 tablespoons of the flour onto work surface; coat sides of half of dough with flour. With rolling pin, roll out dough to 1/4-inch thickness, adding additional flour as needed to prevent sticking.

3 With floured 3-inch heart-shaped cookie cutter, cut out dough hearts. Gently brush excess flour from hearts; place 2 inches apart on ungreased cookie sheets. Repeat with the remaining half of the dough.

4 Bake 7 to 9 minutes or until light golden brown. Cool 1 minute; remove from cookie sheet and place on wire racks. Cool completely, about 15 minutes.

5 In 1-quart saucepan, heat chocolate chips and shortening over low heat, stirring occasionally, until chips are melted and smooth. Remove from heat. Dip half of each cookie into melted chocolate, allowing excess chocolate to drip off; place on waxed paper-lined cookie sheets.

NUTRITION INFORMATION PER SERVING: Calories 150 • Total Fat 8g • Saturated Fat 3g • Cholesterol 5mg • Sodium 65mg • Total Carbohydrate 20g • Dietary Fiber 0g. DIETARY EXCHANGES: 1-1/2 Other Carbohydrate • 1-1/2 Fat.

cook's notes

Look for heart-shaped sprinkles wherever baking supplies are sold.

angel bites

PREP TIME: 20 Minutes ✱ READY IN: 35 Minutes ✱ SERVINGS: 12 Candies

- 6 oz. vanilla-flavored candy coating or almond bark, chopped
- 12 butterfly-shaped crackers
- 12 triangular whole wheat crackers
- 12 bite-sized round butter crackers
- Colored sugar

1 Line cookie sheet with waxed paper. Place candy coating in 2-cup microwavable measuring cup. Microwave on Medium for 2 to 3 minutes, stirring once halfway through melting time. Stir until melted and smooth.

2 To form each angel shape, dip 1 butterfly-shaped cracker in candy coating; allow excess to drip off. Place on paper-lined cookie sheet, wide end up, to form wings. Dip 1 triangular cracker in candy coating; allow excess to drip off. Attach to center of butterfly cracker, pointed side up, to form the skirt.

3 Dip 1 round cracker in candy coating; allow excess to drip off. Attach to butterfly cracker at top of point of triangular cracker to form head. Immediately sprinkle with colored sugar. Let crackers stand at room temperature for 15 minutes or until coating is set.

NUTRITION INFORMATION PER SERVING: Calories 110 • Total Fat 6g • Saturated Fat 3g • Cholesterol 5mg • Sodium 60mg • Total Carbohydrate 13g • Dietary Fiber 0g. DIETARY EXCHANGES: 1/2 Starch • 1/2 Fruit • 1 Other Carbohydrate • 1 Fat.

cook's notes

Cut the candy coating into very small pieces; they will melt quickly without over-cooking.

chocolate-dipped heart cookies

snow globe cookie

snow globe cookie

PREP TIME: 55 Minutes ✱ READY IN: 1 Hour 25 Minutes ✱ SERVINGS: 16 Cookies

- 1/4 cup all-purpose flour
- 1 roll (16.5 oz.) refrigerated sugar cookies
- 1 container (1 lb.) vanilla creamy ready-to-spread frosting
- 5 drops green food color
- 10 drops blue food color
- Assorted small candy sprinkles, edible glitter and/or decorator sugar crystals

1 Heat oven to 350°F. Line large cookie sheet with foil. Sprinkle flour over work surface. Cut roll of cookie dough in half crosswise. Return 1 half to refrigerator.

2 To form top of globe, shape dough into ball; roll in flour to coat. Place on one end of cookie sheet. Press or roll into 10-inch round.

3 Remove remaining half of dough from refrigerator. Cut dough in half. To form base of globe, shape one half into ball; roll in flour to coat. Press or roll into 8-inch round. Cut round in half; place half round next to 10-inch round on foil-lined cookie sheet, rounded edges touching.

4 Bake 7 to 11 minutes or until light golden brown. Cool completely, about 30 minutes. Carefully peel foil from back of cookie; place cookie on tray or foil-covered cardboard.

5 Meanwhile, grease cookie sheet with shortening. Coat remaining dough with flour; roll to 1/8-inch thickness. With floured cookie cutters, cut two 3-1/2- to 4-inch trees, one 2-inch tree, one 3-1/2- to 4-inch snowman and three 1-1/4-inch stars. Bake stars 2 to 3 minutes; trees and snowman 7 to 10 minutes or until light golden brown. Cool 1 minute; remove from cookie sheet. Cool completely, about 30 minutes.

6 Use 1/3 cup vanilla frosting to frost base of globe. Frost stars and snowman with vanilla frosting. In small bowl, blend 2 tablespoons frosting and the green food color. Frost trees. To remaining frosting, add blue food color; blend well. Frost globe.

7 Arrange trees, snowman and stars on blue-frosted globe. Sprinkle glitter or decorator sugar crystals to resemble snow-covered ground; sprinkle some in "sky" for falling snow. Decorate snowman, stars and trees as desired with candy, edible glitter and/or decorator sugar crystals.

HIGH ALTITUDE (3500-6500 FT): In large bowl, break up cookie dough. Stir or knead in 1/4 cup all-purpose flour. Re-shape into 8-inch roll. Continue as directed in Step 1.

NUTRITION INFORMATION PER SERVING: Calories 260 • Calories from Fat 110 • Total Fat 12g • Saturated Fat 3g • Trans Fat 3.5g • Cholesterol 10mg • Sodium 150mg • Total Carbohydrate 38g • Dietary Fiber 0g • Sugars 26g • Protein 1g. DIETARY EXCHANGES: 2-1/2 Other Carbohydrate • 2-1/2 • Fat • 2-1/2 Carb Choices.

cook's notes

Let your creativity shine when decorating the snowman and trees on this large cookie. Miniature chocolate chips, candy-coated chocolate candies, colored sugar and sprinkles are just a few decorative items to try.

craft dough snowmen

PREP TIME: 30 Minutes ✱ READY IN: 1 Hour 45 Minutes

- 2 cups all-purpose flour
- 1 cup salt
- 3/4 cup water
- Acrylic paint or polyurethane

1 Heat oven to 350°F. Grease large cookie sheet. In large bowl, combine flour and salt; mix well. Gradually add water, stirring until a stiff dough forms. If necessary, add up to 1/4 cup additional water to moisten all dry ingredients. Knead dough 5 minutes or until smooth.

2 To make each snowman, shape one 2-inch ball of dough, one 1-inch ball of dough and two 1/4-inch balls of dough. Place 2-inch ball on greased cookie sheet; moisten top edge of ball and place 1-inch ball on it, gently pressing balls together. Moisten 1 edge of each 1/4-inch ball; gently press onto each side of 2-inch ball to resemble snowman arms.

3 Bake for 35 to 45 minutes or until firm to the touch. Turn oven off; let stand in warm oven for 2 hours to finish drying.

4 Spray or brush snowmen with assorted colors of acrylic paint or clear, glossy polyurethane. Let dry completely. Decorate as desired using scraps of fabric or ribbon for scarves. Attach hat and broom from craft store or glue felt circle on snowmen for hats. DO NOT EAT.

kitchen tip

Kids can also roll out and cut this multiuse craft dough with their favorite cookie cutters. For colored dough, add a few drops of food color to portions of the dough and knead to blend.

kitchen tip

Not all graters are alike, and now there are many types available with holes of varying sizes and shapes. A grater with larger holes will give you bigger pieces of white chocolate, just like you see in the picture of this showpiece dessert.

tree-shaped brownie torte

PREP TIME: 40 Minutes ✱ READY IN: 2 Hours 10 minutes ✱ SERVINGS: 18

Brownies
- 1 box (1 lb. 3.8 oz.) fudge brownie mix
- 1/2 cup vegetable oil
- 1/4 cup water
- 2 eggs

Glaze
- 1/2 cup whipping cream
- 1 cup semisweet chocolate chips (6 oz.)

Frosting
- 2 cups powdered sugar
- 1/3 cup butter or margarine, softened
- 1/2 teaspoon vanilla
- 1 to 3 tablespoons milk

Decorations
- 1 (4 oz.) white chocolate baking bar, grated
- 1 chocolate-covered candy bar, cut in half

1 Heat oven to 350°F. Line 13x9-inch pan with foil, extending foil over sides of pan; grease foil with shortening. In medium bowl, stir brownie mix, oil, water and eggs with spoon until well blended. Spread in pan.

2 Bake 28 to 30 minutes or until set. Do not overbake. Cool completely, about 30 minutes. Freeze brownies 30 minutes.

3 Meanwhile, in small saucepan, heat whipping cream to boiling. Remove from heat. Stir in chocolate chips until melted. Let stand about 30 minutes or until spreadable. In small bowl, blend all frosting ingredients, adding enough milk for desired spreading consistency.

4 Using foil, lift brownies from pan; place on cutting board. To cut tree shape from brownies, start at center of 1 short side and make 2 diagonal cuts to corners of opposite short side, forming a triangular piece in center.

5 Place 2 side pieces together on foil-lined serving tray (or piece of heavy cardboard) to form tree shape. Spread with frosting. Top with whole tree shape. Trim if necessary to line up edges.

6 Spread glaze evenly over sides and top of brownie torte. Sprinkle top with grated white chocolate to form garland. Place candy bar half at base of tree for trunk. Let stand 15 minutes or until set.

High Altitude (3500-6500 ft): Follow High Altitude directions on brownie mix box for 13x9-inch pan.

NUTRITION INFORMATION PER SERVING: Calories 390 • Calories from Fat 170 • Total Fat 19g • Saturated Fat 8g • Trans Fat 1g • Cholesterol 40mg • Sodium 160mg • Total Carbohydrate 52g • Dietary Fiber 0g • Sugars 43g • Protein 3g. DIETARY EXCHANGES: 1 Starch • 2-1/2 Other Carbohydrate • 3-1/2 Fat • 3-1/2 Carb Choices.

special touch

If your friends and family like raisins, add 1/4 to 1/2 cup to the dough with the chocolate pieces.

yummy little sandwich cookies

READY IN: 1 Hour ✱ SERVINGS: 30 Cookies

- 1 roll (of a 16.5 oz.) Pillsbury® Create 'n Bake® Refrigerated Sugar Cookies
- 1/2 cup miniature candy-coated semisweet chocolate baking bits
- 3/4 cup white vanilla chips
- 3/4 cup vanilla ready-to-spread frosting (from 16-oz. can)

1 Heat oven to 350°F. In large bowl, break up cookie dough. Stir in baking bits. Shape dough into 3/4-inch balls; place 2 inches apart on ungreased cookie sheets. With glass dipped in sugar, flatten each ball slightly.

2 Bake 8 to 10 minutes or until edges are golden brown. Immediately remove from cookie sheets; place on wire racks. Cool completely, about 15 minutes.

3 In medium microwavable bowl, microwave vanilla chips on High 20 to 30 seconds or until melted, stirring every 15 seconds. Stir in frosting until smooth. For each sandwich cookie, spread 1 to 2 teaspoons frosting mixture on bottom of 1 cookie. Top with second cookie, bottom side down; press gently.

NUTRITION INFORMATION PER SERVING: Calories 150 • Total Fat 7g • Saturated Fat 3.5g • Cholesterol 5mg • Sodium 65mg • Total Carbohydrate 21g • Dietary Fiber 0g. DIETARY EXCHANGES: 1-1/2 Other Carbohydrate • 1-1/2 Fat.

tree-shaped brownie torte

cinnamon polar bears

cinnamon polar bears

PREP TIME: 1 Hour 20 Minutes ✱ READY IN: 2 Hours 20 Minutes ✱ SERVINGS: 48 Cookies

- 1 cup sugar
- 1 cup butter, softened
- 1 egg
- 2-1/4 cups all-purpose flour
- 1 teaspoon cinnamon
- Powdered sugar
- 1 tablespoon (96) miniature semisweet chocolate chips
- 48 red cinnamon candies

1 In large bowl, combine sugar and butter; beat until light and fluffy. Add egg; beat well. Add flour and cinnamon; blend well. Cover dough with plastic wrap; refrigerate 1 hour for easier handling.

2 Heat oven to 350°F. For each cookie, shape dough into 1-inch ball; place 2 inches apart on ungreased cookie sheets. Flatten slightly. Shape dough into 3 (1/4-inch) balls. Place 2 of the balls above and touching larger ball for ears and 1 ball on top to resemble snout. Flatten slightly.

3 Bake for 11 to 15 minutes or until firm to the touch. Immediately remove from cookie sheets. Lightly sprinkle cookies with powdered sugar. Press 2 chocolate chips into each cookie for eyes and 1 cinnamon candy for nose.

High Altitude (3500-6500 ft): Increase flour to 2-1/3 cups. Bake as directed above.

NUTRITION INFORMATION PER SERVING: Calories 80 • Total Fat 4g • Saturated Fat 2g • Cholesterol 15mg • Sodium 25mg • Total Carbohydrate 10g • Dietary Fiber 0g. DIETARY EXCHANGES: 1/2 Starch • 1 Fat.

cook's notes

To ensure that these cookies hold their shape in the oven, work with only a small portion of dough at a time, and keep the rest refrigerated.

macaroonies

READY IN: 1 Hour 5 Minutes ✱ SERVINGS: 36 Cookies

- 2 eggs
- 1/8 teaspoon salt
- 3/4 cup sugar
- 1/2 cup all-purpose flour
- 1 tablespoon butter or margarine, melted
- 2 cups flaked coconut
- 1 cup semisweet chocolate chips (6 oz.)
- 1 teaspoon grated lemon or orange peel
- 1 teaspoon vanilla

1 Heat oven to 325°F. Lightly grease cookie sheets with shortening or cooking spray; lightly flour cookie sheets.

2 In small bowl, beat eggs and salt with electric mixer on medium speed until foamy. Gradually add sugar, beating 5 to 7 minutes or until thick and ivory colored. With spoon, fold in flour and butter until well blended. Stir in remaining ingredients.

3 Onto cookie sheets, drop dough by rounded teaspoonfuls 2 inches apart. Bake 12 to 15 minutes until delicately browned. Cool 1 minute; remove from cookie sheets.

NUTRITION INFORMATION PER SERVING: Calories 80 • Calories from Fat 30 • Total Fat 3.5g • Saturated Fat 2.5g • Trans Fat 0g • Cholesterol 15 mg • Sodium 25mg • Total Carbohydrate 10g • Dietary Fiber 0g • Sugars 8g • Protein 0g. DIETARY EXCHANGES: 1 Other Carbohydrate • 1/2 Fat.

Judith Ann Carlson
Amery, Wisconsin
Bake-Off® Contest 15, 1963

cook's notes

These are great cookies to make in stages. One day, shape and bake the cookies. Cool completely and freeze in a tightly covered container up to 1 month ahead of time. Another day, thaw, frost and decorate the cookies.

cookie skates

PREP TIME: 1 Hour 20 Minutes ✱ READY IN: 1 Hour 50 Minutes ✱ SERVINGS: 30 Cookies

Cookies

- 1/2 roll (of a 16.5-oz. size) refrigerated sugar cookies
- 1/4 cup of all-purpose flour

Frosting

- 1-1/2 cups powdered sugar
- 1/4 cup butter, softened
- 4 to 6 teaspoons lemon juice
- Green food color
- 30 small candy canes

1. In large bowl, break up cookie dough. Add flour; mix with hands until well blended. Shape dough into 10-inch log; wrap in plastic wrap. Freeze 30 minutes.
2. Heat oven to 350°F. Remove dough from freezer. Flatten dough down center with handle of wooden spoon. To form boot shape, with fingers, flatten one side of log until about 3/4 inch thick. (See photo.) Cut log into 3/8-inch-thick slices; place on ungreased cookie sheets. Flatten slightly with fingers.
3. Bake 8 to 11 minutes or until edges are light golden brown. Immediately remove from cookie sheets. Cool completely, about 15 minutes.
4. In small bowl, mix powdered sugar, butter and enough lemon juice for desired spreading consistency. In another small bowl, reserve 1/3 of frosting; add green food color and blend well. Place green frosting in resealable food-storage plastic bag; cut off small corner of bag.
5. Frost cookies with white frosting. Place small amount of white frosting along bottom edge of each cookie; attach candy canes to form "skate blades," breaking off portion of tip on curved end, if necessary. With green frosting, pipe laces and bows on skates.

NUTRITION INFORMATION PER SERVING: Calories 90 • Total Fat 3g • Saturated Fat 1.5g • Trans Fat 0g • Cholesterol 5mg • Sodium 35mg • Total Carbohydrate 14g • Dietary Fiber 0g • Sugars 11 g • Protein 0g. DIETARY EXCHANGES: 1/2 Starch • 1/2 Other Carbohydrate • 1/2 Fat.

kitchen tip

Look for colorful holiday sprinkles in the baking aisle of the grocery store.

cream cheese sugar cookies

PREP TIME: 1 Hour ✱ READY IN: 2 Hours ✱ SERVINGS: 72 Cookies

- 1 cup sugar
- 1 cup butter, softened
- 1 package (3 oz.) cream cheese, softened
- 1/2 teaspoon salt
- 1/2 teaspoon almond extract
- 1/2 teaspoon vanilla
- 1 egg yolk
- 2 cups all-purpose flour
- Colored sugar or sprinkles, if desired

1. In large bowl, beat all ingredients except flour and colored sugar with electric mixer on medium speed until light and fluffy. Beat in flour until well combined.
2. Shape the cookie dough into 3 disks. Wrap the dough disks in plastic wrap; refrigerate 1 hour for easier handling.
3. Heat oven to 375°F. On floured surface with rolling pin, roll out 1 disk of dough at a time to 1/8-inch thickness (keep remaining dough refrigerated). Cut dough with lightly floured 2-1/2-inch round or desired shape cookie cutters; place 1 inch apart on ungreased cookie sheets.
4. Decorate cookies with colored sugar or sprinkles. Bake 6 to 10 minutes or until light golden brown. Immediately remove from cookie sheets.

High Altitude (3500-6000 ft): Increase flour to 2-1/4 cups. Bake as directed above.

NUTRITION INFORMATION PER SERVING: Calories 50 • Total Fat 3g • Saturated Fat 2g • Cholesterol 10mg • Sodium 45mg • Total Carbohydrates 64g • Dietary Fiber 0g • Sugars 3g • Protein 1g. DIETARTY EXCHANGES: 1/2 Starch • 1/2 Fat OR 1/2 Carbohydrates • 1/2 Fat.

cookie skates

Elegant Desserts

Celebrate in style with after-dinner specialties that promise to impress everyone at the table. With this heavenly assortment, dazzling guests has never been easier.

p. 296

p. 293

p. 288

p. 303

p. 290

frozen raspberry delight p. 287

chocolate-caramel satin pie

apricot coconut cream pie

SERVINGS: 8

Harriet Warkentin
San Jacinto, California
Bake-Off® Contest 33, 1988

1 refrigerated pie crust (from 15-oz. pkg.)

Filling

- 1 envelope unflavored gelatin
- 1 cup apricot nectar
- 2 cans (16 oz. each) apricot halves, drained
- 1/2 cup sugar
- 1/4 cup cornstarch
- 1/4 teaspoon salt
- 1-3/4 cups milk
- 4 egg yolks, beaten
- 1 tablespoon butter or margarine
- 1/2 teaspoon vanilla
- 1/2 cup coconut, toasted

Topping

- 1 cup whipping cream
- 1 tablespoon sugar
- 1/4 teaspoon vanilla
- 2 to 3 tablespoons apricot preserves, melted
- 1/2 cup coconut, toasted

1 Heat oven to 450°F. Prepare pie crust according to package directions for one-crust baked shell using 9-inch pie pan. Bake for 9 to 11 minutes or until light golden brown. Cool completely.

2 In small bowl, sprinkle gelatin over 1/4 cup of the apricot nectar; let stand to soften. Set aside. In another small bowl, cut 1 can of the apricot halves into small pieces. Set aside. In blender container or food processor bowl with metal blade, combine remaining 3/4 cup apricot nectar and remaining can of apricot halves. Cover; blend until smooth.

3 In medium saucepan, combine 1/2 cup sugar, cornstarch and salt; mix well. Stir in milk and apricot mixture. (Mixture will look curdled.) Cook over medium heat until mixture thickens and boils, stirring constantly. Boil 2 minutes, stirring constantly. Remove from heat. Blend a small amount of hot mixture into egg yolks. Gradually stir yolk mixture into hot mixture in saucepan. Cook over medium heat until mixture comes to a boil, stirring constantly. Cook 2 minutes, stirring constantly. Remove from heat; stir in butter, 1/2 teaspoon vanilla and softened gelatin. Fold in 1/2 cup toasted coconut. Refrigerate about 30 minutes or until slightly thickened. Fold in apricot pieces. Spoon into cooled baked shell. Refrigerate about 45 minutes or until filling is partially set.

4 In large bowl, beat whipping cream until soft peaks form. Add 1 tablespoon sugar and 1/4 teaspoon vanilla; beat until stiff peaks form. Gently fold in apricot preserves. Pipe or spoon whipped topping mixture over cooled filling.

5 Garnish with 1/2 cup toasted coconut. Refrigerate 3 to 4 hours or until set. Store leftovers in the refrigerator.

NUTRITION INFORMATION PER SERVING: Calories 480 • Protein 7g • Carbohydrate 51g • Fat 27g • Sodium 270mg.

lazy maple crescent pull-aparts

PREP TIME: 15 Minutes ✷ READY IN: 40 Minutes ✷ SERVINGS: 12 Rolls

- 1/4 cup butter or margarine
- 1/4 cup packed brown sugar
- 2 tablespoons maple-flavored syrup
- 1/4 cup chopped pecans or walnuts
- 1 can (8 oz.) refrigerated crescent dinner rolls
- 1 tablespoon granulated sugar
- 1/2 teaspoon ground cinnamon

1 Heat oven to 375°F. In ungreased 8- or 9-inch round cake pan, mix butter, brown sugar and syrup. Heat in oven 2 to 4 minutes or until butter melts; blend well. Sprinkle with pecans.

2 Remove dough from can in 2 rolled sections. Do not unroll dough. Cut each roll of dough into 6 slices. In small bowl, mix granulated sugar and cinnamon; dip both sides of each slice in sugar mixture. Arrange slices over butter mixture in pan; sprinkle with any remaining sugar mixture.

3 Bake 17 to 23 minutes or until golden brown. Cool 1 minute; invert rolls onto serving plate. Serve warm.

NUTRITION INFORMATION PER SERVING: Calories 310 • Total Fat 19g • Saturated Fat 8g • Trans Fat 2.5g • Cholesterol 20mg • Sodium 360mg • Total Carbohydrate 32g • Dietary Fiber 0g • Sugars 16g • Protein 3g. DIETARY EXCHANGES: 1 Starch • 1 Other Carbohydrate • 3-1/2 Fat • 2 Carb Choices.

special touch

Arrange these rolls in a basket lined with a decorative holiday napkin. To keep the rolls warm, cover them with the four corners of the napkin or put another napkin on top.

cook's notes

Remember when you were a kid and cut paper dolls or snowflake designs out of paper? This beautiful pie uses that same idea, except you do the cutting on pie crust instead. No need to be intricate—a simple design will look great.

raspberries and cream snowflake pie

PREP TIME: 45 Minutes ✷ READY IN: 3 Hours 45 Minutes ✷ SERVINGS: 8

Crust

- 1 box (15 oz.) refrigerated pie crusts, softened as directed on box

Filling

- 1 can (21 oz.) raspberry pie filling
- 1 package (8 oz.) cream cheese, softened
- 1 can (14 oz.) sweetened condensed milk (not evaporated)
- 1/3 cup lemon juice
- 1/2 teaspoon almond extract
- 1/2 to 1 teaspoon powdered sugar

1 Heat oven to 450°F. Make pie crust as directed on box for one-crust baked shell, using 9-inch glass pie plate. Bake 9 to 11 minutes or until lightly browned. Cool.

2 To make snowflake crust, unroll remaining crust onto ungreased cookie sheet. Cut crust into 7-1/2-inch diameter round; discard scraps. Fold round in half, then in half again on cookie sheet. With knife, cut designs from folded and curved edges; discard scraps. Unfold. Bake 6 to 8 minutes or until lightly browned. Cool completely.

3 Reserve 1/2 cup raspberry filling; spoon remaining filling into cooled baked shell. In large bowl, beat cream cheese until light and fluffy. Add condensed milk; blend well. Add lemon juice and almond extract; stir until thickened. Spoon over raspberry filling in crust. Refrigerate 1 hour.

4 Spoon reserved 1/2 cup raspberry filling around edge of pie. Place snowflake crust over top. Refrigerate several hours. Just before serving, sprinkle with powdered sugar. Store in refrigerator.

NUTRITION INFORMATION PER SERVING: Calories 650 • Total Fat 25g • Saturated Fat 13g • Trans Fat 0g • Cholesterol 55mg • Sodium 340mg • Total Carbohydrate 99g • Dietary Fiber 0g • Sugars 64g • Protein 6g. DIETARY EXCHANGES: 2 Starch • 4-1/2 Other Carbohydrate • 5 Fat • 6-1/2 Carb Choices.

holiday cherry-chocolate cake

PREP TIME: 35 Minutes ✳ READY IN: 55 Minutes ✳ SERVINGS: 12

Cake

- 1 package (1 lb. 2.25 oz.) devil's food cake mix with pudding
- 2 tablespoons all-purpose flour
- 1-3/4 cups water
- 3/4 cup refrigerated or frozen fat-free egg product, thawed, or 3 eggs

Filling and Topping

- 1 can (21 oz.) cherry pie filling
- 3/4 teaspoon almond extract
- 1 container (8 oz.) frozen light whipped topping, thawed

1 Heat oven to 350°F. Spray 15x10x1-inch baking pan with nonstick cooking spray. Line bottom of pan with waxed paper; spray paper. Prepare cake mix as directed on package using flour, water and egg product. Pour batter into sprayed paper-lined pan.

2 Bake for 18 to 20 minutes or until cake springs back when touched lightly in center. Cool cake in pan on wire rack for 10 minutes. Invert cake onto wire rack; remove pan and paper. Cool 15 minutes or until completely cooled.

3 In small bowl, combine pie filling and 1/2 teaspoon of the almond extract; mix well. Cut cake in half crosswise to form two 10x7-inch layers.

4 Place 1 cake layer on serving platter or tray; spread pie filling mixture over top. Top with remaining cake layer.

5 Stir remaining 1/4 teaspoon almond extract into whipped topping. Spread mixture over top and sides of cake. Serve immediately or refrigerate until serving time. Store in refrigerator.

NUTRITION INFORMATION PER SERVING: Calories 290 • Total Fat 7g • Saturated Fat 3g • Cholesterol 0mg • Sodium 430mg • Total Carbohydrate 52g • Dietary Fiber 2g • Sugars 37g • Protein 5g. DIETARY EXCHANGES: 1-1/2 Starch • 1 Fat • 2 Other Carbohydrates • 3-1/2 Carb Choices.

special touch

If desired, garnish each serving with a maraschino or candied cherry and chocolate curls. Use a vegetable peeler to shave a room-temperature chocolate bar into curls. Try dark, milk or white chocolate, or go for it and try a combo.

easy caramel-pecan bars

PREP TIME: 25 Minutes ✳ READY IN: 2 Hours 15 Minutes ✳ SERVINGS: 36

- 1 package (18 oz.) Pillsbury® Refrigerated Sugar Cookies
- 3/4 cup caramel ice cream topping
- 2 tablespoons all-purpose flour
- 1 cup pecan pieces
- 1 cup flaked coconut
- 1 package (6 oz.) semisweet chocolate chips (1 cup)

1 Heat oven to 350°F. Spray 13x9-inch pan with nonstick cooking spray. Cut cookie dough into 1/2 inch slices. Arrange slices in bottom of sprayed pan. With floured fingers, press dough evenly in pan to form crust.

2 Bake for 10 to 15 minutes or until light golden brown. Meanwhile, in glass measuring cup, combine caramel topping and flour; blend until smooth.

3 Remove partially baked crust from oven. Sprinkle pecans, coconut and chocolate chips over crust. Drizzle with caramel mixture.

4 Return to oven; bake an additional 15 to 20 minutes or until topping is bubbly. Cool 1-1/2 hours or until completely cooled. Cut into bars.

NUTRITION INFORMATION PER SERVING: Calories 140 • Total Fat 7g • Saturated Fat 2g • Cholesterol 0mg • Sodium 85mg • Total Carbohydrate 18g • Dietary Fiber 1g • Sugars 11g • Protein 1g. DIETARY EXCHANGES: 1/2 Starch • 1/2 Fruit • 1-1/2 Fat OR 1 Carbohydrate, 1-1/2 Fat • 1 Carb Choice.

cook's notes

If the caramel ice cream topping is very thick and hard to pour, microwave it, uncovered, in the glass measuring cup for 10 to 15 seconds on High or until it's slightly warmed and pourable.

special touch

Feel free to use whatever cookie cutters you have on hand to make the decorations for this lovely dessert.

three-berry cheesecake

PREP TIME: 45 Minutes ✷ READY IN: 4 Hours 35 Minutes ✷ SERVINGS: 12

- 1 box (15 oz.) Pillsbury® Refrigerated Pie Crusts, softened as directed on box
- 2 tablespoons coarse sugar
- 2 packages (8 oz. each) cream cheese, softened
- 1-1/4 cups granulated sugar
- 1 tablespoon lemon juice
- 1 teaspoon vanilla
- 1 container (8 oz.) frozen whipped topping, thawed
- 1/4 cup seedless raspberry preserves
- 1 can (21 oz.) cherry pie filling
- 3 cups fresh strawberries, each quartered
- 1 cup fresh raspberries

1 Heat oven to 450°F. Remove 1 crust from pouch. Make pie crust as directed on box for one-crust baked shell, using 10-inch glass pie plate. Bake 9 to 11 minutes or until golden brown. Cool completely, about 30 minutes.

2 Meanwhile, to make cheesecake decorations, grease cookie sheet with shortening or cooking spray, or line with parchment paper. Remove remaining crust from pouch; unroll onto cookie sheet. Cut crust into large holly leaves using cookie cutter. Cut small circles for holly berries. Place on cookie sheet; sprinkle with coarse sugar.

3 Bake decorations 8 to 10 minutes or until light golden brown. Carefully remove from cookie sheet to cooling rack. Cool completely, about 15 minutes.

4 In a large bowl, beat cream cheese, granulated sugar, the lemon juice and vanilla with electric mixer on medium speed until fluffy. Fold in whipped topping until well blended. Spread 2 cups cream cheese mixture in cooled baked shell. Gently spoon and spread preserves over mixture. Spread with remaining cream cheese mixture.

5 In medium bowl, mix pie filling, 2-1/2 cups of the strawberries and 1/2 cup of the raspberries. Spoon over cream cheese mixture. Sprinkle with remaining strawberries and raspberries. Refrigerate at least 4 hours or until set. Just before serving, arrange some of the holly leaves and berries on cheesecake. Serve individual slices with additional holly leaves and berries. Store in refrigerator.

NUTRITION INFORMATION PER SERVING: Calories 520 • Total Fat 26g • Sodium 270mg • Dietary Fiber 2g. DIETARY EXCHANGES: 1/2 Starch • 4 Other Carbohydrate • 1/2 Medium Fat Meat • 4-1/2 Fat • 4-1/2 Carb Choices.

streusel pecan pie squares

PREP TIME: 15 Minutes ✷ READY IN: 1 Hour ✷ SERVINGS: 15

CRUST

- 3 cups all-purpose flour
- 3/4 cup packed brown sugar
- 1-1/2 cups cold butter or margarine

FILLING

- 3/4 cup packed brown sugar
- 1-1/2 cups corn syrup or maple-flavored syrup
- 1 cup milk
- 1/3 cup butter or margarine, melted
- 1 teaspoon vanilla
- 4 eggs
- 1-1/2 cups chopped pecans

TOPPING

Whipped cream or ice cream, if desired

1 Heat oven to 400°F. In large bowl, mix all crust ingredients until crumbly. Reserve 2 cups crumbs for filling and topping. Press remaining crumbs in bottom and 3/4 inch up sides of ungreased 15x10x1-inch pan. Bake 10 minutes.

2 In large bowl, mix 1/4 cup of the reserved crumbs and all filling ingredients except pecans. Stir in pecans. Pour over partially baked crust; bake 10 minutes.

3 Reduce oven temperature to 350°F. Sprinkle remaining 1-3/4 cups reserved crumbs over filling; bake 20 to 25 minutes longer or until filling is set and crumbs are golden brown. Serve with whipped cream.

NUTRITION INFORMATION PER SERVING: Calories 590 • Total Fat 32g • Saturated Fat 16g • Trans Fat 1.5g • Cholesterol 115mg • Sodium 230mg • Total Carbohydrate 69g • Dietary Fiber 2g • Sugars 35g • Protein 6g. DIETARY EXCHANGES: 2 Starch • 2-1/2 Other Carbohydrate • 6 Fat • 4-1/2 Carb Choices.

cook's notes

Expect rave reviews for these sensational buttery pecan pie squares! If you're a fan of real maple syrup, by all means, go ahead and use that instead of the corn syrup or maple-flavored syrup.

chocolate crust-orange cheesecake dessert

PREP TIME: 25 Minutes ✱ READY IN: 4 Hours 55 Minutes ✱ SERVINGS: 16

CRUST

1-1/2 cups chocolate cookie crumbs (from15-oz. pkg.)
1/4 cup powdered sugar
1/3 cup butter or margarine, melted

FILLING

1/2 cup orange juice
2 envelopes unflavored gelatin
1/2 cup sugar
2 packages (8 oz. each) 1/3-less-fat cream cheese (Neufchâtel), softened
2 containers (6 oz. each) Yoplait® Original 99% Fat Free mandarin orange yogurt
1 teaspoon grated orange peel
2 cups frozen light whipped topping, thawed
1/2 pint (1 cup) fresh raspberries
Strips of candied orange peel, if desired

1 In medium bowl, combine all crust ingredients; mix well. Press in bottom of ungreased 10-inch springform pan. Press crust mixture in bottom and up sides of pan. Freeze 30 minutes.

2 In small saucepan, combine orange juice and gelatin; mix well. Heat over low heat until gelatin is dissolved, stirring occasionally.

3 In large bowl, combine 1/2 cup sugar and cream cheese; beat with electric mixer at medium speed until light and fluffy. Add yogurt, orange peel and gelatin mixture; mix well. Fold in 1 cup of the whipped topping. Spoon into cooled crust; spread evenly. Refrigerate 4 hours or until set.

4 Remove sides of pan. To serve, cut dessert into wedges; place on individual dessert plates. Garnish each with dollop of remaining whipped topping, raspberries and candied orange peel.

NUTRITION INFORMATION PER SERVING: Calories 240 • Total Fat 14g • Saturated Fat 8g • Cholesterol 35mg • Sodium 230mg • Total Carbohydrate 25g • Dietary Fiber 1g. DIETARY EXCHANGES: 1-1/2 Starch • 2-1/2 Fat.

Kitchen tip

Look for chocolate cookie crumbs in the grocery store baking aisle near the ready-to-use crumb crusts.

chocolate chip gingerbread with orange hard sauce

chocolate chip gingerbread with orange hard sauce

PREP TIME: 15 Minutes ✱ READY IN: 1 Hour 30 Minutes ✱ SERVINGS: 9

GINGERBREAD

- 3 eggs
- 1/2 cup molasses
- 1/4 cup sugar
- 3/4 cup buttermilk
- 1/2 cup butter, melted
- 2 cups all-purpose flour
- 1 teaspoon baking soda
- 1 teaspoon ginger
- 1 teaspoon cinnamon
- 1/2 teaspoon salt
- 1/2 teaspoon cloves
- 1/2 cup miniature semisweet chocolate chips

SAUCE

- 2/3 cup powdered sugar
- 1/3 cup butter, softened
- 1 teaspoon grated orange peel
- 1 tablespoon orange juice

1 Heat oven to 350°F. Grease bottom only of 8- or 9-inch square pan. Beat eggs in large bowl with electric mixer at medium speed for 2 to 3 minutes or until slightly thickened. Gradually add molasses and sugar, beating until well blended.

2 Add buttermilk and melted butter; mix well. Add all remaining gingerbread ingredients except chocolate chips; beat until smooth. Stir in chocolate chips. Pour into greased pan.

3 Bake until toothpick inserted in center comes out clean. For 8-inch pan, bake 43 to 53 minutes; for 9-inch pan, bake 30 to 40 minutes. Cool 20 minutes.

4 In small bowl, combine powdered sugar and 1/3 cup butter; beat with electric mixer at low speed until smooth and creamy. Beat in orange peel and orange juice.

5 To serve, cut gingerbread into squares; place on individual dessert plates. Spoon about 1 tablespoon sauce over each serving.

HIGH ALTITUDE (3500-6500 FT): For gingerbread, decrease sugar to 2 tablespoons; decrease butter to 1/3 cup. For 8-inch pan, bake at 350°F for 42 to 47 minutes. For 9-inch pan, bake at 350°F for 40 to 45 minutes.

NUTRITION INFORMATION PER SERVING: Calories 445 • Total Fat 22g • Saturated Fat 13g • Cholesterol 115mg • Sodium 440mg • Total Carbohydrate 56g • Dietary Fiber 1g. DIETARY EXCHANGES: 2 Starch • 2 Other Carbohydrate • 4 Fat.

cook's notes

In England, traditional hard sauce is flavored with brandy, rum or whiskey. This version is made with orange juice to complement the spicy gingerbread flavors. If desired, try an orange liqueur, such as Grand Marnier.

cook's notes

The fudge can be frozen for up to 3 months. Let it cool after baking, then layer small squares between sheets of waxed paper in an airtight container.

cranberry-walnut white fudge

PREP TIME: 20 Minutes ✱ READY IN: 1 Hour 20 Minutes ✱ SERVINGS: 36

- 1 package (12 oz.) white vanilla chips (2 cups)
- 1/2 cup powdered sugar
- 1/2 cup vanilla ready-to-spread frosting (from 16-oz. can)
- 1 package (3 oz.) cream cheese, softened
- 3/4 cup chopped walnuts
- 1/3 cup sweetened dried cranberries
- 1 teaspoon grated orange peel

1 Line 9-inch square pan with foil so foil extends over sides of pan; spray foil lightly with nonstick cooking spray. Melt vanilla chips in small saucepan over low heat, stirring until smooth. Remove from heat.

2 In medium bowl, combine powdered sugar, frosting and cream cheese; blend well. Stir in melted chips, walnuts, cranberries and orange peel. Spread in sprayed foil-lined pan. Refrigerate about 1 hour or until firm.

3 Remove fudge from pan by lifting foil; remove foil. Cut into squares. Serve fudge at room temperature.

NUTRITION INFORMATION PER SERVING: Calories 110 • Total Fat 6g • Saturated Fat 3g • Cholesterol 5mg • Sodium 15mg • Total Carbohydrate 13g • Dietary Fiber 0g • Sugars 12g • Protein 1g. DIETARY EXCHANGES: 1 Fat • 1 Other Carbohydrate • 1 Carb Choice.

apple nut cookie tart

PREP TIME: 30 Minutes ✱ READY IN: 3 Hours ✱ SERVINGS: 16

- 1/2 cup finely chopped walnuts
- 3 tablespoons sugar
- 3/4 teaspoon cinnamon
- 1/2 teaspoon grated orange peel
- 1 roll (16.5 oz.) Pillsbury® Create 'n Bake® Refrigerated Sugar Cookies, well chilled
- 1/3 cup purchased apple butter
- 1 teaspoon all-purpose flour
- 16 pecan halves
- 32 slivered almonds (1 tablespoon)
- Sweetened whipped cream or vanilla ice cream, if desired

1 Heat oven to 325°F. Place cookie sheet in oven to preheat. Spray 9-1/2-inch tart pan with removable bottom or 9-inch springform pan with nonstick cooking spray.

2 In medium bowl, combine walnuts, sugar, 1/2 teaspoon of the cinnamon and the orange peel; mix well. Set aside.

3 Remove half of cookie dough from wrapper; refrigerate remaining half. With floured fingers, press dough in bottom of sprayed pan. Spread apple butter over dough to within 1/2 inch of edge. Top apple butter with walnut mixture.

4 Place remaining half of dough between 2 sheets of lightly floured waxed paper; roll to 9-1/2-inch round. Peel off top sheet of waxed paper. Carefully invert dough over walnut mixture; remove waxed paper. Press edges to fit pan.

5 In small bowl, combine flour and remaining 1/4 teaspoon cinnamon. Dipping knife in flour mixture before each cut, score top of tart into 16 wedges. Press 1 pecan half in each wedge, centered 1 inch from edge of pan. Press 2 almonds in V-shape just below each pecan.

6 Place tart on heated cookie sheet in oven. Bake for 45 to 55 minutes or until tart is light golden brown and center is set. Cool 15 minutes. Remove sides of pan. Cool 1-1/2 hours. To serve, top with whipped cream. Store in refrigerator.

NUTRITION INFORMATION PER SERVING: Calories 190 • Total Fat 10g • Saturated Fat 2g • Cholesterol 10mg • Sodium 95mg • Total Carbohydrate 24g • Dietary Fiber 0g. DIETARY EXCHANGES: 1/2 Starch • 1 Other Carbohydrate • 2 Fat.

kitchen tip

Use a microplane to grate citrus zest with ease. This tool quickly removes just the colored portion of the peel without any pressure. A microplane can be found at kitchen specialty stores.

pumpkin gingerbread with caramel sauce

special touch

The fudge sauce for this dessert is delicious; try it over sundaes. Instead of spooning the fudge sauce over the dessert, drizzle it on the plate before adding the dessert square.

frozen strawberry-pistachio dessert

PREP TIME: 1 Hour ✱ READY IN: 6 Hours ✱ SERVINGS: 16

CRUST

- 1-1/2 cups chocolate cookie crumbs (from 15-oz. pkg.)
- 1/4 cup powdered sugar
- 1/4 cup chopped pistachios or almonds
- 6 tablespoons butter, melted

STRAWBERRY LAYER

- 1 container (1/2-gallon) strawberry or cherry ice cream

PISTACHIO LAYER

- 1 container (1/2-gallon) vanilla ice cream
- 1 package (3.4 oz.) instant pistachio pudding and pie filling mix
- 1 cup half-and-half

FUDGE SAUCE

- 2 cups powdered sugar
- 1 package (6 oz.) semisweet chocolate chips (1 cup)
- 1/2 cup butter
- 1 can (12 oz.) evaporated milk (1-1/2 cups)
- 1 teaspoon vanilla
- Frozen whipped topping, thawed, if desired
- Fresh strawberries, if desired

1 Line 13x9-inch pan with foil, extending foil over all sides of pan. In medium bowl, combine all crust ingredients; mix well. Press evenly in bottom of foil-lined pan. Freeze 30 minutes. Place strawberry ice cream in refrigerator to soften.

2 Spoon softened strawberry ice cream onto crust; smooth with back of spoon. Freeze 30 minutes. Place vanilla ice cream in refrigerator to soften.

3 Place softened vanilla ice cream in large bowl; stir with spoon until smooth. In small bowl, combine pudding mix and half-and-half; stir until blended. Add to ice cream; mix with electric mixer at low speed until well blended. Spoon over strawberry ice cream. Freeze 4 hours or until firm.

4 Meanwhile, in large saucepan, combine powdered sugar, chocolate chips, butter and evaporated milk; stir to mix. Bring to a boil over medium heat, stirring occasionally. Boil 5 minutes, stirring frequently. Remove from heat. Stir in vanilla. Cool at least 1 hour before serving.

5 To serve, let dessert stand at room temperature for 15 minutes. Cut into squares. Serve each with fudge sauce, whipped topping and strawberries.

NUTRITION INFORMATION PER SERVING: Calories 620 • Total Fat 34g • Saturated Fat 20g • Cholesterol 100mg • Sodium 350mg • Total Carbohydrate 71g • Dietary Fiber 1g. DIETARY EXCHANGES: 2 Starch • 3 Other Carbohydrate • 6-1/2 Fat.

quick bread trifle squares

PREP TIME: 25 Minutes ✱ READY IN: 2 Hours 25 Minutes ✱ SERVINGS: 12

- 2 cups milk
- 1 package (3 oz.) vanilla pudding and pie filling mix
- 1 loaf Pineapple-Cherry Quick Bread
- 3 tablespoons cherry-flavored liqueur or pineapple juice
- 1/2 cup seedless raspberry jam
- 1/2 pint (1 cup) fresh raspberries
- 1 can (8 oz.) pineapple tidbits in unsweetened juice, well drained
- 1 cup whipping cream
- 1 tablespoon powdered sugar
- Fresh raspberries, if desired
- Fresh mint sprigs, if desired

1 In medium saucepan, combine milk and pudding mix; mix well. Cook over medium heat, stirring constantly until mixture boils. Remove from heat. Place plastic wrap directly over pudding. Cool 1 hour or until completely cooled.

2 Trim off short ends of quick bread loaf. Cut loaf into 9 slices. Arrange slices in ungreased 13x9-inch (3-quart) glass baking dish, cutting to fit. Sprinkle liqueur over bread. Spread with jam. Top with raspberries and pineapple. Spread cooled pudding over fruit.

3 Beat whipping cream in small bowl with electric mixer at high speed until soft peaks form. Add powdered sugar; beat until stiff peaks form. Spread over pudding. Cover; refrigerate at least 1 hour to blend flavors. Store in refrigerator. Cut into squares; garnish each with raspberries and mint.

NUTRITION INFORMATION PER SERVING: Calories 580 • Total Fat 22g • Saturated Fat 7g • Cholesterol 95mg • Sodium 390mg • Total Carbohydrate 88g • Dietary Fiber 2g. DIETARY EXCHANGES: 3 Starch • 3 Other Carbohydrate • 4 Fat.

kitchen tip

For extra-rich flavor, prepare the pudding with eggnog instead of milk. No time for baking? Try frozen pound cake in place of the Pineapple-Cherry Quick Bread. Use a 9-inch loaf; thaw the cake before cutting it into 12 slices.

chocolate cheesecake

PREP TIME: 15 Minutes ✱ READY IN: 7 Hours 20 Minutes ✱ SERVINGS: 16

CRUST

- 1 package (9 oz.) thin chocolate wafer cookies, crushed (1-3/4 cups)
- 6 tablespoons butter or margarine, melted

FILLING

- 2 packages (8 oz. each) cream cheese, softened
- 2/3 cup sugar
- 3 eggs
- 1 bag (12 oz.) semisweet chocolate chips (2 cups), melted
- 1 cup whipping cream
- 2 tablespoons butter or margarine, melted
- 1 teaspoon vanilla

1 Heat oven to 325°F. In medium bowl, mix crust ingredients; reserve 1 tablespoon crumbs for garnish. Press remaining crumbs in bottom and 2 inches up side of ungreased 10-inch springform pan. Refrigerate.

2 In large bowl, beat cream cheese and sugar until smooth. Beat in 1 egg at a time until well blended. Add melted chocolate; beat well. Add remaining filling ingredients; beat until smooth. Pour into crust-lined pan.

3 Bake 55 to 65 minutes or until edges are set; center of cheesecake will be soft. (To minimize cracking, place shallow pan half full of hot water on lower oven rack during baking.) Cool in pan 5 minutes.

4 Carefully remove side of pan. Cool completely, about 2 hours. Garnish with reserved crumbs. Refrigerate at least 4 hours or overnight. Store in refrigerator.

HIGH ALTITUDE (3500-6500 FT): Bake 60 to 65 minutes.

NUTRITION INFORMATION PER SERVING: Calories 410 • Total Fat 29g • Saturated Fat 17g • Trans Fat 1g • Cholesterol 105mg • Sodium 210mg • Total Carbohydrate 32g • Dietary Fiber 2g • Sugars 24g • Protein 5g. DIETARY EXCHANGES: 1/2 Starch • 1-1/2 Other Carbohydrate • 1/2 High-Fat Meat • 5 Fat • 2 Carb Choices.

kitchen tip

Chocolate and cheesecake—can't go wrong with that! Don't worry about the center of the cheesecake being soft when you take it out of the oven; it becomes firm as it cools. To cut cheesecake easily, dip the knife into water and clean it off after every cut.

special touch

After a taste of the raspberry sauce, you may want to double the recipe. It's absolutely delicious drizzled over ice cream, pound or angel food cake, or chocolate brownies.

raspberry-sauced fresh pear dumplings

READY IN: 45 Minutes ✷ SERVINGS: 8

DUMPLINGS

- 2 firm ripe pears, peeled, cored and coarsely chopped
- 1/4 cup golden raisins
- 1/4 cup firmly packed brown sugar
- 1 Pillsbury® Refrigerated Pie Crust (from 15-oz. pkg.), softened as directed on package
- 1 tablespoon milk
- 1 tablespoon sugar

SAUCE

- 1 package (10 oz.) frozen raspberries in syrup, thawed
- 3 tablespoons sugar
- 1 teaspoon cornstarch

1 Heat oven to 425°F. In medium bowl, combine pears, raisins and brown sugar; mix well. Remove pie crusts from pouches. Unfold crusts; cut each into quarters. Place about 1/3 cup pear mixture on each crust quarter.

2 Brush crust edges lightly with water. Bring sides of each crust up to top of pears; press edges to seal, making 3 seams.

3 With pancake turner, carefully place dumplings seam side up in ungreased 15x10x1-inch baking pan. Brush with milk. Sprinkle with 1 tablespoon sugar.

4 Bake for 15 to 20 minutes or until deep golden brown. Cool on wire rack for 10 minutes. Meanwhile, place raspberries in food processor bowl with metal blade or blender container; process until smooth.

5 If desired, place strainer over small saucepan; pour raspberries into strainer. Press berries with back of spoon through strainer to remove seeds; discard seeds. Add 3 tablespoons sugar and cornstarch to raspberries in saucepan; cook over medium heat until mixture comes to a boil, stirring constantly. Place in freezer for 5 to 10 minutes to cool quickly. To serve, spoon raspberry sauce evenly onto individual dessert plates. Top each with dumpling.

NUTRITION INFORMATION PER SERVING: Calories 370 • Total Fat 14g • Saturated Fat 6g • Cholesterol 15mg • Sodium 210mg • Total Carbohydrate 59g • Dietary Fiber 3g • Sugars 30g • Protein 2g. DIETARY EXCHANGES: 1/2 Starch • 3-1/2 Fruit • 2-1/2 Fat OR 4 Carbohydrate • 2-1/2 Fat • 4 Carb Choices.

crumbleberry pear pie

PREP TIME: 20 Minutes ✳ READY IN: 2 Hours 25 Minutes ✳ SERVINGS: 12

Crust

1 refrigerated pie crust (from 15-oz. box), softened as directed on box

Filling

1/2 cup butter or margarine, softened
1/2 cup granulated sugar
2 eggs
1 cup finely ground almonds
1/4 cup all-purpose flour
1 large firm pear or apple, peeled, thinly sliced
1 cup fresh or frozen raspberries and/or blueberries, thawed

Topping

3/4 cup all-purpose flour
1/3 cup packed brown sugar
1/2 teaspoon almond extract
1/3 cup butter or margarine

1 Heat oven to 350°F. Place pie crust in 9-inch glass pie plate as directed on box for one-crust filled pie.

2 In large bowl, beat 1/2 cup butter and the granulated sugar until light and fluffy. Beat in 1 egg at a time until well blended. Stir in almonds and 1/4 cup flour just until evenly moistened. Spread mixture in crust-lined pan. Arrange pear slices on top of filling, overlapping slightly. Bake 20 to 30 minutes or until filling and pears are light golden brown.

3 Meanwhile, in medium bowl, mix 3/4 cup flour, the brown sugar and almond extract. Using pastry blender or fork, cut in 1/3 cup butter until mixture resembles coarse crumbs.

4 Sprinkle raspberries over pear; sprinkle with topping. Bake 18 to 28 minutes or until topping is golden brown. Cool 1 hour. Serve warm. Store in refrigerator.

NUTRITION INFORMATION PER SERVING: Calories 370 • Total Fat 23g • Saturated Fat 10g • Trans Fat 1g • Cholesterol 70mg • Sodium 180mg • Total Carbohydrate 37g • Dietary Fiber 2g • Sugars 17g • Protein 4g. DIETARY EXCHANGES: 1 Starch • 1-1/2 Other Carbohydrate • 4-1/2 Fat • 2-1/2 Carb Choices.

kitchen tip

Grind almonds in a food processor or in batches in a blender. Use short on/off bursts to grind them evenly, stirring once or twice. If you grind them too much, the mixture will turn into a paste.

white chocolate-cranberry-pecan tart

PREP TIME: 30 Minutes ✳ READY IN: 3 Hours 15 Minutes ✳ SERVINGS: 12

Crust

1 refrigerated pie crust (from 15-oz. box), softened as directed on box

Filling

1 cup fresh or frozen cranberries
1 cup pecan halves
1 cup white vanilla baking chips
3 eggs
3/4 cup packed brown sugar
3/4 cup light corn syrup
2 tablespoons all-purpose flour
1 teaspoon grated orange peel

Topping

Whipped cream, if desired

1 Place cookie sheet in oven on middle oven rack. Heat oven to 400°F. Place pie crust in 10-inch tart pan with removable bottom as directed on box for one-crust filled pie.

2 Layer cranberries, pecans and baking chips in crust-lined pan. In large bowl, beat eggs. Add brown sugar, corn syrup, flour and orange peel; blend well. Pour over cranberry mixture.

3 Place tart on cookie sheet in oven. Bake 25 minutes. Cover tart loosely with foil lightly sprayed with nonstick cooking spray; bake 10 to 20 minutes longer or until crust is golden brown and filling is set in center. Remove foil; cool completely, about 2 hours. Serve with whipped cream. Store in refrigerator.

High Altitude (3500-6500 ft): In Step 3, after adding foil bake 10 to 15 minutes longer.

NUTRITION INFORMATION PER SERVING: Calories 390 • Total Fat 17g • Saturated Fat 7g • Trans Fat 0g • Cholesterol 55mg • Sodium 160mg • Total Carbohydrate 54g • Dietary Fiber 1g • Sugars 34g • Protein 4g. DIETARY EXCHANGES: 1 Starch • 2-1/2 Other Carbohydrate • 3-1/2 Fat • 3-1/2 Carb Choices.

cook's notes

This dessert can be made in a 9-inch glass pie plate. When mixing the filling, increase the flour to 3 tablespoons.

For breakfast or brunch, prepare the kringle the night before. Let the drizzle set before covering it; invert a deep baking pan over it to keep it from drying out.

easy danish kringle

PREP TIME: 15 Minutes ✱ READY IN: 1 Hour 15 Minutes ✱ SERVINGS: 8

- 1 Pillsbury® Refrigerated Pie Crust (from 15-oz. box), softened as directed on box
- 2/3 cup chopped pecans
- 1/3 cup firmly packed brown sugar
- 3 tablespoons butter or margarine, softened (do not use margarine spread)
- Water
- 1/2 cup powdered sugar
- 1/4 teaspoon vanilla
- 2 to 3 teaspoons milk
- 3 tablespoons chopped pecans, if desired

1 Heat oven to 375°F. Remove crust from pouch; place on large ungreased cookie sheet. In medium bowl, combine 2/3 cup pecans, brown sugar and butter; mix well. Sprinkle over half of pie crust to within 3/4 inch of edge.

2 Brush edge with water; fold pie crust over filling. Move kringle to center of cookie sheet. Press edges with fork to seal. Prick top with fork. Bake for 17 to 22 minutes or until golden brown. Cool 5 minutes.

3 In small bowl, combine powdered sugar, vanilla and enough milk for desired drizzling consistency; blend until smooth. Drizzle icing over kringle. Sprinkle with 3 tablespoons pecans. Cool 30 minutes or until completely cooled. Cut into wedges.

NUTRITION INFORMATION PER SERVING: Calories 295 • Total Fat 18g • Saturated Fat 6g • Cholesterol 17mg • Sodium 140mg • Total Carbohydrate 31g • Dietary Fiber 0g. DIETARY EXCHANGES: 1 Starch • 1 Fruit • 2 Other Carbohydrate • 3-1/2 Fat.

irish cream chocolate tart

PREP TIME: 15 Minutes ✱ READY IN: 4 Hours 5 Minutes ✱ SERVINGS: 12

Tart

- 1 Pillsbury® Refrigerated Pie Crust (from 15-oz. box), softened as directed on box
- 1-1/2 cups semisweet chocolate chips
- 1 can (14 oz.) sweetened condensed milk
- 1/3 cup Irish cream liqueur or whipping cream
- 2 eggs

Topping

- 1/2 cup powdered sugar
- 1/3 cup unsweetened baking cocoa
- Dash salt
- 1-1/2 cups whipping cream
- 1 teaspoon vanilla
- Additional unsweetened baking cocoa, if desired
- White chocolate curls, if desired

1 Heat oven to 425°F. Remove crust from pouch; press in bottom and 1-1/2 inches up side of 9-inch springform pan. Bake 9 to 11 minutes or until golden brown.

2 Place chocolate chips in medium microwavable bowl. Microwave on High 40 seconds. Stir; microwave 5 to 15 seconds longer or until chocolate is melted and smooth. Cool 3 minutes.

3 In large bowl, beat condensed milk, liqueur, eggs and melted chocolate with electric mixer on medium speed until smooth. Pour into cooled baked shell.

4 Bake 15 minutes. Reduce oven temperature to 350°F; bake 20 to 30 minutes longer or until center is set. Cool completely on cooling rack, about 1 hour. Refrigerate 2 hours.

5 In medium bowl, beat all topping ingredients except additional cocoa and chocolate curls with electric mixer on high speed until stiff peaks form. Spread topping over tart; sprinkle with additional cocoa and garnish with chocolate curls. Store in refrigerator.

High Altitude (3500-6500 ft): Place pan of water on oven rack below the rack tart will be baked on. In Step 3, add 1/4 cup all-purpose flour to ingredients in bowl. In Step 4, increase second bake time at 350°F to 25 to 35 minutes.

NUTRITION INFORMATION PER SERVING: Calories 440 • Total Fat 25g • Saturated Fat 14g • Trans Fat 0g • Cholesterol 85mg • Sodium 150mg • Total Carbohydrate 48g • Dietary Fiber 2g • Sugars 36g • Protein 6g. DIETARY EXCHANGES: 1/2 Starch • 2-1/2 Other Carbohydrate • 1/2 Medium-Fat Meat • 4-1/2 Fat • 3 Carb Choices.

easy danish kringle

praline cream puffs

praline cream puffs

PREP TIME: 30 Minutes ✻ READY IN: 1 Hour 30 Minutes ✻ SERVINGS: 12 Cream Puffs

Cream Puffs

- 1 cup water
- 1/2 cup butter or margarine
- 1 cup all-purpose flour
- 1/2 teaspoon salt
- 4 eggs

Toasted Pecan Sauce

- 1/2 cup butter or margarine
- 1-1/4 cups packed brown sugar
- 1/4 cup corn syrup
- 1/2 cup whipping cream
- 1 cup chopped pecans, toasted

Filling

- 1 quart (4 cups) vanilla or butter pecan ice cream

1 Heat oven to 400°F. Grease cookie sheets with shortening. In medium saucepan, heat water and 1/2 cup butter to boiling over medium heat. Stir in flour and salt; cook, stirring constantly, until mixture leaves side of pan in smooth ball.

2 Remove from the heat. Beat in 1 egg at a time until the mixture is smooth and glossy. Do not overbeat.

3 Spoon 12 mounds of dough (about 1/4 cup each) 3 inches apart onto cookie sheet. Bake 30 to 35 minutes or until golden brown.

4 Prick the puffs with a sharp knife to allow the steam to escape. Remove from cookie sheets; cool completely.

5 To make sauce, in medium saucepan, melt 1/2 cup butter. Stir in brown sugar and corn syrup. Heat to boiling; boil 1 minute, stirring constantly. Gradually stir in whipping cream; return to boiling. Remove from heat. Stir in pecans. Keep warm.

6 To serve, place each puff on serving plate; slice in half horizontally. Spoon about 1/3 cup ice cream into bottom half of puff. Replace top half of puff; drizzle with sauce.

7 To toast pecans, bake uncovered in ungreased shallow pan in 350°F oven 6 to 10 minutes, stirring occasionally, until light brown. Or cook in ungreased heavy skillet over medium heat 5 to 7 minutes, stirring frequently until nuts begin to brown, then stirring constantly until light brown. Sprinkle over sauce.

NUTRITION INFORMATION PER SERVING: Calories 510 • Total Fat 32g • Saturated Fat 16g • Trans Fat 1g • Cholesterol 145mg • Sodium 290mg • Total Carbohydrate 49g • Dietary Fiber 2g • Sugars 34g • Protein 6g. DIETARY EXCHANGES: 1 Starch • 2 Other Carbohydrate • 1/2 High-Fat Meat • 5-1/2 Fat • 3 Carb Choices.

Kitchen tip

Cream puffs may seem like a hard-to-make mystery, but no special ingredients or equipment are required—just flour, water, butter, salt and eggs. Bake them in the oven and voilà, they're ready to fill!

cook's notes

Frozen strawberries are not recommended for this recipe because they will add too much moisture.

rustic strawberry tart with strawberry cream

READY IN: 35 Minutes * SERVINGS: 8

- 1 Pillsbury® Refrigerated Pie Crust (from 15-oz. box), softened as directed on box
- 2 tablespoons granulated sugar
- 1 tablespoon cornstarch
- 3-1/4 cups coarsely chopped fresh strawberries
- 1 teaspoon granulated sugar
- 1/2 cup whipping (heavy) cream
- 1 tablespoon powdered sugar
- Fresh mint, if desired

1 Heat oven to 450°F. Lightly spray cookie sheet with nonstick cooking spray. Remove pie crust from pouch; unroll on cookie sheet.

2 In medium bowl, mix 2 tablespoons granulated sugar and the cornstarch. Gently stir in 3 cups of the strawberries. Spoon onto center of crust, spreading to within 2 inches of edge. Fold 2-inch crust edge up over filling, pleating decoratively.

3 Brush crust edge with water; sprinkle with 1 teaspoon granulated sugar. Bake 15 to 20 minutes or until crust is golden brown.

4 Meanwhile, in small bowl, beat whipping cream and powdered sugar with electric mixer on high speed until stiff peaks form. In another small bowl, mash remaining 1/4 cup strawberries; fold into whipped cream. Serve tart with strawberry whipped cream. Garnish with fresh mint.

NUTRITION INFORMATION PER SERVING: Calories 210 • Total Fat 12g • Saturated Fat 5g • Cholesterol 20mg • Sodium 115mg • Total Carbohydrate 24g • Dietary Fiber 2g. DIETARY EXCHANGES: 1-1/2 Other Carbohydrate • 2-1/2 Fat.

peanut butter-candy tart

PREP TIME: 10 Minutes ✳ READY IN: 30 Minutes ✳ SERVINGS: 10

- 1 Pillsbury® Refrigerated Pie Crust (from 15-oz. box), softened as directed on box
- 1/2 cup powdered sugar
- 1/2 cup creamy peanut butter
- 2 to 3 tablespoons milk
- 3 bars (2.07 oz. each) milk chocolate-covered peanut, caramel and nougat candy, unwrapped, chopped
- 2 tablespoons chocolate topping, heated
- 2 tablespoons fat-free caramel topping, heated

1 Heat oven to 450°F. Remove pie crust from pouch; unroll on ungreased large cookie sheet. If desired, flute edge. Generously prick crust with fork. Bake 8 to 10 minutes or until lightly browned. Cool completely, about 15 minutes.

2 Meanwhile, in small bowl, mix powdered sugar, peanut butter and enough milk until smooth and desired spreading consistency.

3 Spread peanut butter mixture over cooled baked crust. Sprinkle evenly with chopped candy; drizzle with chocolate and caramel toppings. Cut into wedges to serve.

NUTRITION INFORMATION PER SERVING: Calories 310 • Total Fat 16g • Saturated Fat 6g • Cholesterol 0mg • Sodium 210mg • Total Carbohydrate 36g • Dietary Fiber 2g. DIETARY EXCHANGES: 1 Starch • 1-1/2 Other Carbohydrate • 3 Fat.

cook's notes

Make this yummy treat up to six hours ahead but cut it into wedges just before serving.

raspberry truffle tart

pear upside-down cake

PREP TIME: 30 Minutes ✻ READY IN: 1 Hour 35 Minutes ✻ SERVINGS: 12

Cake

- 2 cups powdered sugar
- 3/4 cup butter, softened
- 3 eggs
- 1 teaspoon vanilla
- 1 cup all-purpose flour
- 1/2 cup cornmeal
- 1 teaspoon baking powder

Topping

- 1/4 cup butter
- 3/4 cup firmly packed brown sugar
- 2 firm ripe pears, peeled, thinly sliced
- Whipped cream, if desired

1 Heat oven to 350°F. In medium bowl, combine powdered sugar and 3/4 cup butter; beat at low speed until crumbly. Add eggs, one at a time, beating well at medium speed after each addition. Add vanilla; beat well. Add flour, cornmeal and baking powder; mix well.

2 Place 1/4 cup butter in 9-inch round cake pan. Heat in oven for about 4 minutes or until butter is melted. Sprinkle brown sugar evenly over butter. Arrange pear slices over mixture in pan, slightly overlapping. Spoon and carefully spread cake batter over pears.

3 Bake for 55 to 65 minutes or until toothpick inserted in center comes out clean. Cool in pan on wire rack for 5 minutes. Invert onto serving plate. Serve warm or cool alongside whipped cream.

High Altitude (3500-6500 ft): Increase flour to 1 cup plus 2 tablespoons. Bake as directed above.

NUTRITION INFORMATION PER SERVING: Calories 440 • Total Fat 23g • Saturated Fat 13g • Cholesterol 115mg • Sodium 230mg • Total Carbohydrate 53g • Dietary Fiber 1g. DIETARY EXCHANGES: 1 Starch • 2-1/2 Fruit • 3-1/2 Other Carbohydrate • 4-1/2 Fat.

Kitchen tip

Even the recipe for upside-down cake is upside-down–it begins with the topping. Sugar is sprinkled over melted butter in the pan bottom, then fruit is decoratively arranged over it. The batter is spooned on top. In the oven, the butter, sugar and fruit juices bake into caramel. When done, the hot cake is inverted so the glazed fruit becomes the topping.

candy bar pie

candy bar pie

PREP TIME: 25 Minutes ✱ READY IN: 6 Hours 5 Minutes ✱ SERVINGS: 10

CRUST

1 Pillsbury® Refrigerated Pie Crust (from 15-oz. box), softened as directed on box

FILLING

5 bars (2.07 oz. each) milk chocolate-covered peanut, caramel and nougat candy, unwrapped

1/2 cup sugar

4 packages (3 oz. each) cream cheese, softened

2 eggs

1/3 cup sour cream

1/3 cup creamy peanut butter

TOPPING

3 tablespoons whipping cream

2/3 cup milk chocolate chips

1 Heat oven to 450°F. Place pie crust in 9-inch glass pie pan as directed on package for one-crust filled pie. Bake for 5 to 7 minutes or until very light golden brown. Remove from oven; cool. Reduce temperature to 325°F.

2 Cut candy bars in half lengthwise; cut into 1/4-inch pieces. Arrange candy bar pieces over bottom of partially baked crust. In small bowl, combine sugar and cream cheese; beat until smooth. Add eggs, one at a time, beating well after each addition. Add sour cream and peanut butter, beating until mixture is smooth. Spoon over candy bar pieces.

3 Bake at 325°F for 30 to 40 minutes or until the center is set. Cool 2 hours or until the pie is completely cooled.

4 Heat whipping cream in small saucepan until very warm. Remove from heat. Add chocolate chips; stir until melted and mixture is smooth. Spread over top of pie. Refrigerate 2 to 3 hours before serving. Store in refrigerator.

NUTRITION INFORMATION PER SERVING: Calories 560 • Total Fat 36g • Saturated Fat 19g • Cholesterol 100mg • Sodium 310mg • Total Carbohydrate 49g • Dietary Fiber 1g. DIETARY EXCHANGES: 3 Starch • 3 Other Carbohydrate • 7 Fat.

Kitchen tip

Freeze refrigerated pie crust dough for long storage. Remove only what you need and thaw it in the refrigerator before you use it.

delicious apple cream pie

PREP TIME: 35 Minutes ✱ READY IN: 2 Hours 25 Minutes ✱ SERVINGS:8

CRUST

1 box (15 oz.) refrigerated pie crusts, softened as directed on box

FILLING

3/4 cup granulated sugar

3 tablespoons all-purpose flour

1 teaspoon ground cinnamon

6 cups thinly sliced peeled apples (6 medium)

1/2 cup whipping cream

1 teaspoon vanilla

TOPPING

1 egg white, beaten

1 tablespoon coarse white sparkling sugar or granulated sugar

1 Heat oven to 400°F. Make the pie crusts as directed on box for two-crust pie, using 9-inch glass pie plate.

2 In large bowl, mix granulated sugar, flour and cinnamon; gently stir in apples. In small bowl, mix whipping cream and vanilla. Pour over apple mixture; stir gently to mix well. Spoon into crust-lined pan.

3 Top with second pie crust; seal edge and flute. Cut slits or shapes in several places in top crust. Brush top with egg white; sprinkle with coarse sugar. Cover edge of pastry with 2- to 3-inch strip of foil to prevent excessive browning; remove foil for last 15 minutes of baking.

4 Bake 40 to 50 minutes or until apples are tender and crust is golden brown. Cool completely, about 1 hour.

NUTRITION INFORMATION PER SERVING: Calories 410 • Total Fat 19g • Saturated Fat 8g • Trans Fat 0g • Cholesterol 25mg • Sodium 230mg • Total Carbohydrate 60g • Dietary Fiber 1g • Sugars 29g • Protein 1g. DIETARY EXCHANGES: 1 Starch • 1/2 Fruit • 2-1/2 Other Carbohydrate • 3-1/2 Fat • 4 Carb Choices.

Kitchen tip

Try this nifty trick to give regular granulated sugar a decorator look. Moisten fingertips with water, shaking off excess. Dip fingertips into sugar and sprinkle on top of pie. The water on your fingertips will cause the sugar to clump a little, so it adds a nice textured look to the top of the pie.

special touch

To make white chocolate curls, pull a vegetable peeler against the long side of the bottom of a block of vanilla-flavored candy coating (almond bark). If the curls break, place the block in a warm place for about 20 minutes to soften it for better curls.

chocolate-cherry truffle cake

PREP TIME: 25 Minutes ✵ READY IN: 2 Hours 20 Minutes ✵ SERVINGS: 12

Filling

- 1 cup semisweet chocolate chips (from 12-oz. bag)
- 2/3 cup sweetened condensed milk (from 14-oz. can)
- 1/4 teaspoon almond extract

Cake

- 1 box (18.25 oz.) chocolate fudge cake mix with pudding in the mix
- 1 cup water
- 1/2 cup vegetable oil
- 1/2 teaspoon almond extract
- 4 eggs
- 1 box (4 serving size) chocolate instant pudding and pie filling mix
- 1 jar (10 oz.) maraschino cherries, drained on paper towel, chopped (3/4 cup)

Glaze

- Remaining sweetened condensed milk (from 14-oz. can)
- 3/4 cup semisweet chocolate chips (from 12-oz. bag)
- 2 tablespoons corn syrup
- 1 teaspoon milk, if needed

Garnish, If Desired

- 8 oz. vanilla-flavored candy coating
- Maraschino cherries with stems, drained on paper towel

1 Heat oven to 350°F. Grease with shortening and lightly flour 12-cup fluted tube pan. In medium microwavable bowl, mix filling ingredients. Microwave on High 25 to 35 seconds, stirring every 15 seconds, until melted and smooth; set aside.

2 In large bowl with electric mixer, beat cake mix, water, oil, 1/2 teaspoon almond extract, the eggs and pudding mix on low speed about 1 minute, scraping bowl constantly. With rubber spatula, fold in cherries. Spoon batter into pan; spread evenly. Carefully spoon filling in ring over batter (do not let filling touch side of pan).

3 Bake 45 to 50 minutes or until toothpick inserted 1 inch from inside edge of pan comes out clean, top of cake feels firm to the touch and cake pulls away slightly from side of pan. Cool 15 minutes.

4 Place heatproof serving plate over pan; turn plate and pan over. Remove pan. Cool cake completely, about 1 hour.

5 In 1-quart saucepan, heat all glaze ingredients except 1 teaspoon milk over medium-low heat, stirring occasionally, until chocolate is melted and mixture is smooth. Stir in up to 1 teaspoon milk if necessary for glazing consistency. Pour glaze over cake, allowing some to drizzle down sides. Store loosely covered in refrigerator.

High Altitude (3500-6500 ft): Heat oven to 375°F. In Step 2, beat on low speed 30 seconds then on medium speed 2 minutes.

NUTRITION INFORMATION PER SERVING: Calories 600 • Total Fat 25g • Saturated Fat 10g • Cholesterol 80mg • Sodium 530mg • Total Carbohydrate 85g • Dietary Fiber 3g. DIETARY EXCHANGES: 2 Starch • 3-1/2 Other Carbohydrate • 5 Fat.

chocolate-cherry truffle cake

perfect apple pie

perfect apple pie

PREP TIME: 30 Minutes ✷ READY IN: 1 Hour 15 Minutes ✷ SERVINGS: 8

CRUST

1 package (15 oz.) Pillsbury® Refrigerated Pie Crusts, softened as directed on package

FILLING

3/4 cup sugar

2 tablespoons all-purpose flour

3/4 teaspoon cinnamon

1/4 teaspoon salt

1/8 teaspoon nutmeg

1 tablespoon lemon juice, if desired

6 cups (6 medium) thinly sliced, peeled apples

1 Heat oven to 425°F. Prepare pie crusts as directed on package for two-crust pie, using 9-inch glass pie pan.

2 In large bowl, combine all filling ingredients except lemon juice and apples; mix well. Add lemon juice and apples; toss gently to mix. Spoon into crust-lined pan. Top with second crust; seal edges and flute. Cut slits or shapes in several places in top crust. Bake for 40 to 45 minutes or until apples are tender and crust is golden brown.

NUTRITION INFORMATION PER SERVING: Calories 370 • Total Fat 14g • Saturated Fat 6g • Cholesterol 15mg • Sodium 270mg • Total Carbohydrate 59g • Dietary Fiber 2g • Sugars 30g • Protein 2g. DIETARY EXCHANGES: 1 Starch • 3 Fruit • 2-1/2 Fat OR 4 Carbohydrate • 2-1/2 Fat • 4 Carb Choices.

special touch

For extra flair, drizzle the pie with 1/3 cup caramel ice cream topping as soon as it comes out of the oven. Top it with chopped pecans.

chocolate-cashew pie

PREP TIME: 25 Minutes ✷ READY IN: 3 Hours 45 Minutes ✷ SERVINGS: 10

CRUST

1 refrigerated pie crust (from 15-oz. pkg.), softened as directed on package

FILLING AND TOPPING

3/4 cup light corn syrup

1/2 cup sugar

3 tablespoons butter, melted

1 teaspoon vanilla

3 eggs

1 package (6 oz.) semisweet chocolate chips (1 cup)

1 cup cashew halves

10 whole cashews

Whipped cream, if desired

1 Place the pie crust in 9-inch glass pie pan as directed on package for one-crust filled pie. Heat oven to 325°F.

2 In large bowl, combine corn syrup, sugar, butter, vanilla and eggs; beat with wire whisk until well blended. Reserve 2 tablespoons chocolate chips for topping. Stir remaining chocolate chips and cashew halves into corn syrup mixture. Spread evenly in crust-lined pan.

3 Bake for 45 to 55 minutes or until pie is deep golden brown and filling is set. Cover edge of crust with strips of foil after 15 to 20 minutes of baking to prevent excessive browning. Cool 2-1/2 hours or until completely cooled.

4 Meanwhile, line cookie sheet with waxed paper. Place reserved 2 tablespoons chocolate chips in small microwavable bowl. Microwave on High for 45 to 60 seconds or until stirred smooth. Dip each whole cashew in chocolate; place on paper-lined cookie sheet. Refrigerate 15 to 20 minutes or until chocolate is set.

5 Just before serving, garnish pie with whipped cream and chocolate-dipped cashews. Store leftovers in refrigerator.

NUTRITION INFORMATION PER SERVING: Calories 445 • Total Fat 23g • Saturated Fat 9g • Cholesterol 75mg • Sodium 250mg • Total Carbohydrate 54g • Dietary Fiber 1g • Sugars 30g • Protein 6g. DIETARY EXCHANGES: 2 Starch • 4-1/2 Fat • 1-1/2 Other Carbohydrates • 3-1/2 Carb Choices.

special touch

If you're nuts for almonds, use toasted slivered almonds in place of the cashews and stir 1 tablespoon of amaretto into the filling. Garnish with whole blanched almonds dipped in melted chocolate.

general recipe index

alphabetical recipe index